JOHN H. OAK

HEALTHY CHRISTIANS

MAKE A

HEALTHY CHURCH

Translators

Rev. Sam Ko, a Korean-Canadian, serves as the International secretary and assistant to Dr. John H. Oak. A Graduate of Westminster Theological Seminary, Rev. Ko has extensive pastoral experience in Canada, the United States and Korea. He pastors the English speaking community at SaRang, and handles all of the international correspondence of SaRang. He has two sons with his wife Jennifer.

Rev. Jerry Vreeman has been involved in international media ministries since he graduated from Calvin Theological Seminary. He has extensive experience in radio and television. He is an ordained minister in the Christian Reformed Church of North America. He and his wife Cori have four daughters, two sons and two grandchildren.

© John H. Oak

ISBN 1 85792 869 5

Published in 2003
by
Christian Focus Publications,
Geanies House, Fearn,
Ross-shire, IV20 1TW, Scotland

www.christianfocus.com

Cover design by Alister MacInnes

Printed and bound by
Cox & Wyman, Reading, Berkshire

JOHN H. OAK
FOREWORD BY RICK WARREN

HEALTHY
CHRISTIANS
MAKE A
HEALTHY
CHURCH

352 pp - 60g/m²
ISBN 1-85792-869-5

CHRISTIAN FOCUS PUBLICATIONS

About the Author

John Han Hum Oak grew up in a Christian home and wrestled for many years with a call to the ministry. It was only after marriage to Young Soon Kim that he entered seminary and prepared to become a pastor.

While serving several churches and college ministries, John Oak became increasingly interested in discipleship training as the key to growing a healthy and vibrant church. At deep personal and family sacrifice he studied for three years in the U.S. at Calvin and Westminster Theological Seminaries, gradually forming his own unique method of building a healthy church through discipleship.

Returning to Seoul in 1978 he founded SaRang Community church with 9 people through his newly developed discipleship training model. Today with 30,000 members and the same training program, the church continues to grow and birth new communities of believers. Dr. Oak's three-fold vision: to train the laity, to reach out to young people and to evangelize communist countries remain the driving force behind the remarkable story of SaRang.

Dr Oak remains the senior pastor of SaRang Community Church, aided by his faithful wife and ministry partner, Young Soon. He is one of the most recognized church leaders and authors in Korea, serving leadership roles in numerous ministry organizations and educational institutions. Though wrestling with health issues all his ministry life, he has travelled extensively throughout the world teaching church leaders his methods of discipleship training. He has been blessed with three sons and four grandchildren.

This book is dedicated
to all my brothers and sisters in Christ
who devoted their time, money and energy
for the sole purpose of making
true disciples
of
Jesus Christ

contents

contents

ACKNOWLEDGEMENTS

I didn't complete this book all by myself. As I publish this book in English I can't ignore the fact that there are many people whom I wish to thank from the bottom of my heart.

First of all, with deep love and appreciation, I'd like to acknowledge my wife. I am who I am because of my wife and was able to complete this book only through her support. While I was studying in the United States for three years, she raised our three sons all by herself through extreme financial difficulties and loneliness. She has quietly and joyfully shared my cross ever since SaRang church was planted. Today she is still my most faithful co-worker in Christ who kneels down in prayer for me every morning. I am truly a blessed man to have her as my life's partner.

I also cannot forget the many co-workers who have given their sweat and tears for over twenty years to equip the laity for true discipleship in Christ. They are the pioneers who captured the vision and philosophy of my ministry and who have night and day been faithfully training and discipling the laity. I am very proud of them. Without them I would never have been able to describe the abundant fruits that come from discipleship training.

In addition, I'd like to express my utmost thanks to the thousands of lay leaders who through SaRang Community Church have treasured as their life's most precious vision becoming Jesus' disciples. They are the living proof of the power of discipleship training. Because so many of them are serving in every area of our church's ministry, I can confidently shout from the roof tops that discipleship is the biblical answer to transform the hearts of God's people and grow the church. These living disciples around me at church and in the marketplace continue to inspire and motivate me. They are beautiful examples of Christ. I am so proud and thankful for them.

Next, I just don't know how to express my deepest appreciation for my friend, Rev. Jerry Vreeman, who played a major role in publishing this book in English. For the past sixteen years, this book has been equipping churches in Korea. It has influenced and challenged many pastors and lay people to reform the Korean church, make it healthier, and enable it to grow. Guided by a deep spirituality and distinctive theological perspective, Jerry has done his best to make the content acceptable in the American context. I thank him for his friendship and his efforts, and I thank God for bringing him into my life.

I also wish to express my special appreciation to Rev. Rick Warren at Saddleback Community Church. Although he is a busy pastor with one of the largest churches in America, he gladly gave his time to write the preface of this book. Rick's church and ministry have been role models to churches all over the the world demonstrating the potential and power of a purpose equipped laity. He shares my passion that the laity must be trained as Jesus' disciples so His Kingdom can come and His will be done on this earth that Christ may receive the glory and honor and praise.

Finally, I express my love to Pastor Sam Ko who has faithfully served beside me for the past seven years. He has poured out his heart and abilities to translate my book. I couldn't possibly have thought of publishing this book in English without his dedication and commitment.

Foreword

How do you turn the members of your church into mature lay ministers? That is one of the most critical questions in church health and growth today.

It's not enough just to hope and dream that people will get involved in serving Jesus. Your church needs an intentional strategy for leading people to deeper commitment and greater service for Christ. At Saddleback Church, in Lake Forest, California we've been able to commission literally thousands of lay ministers through a strategy of consistent communication, a practical process, and a simple structure. Your church can use these same elements to mobilize your members for ministry.

First, continually teach what the Bible says about the church, about spiritual growth, about serving and about spiritual giftedness. Next, set up a process for uncovering your members' gifts and talents and finding the best place for each one to serve. Then organize the structure of your church in a way that minimizes maintenance and maximizes ministry. That's what this book is all about!

My good friend, Dr. John Oak has written an outstanding

manual on discipleship and equipping. It is full of wisdom that comes from serving Christ for many years. What Pastor Oak shares in the book is not mere theory. It works! It had proven to be effective in SaRang Community Church. God has used the principles in the book to build a church that is both balanced and healthy, not just large.

The starting point in leading members to maturity, ministry and mission is to invest time in teaching your members what the Bible says about these issues. You must lay the biblical foundation. Teach it in classes, sermons, seminars, home cell groups, and every other way you can emphasize it. You should never stop teaching on the importance of every Christian having a ministry. This book can be your guide.

Jesus said, "For even the Son of Man did not come to be served, but to serve, and to give his life as a ransom for many." (Mark 10:45) Serving and giving are the defining characteristics of the Christ-like lifestyle. If we are going to be like Christ, we must learn to serve and to give. We must put the Word into practice, not just listen to it. My prayer is that God will use this book to produce an entire generation of believers who are committed to serving and sharing the eternal purposes of God!

Dr. Rick Warren
Saddleback Valley Community Church, California
Author, *The Purpose Driven Church*

Preface

L ooking back in history, the church has had the stereotype of having to engage in cautious change, for each step is like treading on icy ground. When church influence declines, the church goes through many hardships, such as self-blaming and suffering due to the tensions of the era.

Yet, in times of spiritual revival, the church can't stop concerning itself about the decay and secularization of its surroundings. We are now living in an age of instability. In order for the church to function as salt and light in an evil world, I believe the Holy Spirit initiates a certain amount of unrest and grief within the church. As long as a church is alert to these things, then there is no such thing as a sleeping church.

In order for church leaders to rediscover the role of the laity, it requires remodeling the basic framework of the prior ministry. This can lead to a heavy burden on a church leader. Although many ministers have great interest in the role of laymen, they find it difficult to put it into practice because it may cover a sensitive matter in the original ministry model.

As we all know, reformation is not an easy process to initiate or complete. Having insight to recognize the importance of the laity departs from the prejudice and introverted thinking among many traditional church leaders. This calls for a reformation of the minister first, rather than the church. In fact, throughout history, there have been many cases where the reformation of the church and minister were one and the same. It is almost impossible to reform the church without first seeing a change in the minister.

Hendrik Kraemer correctly points out the need for that renewal, in the sense of a perennial imperative which is always accompanied by the life of the Church.

> *In this sense the imperative is equally imperious for every kind of Church; the flourishing and the decadent ones, the self-complacent and the despondent. In the light of this rule of the perennial, constantly valid law of renewal, the laity, as said already, gets its essential place and meaning, because the whole Church is constantly called to renewal.* [1]

In **Part 1**, the focus is on the current issues facing the church. Through an old proverb, we are reminded that knowing the real problem is the first step in solving the problem. For this purpose, it is important to admit whatever seems to be a problem within a church.

Part 2 describes the new meaning of a Christian community. It is not restricted to the definition of a group of worshippers, but has broadened to a witnessing community of the laymen. For our purpose it is necessary to mention the concepts of the apostolic character of church-the priesthood of all believers and being part of a body. Re-asserting the role of laymen is not an outcome of a temporary theological trend, but, as revealed in the Scriptures, it is a genuine calling. We must rediscover the role of the laity.

Why do churches exist in the world? What are the roles of the laity and the church in the world? To answer these questions, we must go to the scripture. Many times we look at what a pastor conveys in order to make certain deductions. Thus, a pastoral philosophy is the pastor's thoughts about the church's ministry.

Unfortunately, many of us have been brought up in an atmosphere where the concepts of the apostolic character of the church and of the laity were neglected. I believe ministers have to be born again in order to be responsible leaders in the church.

Part 3 is about discipleship. Discipleship is a fundamental biblical strategy, which is a key element in building up self-esteem for a lay person. Discipleship is an ideal model for a layman. Our guide is Jesus who taught us the importance of discipling the laity. In this sense, a focus on discipleship leads to the clear direction of rediscovering the lay people of the church.

Part 4 deals with the practical principles and methods of discipleship training for the development of the laity. Once we establish the pastoral philosophy and strategy it demonstrates that it's not too difficult to find the most ideal method.

We could say that discipleship training itself, regardless of how it is done, is the answer. But by far, the most effective method of education is in the setting of a small group, which Jesus Himself used. It will be helpful to review all these main thoughts and adapt them into the ministry field.

Part 5 shows the ministry field where discipleship training is taking place to develop leaders in the local church. It analyzes both the advantages and disadvantages of discipleship training. It establishes the basis on which to propose the possibility of creating lay disciples within local churches.

Introduction

"And break up your unplowed ground; for it is time to seek the Lord, until he comes and showers righteousness on you." (Hosea 10:12b)

When I have the rare opportunity to get outside of the huge city of Seoul and drive through the agricultural communities which skirt the city, I often see farmland which has been untouched for a long time. Where there once were carefully plowed and cultivated fields there are now only dense weeds and twisted thorn bushes. It is absolutely absurd to scatter seed on such fields in order to reap a harvest of any kind. While the nearby healthy fields turn from fertile brown to a blue green glow and again to a radiant golden color, the unplowed ground always remains desolate, overgrown, and the same in appearance. It is almost impossible to even imagine that unplowed ground could sprout seed and bring grain to grow and ripen. There is a covering of vegetation over such land, but no anticipation of a miracle of new growth or an abundant harvest.

That's the ground I see as I read Jesus' parable of the Sower. When he describes hearts that allow the cares and concerns of one's environment to crowd out of the powerful seed of the Word of God, I imagine those unplowed fields. There could be a magnificent crop if only someone would turn over the soil and plant the seed.

As a pastor I realize there are many people in the church who have hearts like unplowed ground. When such people increase in number then the church itself becomes like those fertile but useless fields. These people may boast about the past life, be completely satisfied in the present, and not see the future. Naturally, such a church does not change. While there is still a form of life, it fears challenge, commitment, and calling. According to A.W. Tozer, many have forgotten that idleness is a fatal enemy of the church. They have forgotten that to neglect the plow or to be afraid of turning over the soil is the same as erecting one's own tombstone.

Sadly, my experience has shown that it is often those with hearts like unplowed ground who are the leaders of the church, or who belong to the core group. This situation is not unique to Korea nor America nor Europe. Wherever the Church avoids the hard work, the sweat and strain of plowing and hoeing, it loses its ability to burst forth an abundant harvest.

Why are many traditional churches unhealthy? Why are they not growing? I believe that when we take time to examine the disease, we will find not a toxic virus nor an outside threat, but vast unplowed hearts. Such hearts are destroying the well being of the church. They are the stumbling block which prevents church growth. They are breaking the morale of thousands of pastors, and letting leadership burn out without ever raising their hands.

The Pastor's dilemma

Before we blame an apathetic or uncultivated laity for the problems of the church, however, let me point out that the situation has often been caused by well meaning clergy themselves. Many pastors fall into the dilemma of working extremely hard with very little results. Why? I believe it is because they have failed to break up the unplowed soil - to turn over weed cluttered hearts in the church.

The reality is that most pastors have ministered by devoting their whole lives to a church of long standing doctrines and traditions without ever seeing real growth or abundant harvests. Even when founding a new church, they have often begun the work centered around believers who have long-term experience in churches which have for many years been unplowed. And so the dilemma remains. The pastors never realize their dreams because they have failed to do the most basic task first - breaking up and turning over the unplowed soil in the church.

Meanwhile, there is a truth we cannot deny. We cannot anticipate building a healthy church or watching it grow by pushing aside the traditional believers whose hearts may be unplowed ground. This is the reality of the churches in which most of us who are professional pastors minister. The irony is that while these believers are the epicenter of the sickness and the cause for the church's lack of growth, the key to recovery and harvest is also in their hands. No pastor, therefore, can turn away from them and remain in ministry. A ministry that evades these problems cannot be a true pastoral ministry. We must honestly examine this reality in our churches and come up with the most fitting prescription. Put another way, we must not make the erroneous diagnosis that this patient only has a cold when she actually suffers from lung cancer.

The core of the problem in today's church is leadership. No matter how much a church is like an unplowed field, if it meets the right leader, amazing things can happen. A church needs a great leader who has the courage to do the plowing with a vision of gathering the fascinating harvest afterwards. It needs a healthy spiritual leader heralding a bright future for the church, who can dig up the spiritual potential of the lay members, and develop them into dedicated believers propelled by their own calling.

What brings us into tension is the fact that it is definitely not easy to 'plow up' a church. It cannot be done by one or two sermons. Interesting and diverse programs are also not the keys to solving the basic problem. How about a Bible Study? Unfortunately, seasoned believers today have been through a plethora of Bible Studies for a long time. It is a paradox but not really an exaggeration to say that the trouble is from doing too many Bible studies. Their hearts have shrunk and their heads have swelled.

The ministry of discipleship training breaks up the unplowed ground of the heart

To bring church members to change and to awaken their potential, a pastor has to have an unusual daring, no, a determination to die. As the Apostle Paul said, one has to make the resolution to 'carry the cross' of teaching each person for up to three years without rest and with many tears. This is the pastoral ministry of 'discipleship training' I am referring to. Discipleship training is to break up the 'unplowed ground of the heart' of the lay member who has been saturated in the church culture for too long, who exhibits a temporary reaction no matter how moving a sermon message is, and who shows little change in character or daily life. Such work is never an easy task. It needs an Esther-like determination of 'If I perish, I perish'. I believe that for today's pastors this work has priority over evangelizing to unbelievers. How can one lead people to a sick church? If we, while doing pastoral ministry, avoid difficult and dangerous roads and only select the shortcuts and comfortable paths, the results we will gain are only too clear. We will still see an unchanging church.

There is a popular saying among church growth experts today. "A healthy church will naturally grow." Before discussing church growth, therefore, one needs to make a careful spiritual diagnosis first. In his book, *The Purpose Driven Church*, Rick Warren shocked and challenged many pastors when he stated that in the 21st century our problem is not growth but health. To be honest, nine out of ten pastors are ministering in an unhealthy church. To be even more direct, we're talking in most cases about churches suffering from a serious illness. To make a fitting comparison, 90% of pastors are like doctors wrestling with cancer patients. It's tough, and the outlook is not too bright.

Perhaps that is the reason many pastors are afraid of the expensive sacrifice needed to develop each member of their church as a whole person in Christ. Put another way, it often feels rewarding to give a sermon message to an audience of hundreds of people, but it is miserable to go through the pains and labor of childbearing for a few people. It is also regrettable that many try to apply to the setting of the pastoral ministry the economic principle of gaining huge profits with as little expense as possible.

Revealing Isaiah's vision

Today's church often makes extraordinary efforts at great expense to introduce a splendid new program or to prepare an interesting event, but it does not have much concern to see the fulfillment of the vision Isaiah saw regarding one lay person - "The least of you (lay person) will become a thousand, the smallest a mighty nation." (Isaiah 60:22) I believe this is the root cause for our failure for so long to break up the unplowed ground of church.

Here, however, we also need to remember what the Lord Jesus said. "Whoever finds his life will lose it, and whoever loses his life for my sake will find it." (Matthew 10:39) "So in everything, do to others what you would have them do to you..." (Matthew 7:12a)

It is the promise of our faithful God that when a pastor first makes sacrifices and serves the laity, then surely he will receive a valuable reward. I know many pastors around me who have sacrificed themselves and 'died' like a kernel of wheat to revive a long-time stagnant church. Among them is a pastor who was so excited about the blessing his church received that he devoted himself to discipleship training without giving consideration to his own health. He soon went to be with the Lord. I know another pastor who labored even with a severe thorn in the flesh. Though he experiences deep physical agony he has not given up discipleship training. His simple faith is that it is better for him to be ill than for the church itself to become sick.

Some people think that discipleship training is a method of pastoral ministry that has lost its effectiveness. During my study in the United States I often met professors and seminary students who thought that discipleship training was out dated and ineffective. Before returning to Korea I traveled from the east to the west for about three months to research discipleship training. It was my goal to see healthy churches growing out of discipleship training. I found a few great churches in several places. Though there were differences in the methods, pastors who succeeded in breaking up the unplowed ground were all serving in ministry joyfully. However, there weren't as many churches like these as I had expected. This finding made me very sad.

I don't want to claim that discipleship training is the whole of pastoral ministry. Broadly speaking, a pastor's hard effort day and night, his whole ministry work is to make disciples. No effort to accomplish that end is useless. However, when determining the efficiency for making disciples, not all methods are good or beneficial. The Apostle Paul said, "Everything is permissible for me but not everything is beneficial" (I Corinthians 6:12). No matter how right and long standing, if it is not effective in changing the structure of an unhealthy church to a healthy one and raising up lay members to be co-workers, then that method should be eliminated. It is foolish to whip a dead horse repeatedly. Get on another horse fast!

Understanding the problem of the traditional church

I was born in a family where my great grandfather who had received the Gospel through a missionary from the United States risked all sorts of persecution in his hometown to found a church. My mother especially influenced my faith. I was very devoted as a young boy, following my mother to the early dawn services, the pride of the Korean church. Before reaching my teen years, I had already experienced the joy of being born again, and never let the Bible out of my hands.

In my early twenties I received a calling from the Lord to full time pastoral ministry and, accordingly, went to college and seminary. During those years there was a nagging question that would not leave my mind. The churches I had served during my lay and seminary years as assistant pastor had brought me an amazing disappointment. Almost all churches I knew were suffering from a serious spiritual illness. (Now I know that the source of that illness was the large mass of tradition bound believers whose hearts were unplowed ground). The problem included the elders, those who were exclusively holding on to all of the important church offices and duties. Naturally, the atmosphere of the church was cool and indifferent. There wasn't much difference in church membership between the present and ten years ago. Everywhere I went, I saw pastors who in their desire to maintain 'peace' in the church were abandoning any challenge for creating change. I could not believe that the Lord Jesus wanted such a pastoral ministry for me.

Three disappearing factors
in a traditional church - Gospel, Training, Vision

Shortly after graduating from seminary something happened that brought a great turning point in my pastoral ministry. I came to lead the college 'group' in a church in Seoul that only had one student remaining. This was both a crisis and an opportunity for me at the same time. The Korean church college groups in the early 70s were rapidly in decline. Young adults were running out of the church. During that time, the question, "Why are the young adults leaving the church?" never left my mind. It was while wrestling with this question that my eyes were finally opened to discipleship training. Along with that I discovered the fact that in a traditional church there was no gospel, no training and no vision. This discovery was a great shock to me. As I explored it further, it seemed clear to me that the general situation in the traditional church was that there was great doctrine but no gospel. There were many meetings but no training. And there were diverse programs but no vision to capture the people's imagination. I concluded that it was, perhaps, a natural result for young adults to turn their backs on such churches.

Not three years later the college group that I was entrusted with became a gathering of the largest number of Christian students in Korea. The spiritual change and power happening to them through discipleship training was as good as a miracle. God allowed me to see with my own eyes what a healthy community was.

At that time I still did not know the theological foundation for discipleship training. It was while studying in Calvin Seminary and at Westminster Theological seminary in the United States for three years that my eyes were opened. Through a concentrated study and much prayer I came to understand that at the center of the structure of church is apostolicity. The discovery of apostolicity was a radiant sunbeam that penetrated and swept away the dense fog in my mind. Why does the church exist on earth? Why is a lay person one with a calling? Why train the laity and make each a co-worker in the ministry? In other words I came to know clearly why making a lay member into a disciple of Christ is the substance of pastoral ministry.

The remaining task was to return to Korea and experiment with discipleship training in the setting of a local pastoral ministry. The general atmosphere of the Korean church at the time was the misunderstanding that discipleship training was basically for the young adult's ministry. In some regions there was even the fear that discipleship training had a cultic element to it.

The founding of SaRang Church

So, I founded a church based on what I was learning about discipleship. The nine brothers and sisters who agreed to help me were believers with long-standing traditional Christian backgrounds. Their spiritual hearts were largely like the unplowed ground. Other than habitually coming to church on Sundays they were not very interested in spiritual things. They thought it was very fortunate that they were lay members, not like the clergy with a calling and a responsibility for the church.

As the church grew I grew in my willingness to make sacrifices. Yet, the more I committed myself, my studies, my teaching, and my time to discipleship, the more joy I found. I was engrossed in that work and forgot about everything else.

I placed the priority of my pastoral ministry on discipleship training and worked day and night. My goal was to make the traditional believers into disciples of Jesus and send them out to the world. I consistently shared the Word with about ten people in a small group meeting. We met at least once each week for about three hours. We trained this way for over a year. At first, it felt discouraging, but I did not give up until they began to show certain changes and started bearing fruit. After a while, as the church grew, I had to willingly make sacrifices to lead a group everyday during the week. But my joy in ministry only grew. In fact, I was overjoyed. Nothing else seemed to matter to me. The joys I experienced and the blessings of everyday grace are difficult to express fully in writing.

Today, SaRang Community church is a community of ministry where more than two thousand lay leaders, trained directly by their pastors, are working. Every year we train over 400 new lay leaders. Our Sunday worship attendance increases by over a thousand people each year, an extraordinary rate of growth that has continued now for over ten years. 40%-50% of those attending the church for the first time are new believers. This amazing story is the proof of what can happen from a very humble beginning when lay people are trained to become disciples of Jesus and co-workers in the ministry.

Fifteen years ago as a result of requests from many churches, SaRang Community church began a training seminar that simply opened our doors for others to observe, examine, and learn from what God is doing. As of this writing, more than five thousand pastors from the Korean church, the Japanese church, and the Korean American church have gone through this carefully designed training. I am thrilled to see that many pastors have succeeded in breaking up unplowed ground. Through their dedication and commitment to Biblically directed discipleship principles, they are turning over the fertile soil, and the hearts and lives of many in their churches are now reaping a great harvest. By God's grace, most of these churches, too, have experienced amazing growth.

The goal of this book is not to discuss every detail and methodology of discipleship training as we understand it. After meeting with many pastors over a long period of time, I came to the conclusion that the fundamental reason many pastors don't do discipleship training is not that they don't know the concrete methods. Rather, they lack the clear knowledge and conviction to answer the question, "Why should we do discipleship training?" Pastors need an understanding, a vision, a pervasive mentality to move their ministry forward. In other words, they need to develop the philosophy of pastoral ministry which, though it may be unclear to the outside eye, is embedded in every method and structure of their church. My priority, therefore, in this book is to simply explain why I believe discipleship training is the essence of pastoral ministry. In the process you, too, can confirm the amazing fruits of discipleship training by analyzing the setting of SaRang Community Church and exploring how any church rooted in the pastoral ministry of discipleship training can be revitalized.

I want to shout to every pastor not to give up or be disappointed with the traditional church. I want to emphasize as strongly as I can that once traditional lay believers are showered with grace and begin to revive they will reap an abundant harvest far beyond what we can expect to reap from new believers alone.

An Opportunity Still Remains!

The Church is renewed when people are renewed. For a church to become healthy people must become healthy. Changing the organization, constructing a new building, and introducing diverse programs are all important. But please remember that they are not the key to change a church into a healthy vibrant organism and structure. I believe discipleship training is the most biblical prescription to break up the unplowed ground of the church and allow God's Spirit to make change possible.

I speak now to pastors. What remains is your decision. Let's not reproach the laity. Let's not blame 'the church.' Consider the fact that we ourselves are the problem. But when a leader desires to become a disciple of Jesus and is ready to sacrifice his life for others, then no one will be able to stop him. The church can surely be born again through God's Spirit at work in the hands of a committed leader. The Lord is not a heartless master who demands that we do the impossible. He commands us to do what we can. The rest is up to Him. No matter how deeply rooted in traditions, customs, and structures, there isn't a church so hopelessly sick that it cannot be broken up with the plow of the Word and the power of the Holy Spirit.

The Lord's promise, "those who sow in tears will reap with songs of joy," is still available to all churches. It is never too late. Even now, as many churches are being changed through discipleship training, God is demonstrating that the hope of the 21st century is the church. If we have the ears to hear his voice and desire and willingness to obey, then still there remains a limitless opportunity. Soli Deo Gloria!

PART ONE

TODAY'S CHURCH
AND THE LAITY
PP29 - PP64

Chapter 1: What is the Problem?

Explosive Church Growth

The churches in Korea have become the object of worldwide attention. The explosive growth of the Korean churches has brought about numerous compliments. Many words of encouragement have been written about South Korea being the nation with some of the world's largest churches and the most fervent believers. A former missionary to Japan has referred to the revival in the Korean churches as a great drama unfolding in today's mission phenomenon. 1

Horace Allen and Horace Underwood, who were missionaries from America, started their mission endeavors in Korea in 1884 and finally saw their first convert 2 years later in 1886. From that small beginning Christianity grew. A century later, approximately 6 hundred thousand believers were added in 1983 alone. According to one survey, the churches in Korea have seen a 13-15% growth in membership every year. This is 600-700% higher than the national annual population growth rate which is only 2%.

Since the mid 1970s, South Korea has seen an amazing

proliferation of church growth. Nearly four thousand new churches are planted every year, nearly 10 new churches every day.[2] One hundred years of mission efforts in Korea has seen such marvelous achievements that today it can boast that one out of every four in South Korea's population of 40 million is a Christian. For this reason, the centennial year of the mission in Korea which took place in 1984 was cause for a great celebration.

Several underlying causes can easily be identified to explain the rapid growth of the Korean churches. These causes are still prevalent today. A primary cause is ongoing evangelization by evangelical mission organizations. Such efforts have helped propel the church into the world of our alienated young people. With only a Bible in their hands, for the last 20 years, youth evangelists have ignited the flame of the gospel in the hearts of our youth. In addition, the Pentecostal movement has made a powerful impact in South Korea by spiritually awakening many churches. These are some of the external factors that one can identify to account for the rapid growth of the Korean churches.

I, however, would like to make one additional comment. I believe one of the most significant reasons for the rapid growth of the church is the social instability that was brought on by the state of affairs in Korea.

The Korean Christian church has been purified as if through a burning furnace of social unrest. This process of purification has led Korean churches to bear plenty of fruit. In the midst of suffering, the abundance of God's blessings was made clear. For this reason, I stress the fact that the Korean church has not been established in a day.

Controversial Issues of Revival

Currently, a large number of people are voicing either praise or criticism of the churches in Korea. We, ourselves, have been sensing some alarming symptoms which cause concern for the long term health of the Korean church. These observations, admittedly, come from a subjective point of view.

Frankly speaking, I believe that our views of the church should be optimistic because through the resurrection of Jesus Christ the battle has been won. A pessimistic view of the church would be considered unfaithful. Additionally, the growth of the Korean church has always been spoken of in a positive manner. "The Korean church will surely face a second revival." God will use the Korean church in facing the 21st century. "And to accomplish this plan, God will also give the economic growth in Korea so as to support many missionaries." Hearing statements like this, everyone should be encouraged.

But the real problem is that most often the Korean church only focuses on quantitative growth. It is very serious to take no time to evaluate the optimistic view associated with this situation. It doesn't mean that the growth of the church has stopped or that the church is about to close its doors. Rather, these are like symptoms that a patient with heart disease can only feel. What I am concerned with is not the subjective symptoms, but the disease itself. I am compelled to ask, 'Why doesn't revival happen in our days?' Ironically, the answer is, 'Because of the church.' I believe the church itself is the stumbling block to revival.

Korean churches, along with the modernization of Korea, have grown hand in hand over the past 30 years. During this time, the emphasis was on the economic growth of our country. Concerns about moral ethics decreased when they compromised the goal at hand. The ends were more important than the means. Such actions reinforced rumors that Koreans are some of the most dishonest people in the world, scapegoats of mammonism. Korea has lost as much as it has gained because the image of this society reflects bribery and corruption. 'The International Transparency Head Quarters', a private corruption control organization, has reported in Washington that the International Corruption Index showed that in 1996, Korea was ranked 27 out of 54 countries. This is where we stand. Now we are trying to overcome all the economic turbulence which is the result of our high speed development policy.

But how can we be assured that this is only the case in economics? In the church setting, there are similar things from which to rid ourselves. We have considered revival or growth in terms of the quantitative concept. Due to this view, our focus has been on the quantity of people that came to the meetings, how large the building was, and how much revenue was collected. Some church leaders disregarded pastoral ethics to accomplish the quantitative goal and adapted business marketing strategies without testing them; sometimes even introducing shamanism which causes spiritual confusion.

Indeed the scripture reveals that revival includes both quantity and quality. The real meaning of revival is not to lose equilibrium. One aspect that balances a revival is where the quality determines the quantity. But we ought to realize that when the case is vice versa, it goes beyond the essence of Christianity.

Three Absence Phenomenon
The most serious problem caused by the quantitative growth, is

what I call the 'Three Absence Phenomenon'. What is it? It is 1) imaginary quantity, 2) bluff, and 3) virtual image.

Imaginary quantity refers to the falsehood of the Korean churches statistics. We can only guess how serious this problem really is, since church leaders are the last ones to believe in those statistics. To explain this imaginary quantity a bit, here are some analogies. When a man earns 1,000,000 Won but embellishes the truth by saying he makes 3,000,000 Won, we see that his word is not the truth. Another case is a person who lives in a 1000 square feet apartment, but again misconstrues the truth by implying she lives in a very large apartment. Because on each occasion the facts were misrepresented, the person here cannot be trusted.

In Korean churches the fact is that we are not ashamed of exaggerating the numbers in our congregations. Some make excuses by relating it to faith. This may be the case, but what is the real problem? The real problem is that something happened to our conscience - it has been contaminated by materialism. The underlying reason usually relates to the desire to show off. If the un-churched knew about this, than who would ever believe in Jesus?

If we view the church exclusively in terms of size, then we can only perceive that a ministry is successful when there is quantity. This creates a blind spot. In reality, only five percent of churches are considered to be quantitatively successful in ministry. This is clearly only a small portion of the whole. To such statistics, Pastor Bill Hull responds:

Let me be clear: I don't expect to reach the upper five percent of evangelism. Highly talented and creative entrepreneurial pastoral models dominate the upper five percent. They are very effective,

God greatly uses them to minister to the masses, and they can offer a few principles and hints that can assist others in their work. But as models, they do more harm than good. Most pastors would do better if they had never heard of or been exposed to the upper five percent. The upper five percent present the average pastor with an unrealistic, unreachable, guilt-producing model that threatens his ministry. Pressure to be like them has destroyed many.[3]

Church leaders who don't present imaginary quantities, however harsh the criticism, should take those words as bitter medicine which is good for the health. God perceives one soul to be as precious as a thousand. Real revival begins with acknowledging the worth of one soul. We shouldn't forget that the true church has nothing to do with its size. In this sense, the Korean church should hold a campaign to act according to our conscience by transforming imaginary quantity into an actual number.

Secondly, the bluff indicates the weak influence of Christians in society, even though they are found all over in supreme positions of government, high ranking administrative positions, in the financial world, educational world, etc.

A recent newspaper article states that 67.8% of those who were appointed government ministers during 1993 to 1997 were Christians. Despite that fact, our society has gone from bad to worse mentally and morally. A good case in point is when the elders of the church become involved in scandals. What does that say? It's a sign that Korean churches aren't playing the proper role in this society. If Christians cannot be the salt in this world, then it is a bluff. The facts above, showing the impact of the church, are a heartbreak. So, if we really want a revival of the church, we must quickly focus on changing the bluff into real influence. This means repentance and self evaluation.

Lastly, virtual image refers to a Christian's failure to live a life distinctive from the non-believer. Many Christians fail to practice their faith in daily living. There seems to be no difference, therefore, between them and the world. The real lifeblood of Christianity is when faith convicts our personality and life. Thus, believing means acting.

Unfortunately, the Korean church is not considered any different from the rest of our society. Yet, what we have inherited from the tradition of the reformers is to reject any dualism that separates personal faith and social life. Christians must seek a balanced spirituality which is in the world but doesn't belong to the world.

It is only in knowing God that we come to know ourselves- although, as Calvin pointed with equal vigor, "it is only knowing ourselves fully we come to know God fully". Knowledge of ourselves and knowledge of God are given together or they are not given at all. [4]

If our activities of faith are restricted to the church settings, then we are running away from the world which God created. Faith is related to recovering the relationship between God and His corrupted creatures. Believers are to take the important role in this recovering process. Thus, Christians should show respect, interest and dedication to the world, because of their faithfulness, obedience and love for God the Creator. It seems, however, that we are not very good at maintaining the traditions of the reformers. Korean churches have failed to make disciples. In

Korea, many gather to obtain the essentials of life, for example food and health, but there are not many faithful followers of Jesus. Crowds are a virtual image. Thus, we must develop disciples who can prove faith is life and life is faith. That is the sure way to change the virtual image of church to actual circumstances.

Since Christians are becoming the majority of our society, now is the time when people want to see the real characteristics of the church! They want the church to solve their problems. They are waiting for answers not from international affairs but from the living character and life of the layman in their daily lives. But they are being disappointed more and more. Just as if salt loses its taste and is thrown away, the church is becoming the target of people's criticism as useless to society.

Quantitative Expansion Could Be a Momentary Phenomenon

We witness many young people who have been disappointed by the beliefs of the church leaving to find truth in other religions. Every Christian denomination is showing a decrease in growth rate. Ironically, our strategy to increase growth has become the cause of a decline in membership. This creates a contradiction. Yet these side effects to our multiplication efforts have been continuous, though they have not been seen much in developed countries.

I believe that there is validity in the warning issued by Howard Butt. He contends that although America may be ahead of England in many technological spheres, England is ahead in the religious realm. He uses England as an example to keenly analyze the current status of the American churches.

Fifty years ago our English churches were full like your American churches are today. But we were satisfied with big congregations that focused on the pulpit, routine attendance in the pew... and our shallowness. Consequently, people became disillusioned by an ineffectual church and indifferent to her message. And today our churches are empty. Your American churches are crowded with people today, but there is no Biblical or spiritual depth among your laymen. Religion is largely a sentimental Sunday affair which does not radically influence daily life. If something doesn't change fifty years from now your churches will be empty as ours today. If I were an American minister, rather than concentrating on the people outside the church, I would spend all my time seeking the conversion and deepening those who are already church members.[5]

We are well informed of the fact that Green's prophecy has been proven true in the American church within half of a century. There is no guarantee that the Korean churches will not share the same fate as the English churches.

Cultural anthropology professor Kil Sung Choi, contends that the mass swarming into today's churches could always go the other way someday.

I see the surprising growth in Christianity as due to unaffiliated believers being able to accommodate Christianity, not as a result of overwhelming endeavor on the part of the Church nor as a phenomenon of Christian religion becoming indigenous. It is correct to view the occurrence of the revival in the Korean churches retaining a strong possibility of secularization or reversal of the believers who have converted into Christianity.[6]

The Church Growth Research Institute, attached to Kukmin Il Bo, in a November 1997 article, supported doctor Choi's stated concerns of the church 15 years ago. Korean churches showed a growth rate of 41.2% during 1960-70, 12.5% during 1970-80, 4.4% during 1980-90 and from 1991, the growth rate steadily decreased. The growth rate of congregations during 1990-95 was as follows: Full Gospel Kihasung is 0.5%, Presbyterian Tonghap is 0.45%, Methodist is 0.4%, Presbyterian Hapdong is 0.06%. In the interests of accuracy it should also be noted that this growth index doesn't reflect an increase, but rather a decrease if we consider the imaginary quantity of church statistics.

It is true that a revival usually brings quantitative growth. But, as history shows, some have not resulted in a quantitative increase. This is not necessarily a bad thing. For the kingdom of God is like the mustard seed which grows to be a huge tree filling the world.

There is one negative aspect, however, to revivals. It is when a church leader, blind to seeing the worth of one soul, gives in to materialism. God is more interested in the one lost sheep than the rest of 99 sheep. In some sense, God is not pleased with the majority (I Cor. 10:5). If the majority identify the glory of God with their work, then God will be displeased with them for sure. God was not pleased with David when he wanted to take a census of the population and He is the same today (I Chron. 21).

Weber describes the different ways of counting between God and man in this way:

The result of true evangelism may be the cutting down of the number of church members discovering the cost of discipleship often results in a decline in church membership mission in the New Testament is not connected with statistics, but with sacrifices. [7]

I believe that it will benefit Korean churches to listen attentively to what is really being said.

In order for a revival not to turn into a futile attempt, the Korean churches must advance with the knowledge of a greater vision of God. Churches need to change their clothes. It is time to clothe ourselves with the Lord Jesus Christ and not the desires of the sinful nature (Romans 13:4, NIV). Our problems will not be resolved by rebuilding the church structure in a western architectural design nor will they be settled by sewing another red stripe on the sleeve of a pastor's gown. I am convinced that there is no other way than to teach and train the laity, who are the faces and the essence of the church. They need to be trained to become better disciples of Jesus. The life of our churches is hanging on this. It has become a life or death issue

Didn't the problems facing the church of Jerusalem cause a layperson to become the great leader (Acts 6:1-7)? There is always an opportunity for us, too, for God can turn misfortune into a blessing.

Chapter 2: Rediscovering the Laity as God's Will for the Church

In the twentieth century, if there has been an awakening that threw new light into the church, it is the lay movement. After World War II, this movement sprang up everywhere. Research theses on this subject have burst forth on a torrential scale and practical lay training manuals have stacked up in bookstores. It is even said that the twentieth century movement in rediscovering the laity can be comparable in size and impact to the Reformation of the sixteenth century. This should not be treated as an exaggerated opinion but rather a revelation of the strong will behind the lay movement. If the Reformation rejuvenated the true image of the church for God, then the lay movement can restore the true image of the church to the world.

Kraemer attributes two practical motives as to why there has been a sudden move to awaken the laity.[8] One was a strong effort on the part of laymen to practically apply the latent powers within to be witnesses in a modern society that was expanding at an exponential rate. The other cause was the ecumenical movement.

If the arousing of the laymen is entirely due to the needs of the times, however, then it becomes nothing more than a one-sided bread and butter theory. The call and roll of the laymen must be regarded as a biblical mandate, superceding the needs of the times. Observation of many evangelical mission organizations with no direct connections to the ecumenical movement reveals that they are convinced the laymen's call toward the world is the voice of God from the Bible. Our exclusive foundation for reformation is the Bible. When the truth that is hidden in the Word becomes understandable, under the guidance of the Holy Spirit, it addresses needs. This is the point of contact between truth and the realities of life. This is how we know the will of God. In this regard, I believe what John Stott says here to be very pertinent.

> The real reason for expecting the laity to be responsible, active and constructive church members is biblical not pragmatic, grounded on theological principle, not on expediency. It is neither because the clergy need the laity to help them, nor because the laity want to be of use, nor because the world thinks this way, but because God Himself has revealed it as His will. Moreover, the only way in which the laity will come to see and accept their inalienable rights and duties in the Church is that they come to recognize them in the Word of God as the will of God for the people of God.[9]

The Pulse of Church History

If we look back into the history of the church, we see that in the initial stages of the church, laymen kept their position intact.

In the New Testament Church era and for the next centuries, the focus of the church was on the laity. An ancient church historian, Harnack, has concluded that,

It is impossible to see in any one class of people inside the Church chief agents of the Christian propaganda... we cannot hesitate to believe that the great mission of Christianity was in reality accomplished by means of informal missionaries (the laity).[D]

Although the early life of the church, which was characterized by laymen functioning in their rightful place, was cut short and the Dark Ages took over, throughout its history the torches of reformation that often lit the darkness of the night were usually carried in the hands of the laity. This is especially true of the Wycliff movement in the fourteenth century and Martin Luthers religious reformation which was a wake up call of the period. Periods of reformation and revival were usually a time of restoration for the laymen while eras of stagnation and corruption were usually the times of tyranny by the clergy.

In fact, a church whose lay members are either in slumber or in a state of standstill cannot be said to be healthy. In some sense, when the line dividing clergy and laymen becomes blurred, it can foster greater works of the creative ministry of the Holy Spirit. It might even sound radical, but it is imperative that we search deeply the truth of the following opinion:

The first reformation took the Word of God exclusively out of the hands of the clergy and put it into the hands of the people. The second reformation is to get the ministry exclusively out of the hands of the clergy and into the hands of the people, where it rightly belongs.[■]

44

It is very encouraging to observe that there is a recent increase in the recognition and study of the importance of the laity by the leaders of the Korean churches. Although the change may be a little late, with firm conviction and greater investment in the laity, we could see a reformation and find solutions to the problems that we originally faced with apprehension. This would bring about a renewal to the character of the church. Rediscovering the laity should not be consigned to any mission organization or any international bodies. It is the call of the times for local pastors who, in their sweat and tears, must dedicate themselves to develop the potential of their lay members.

If we continue to avoid developing laypeople into better disciples of Christ, and keep the church clergy-centered with all our attention to worship and rituals, we might succeed in increasing our quantity, but we will fail to increase quality. The result will be a stagnant church.

I do not believe that this is what our Lord Jesus Christ, the head of the church, would wish. The mob that disappointed the heart of Jesus in Galilee cannot be left to raise its voice inside the present church. Pure Christianity is found in one or two spoonfuls of leaven rather than in many bags of flour. This, I believe, is one of the greatest lessons that can be learned by daily reflecting on the 2000 years of church history.

Fortunately, a growing number of church leaders are perceiving the significance of properly developing and fully mobilizing the laity. This is an effective way for the church to operate if it is to accomplish its role as a leaven in our ever-changing, twentieth century society.

Chapter 3: Who are the Laity

The Principal Form of the Church

Laikos, the Hebrew word for laymen or the laity, is not found in the New Testament. However, the meaning is same as the word laos which does appear frequently in the Bible. The word simply means 'people', a 'people group', or a 'mob of people'. In secular terms, it was used to describe the population in the Hellenistic world. In biblical terms, it was first used to distinguish the Jews from the non-Jews (Acts 4:10). Later, it came to mean the New Israel, including the foreigners who believed in Christ, or, in other words, the Church in the last days (Acts 15:14). There is, however, no instance of it being used in the Bible to point out a special portion of people within a group. It is always used as a general term including all the people of a group.[2] Therefore, keep in mind that the original meaning of laymen refers to chosen people having Christ in their hearts (also Christians, disciples), or to the whole Church which is the body of the believers. Furthermore, the meaning of the word laymen does not include a divisive line between the clergy and the rest of the believers. As John Stott

46

has pointed out, the only time it is used in the Bible to differentiate between people is when it is used to set the children of God apart from the world.[B] In other words, there is no base for dividing the children of God within the church. Therefore, even the office of the clergy itself does not constitute a different status from the rest of the believers.

For clarification, it would be helpful to delve into a few basic concepts of the church. The Bible reveals a few ideas on the character of the Church; such concepts as, the people of God, the temple of the Holy Spirit, and the body of Christ. These explain the reasons for designating each and every layperson as the principal form of the Church and provide answers to why there is no positional status difference between the clergy and the laity.

Let me first explain the concept of the Church as the gathering of God's chosen people. All who believe in Jesus Christ are God's people chosen by Him. There can be no difference between the clergy and the laity relative to being chosen, since all have been called out by grace. This emphasizes the fact that there is no room for special status or position within the Church.

"The Church is always and in all cases the whole people of God, the whole ecclesia, the whole fellowship of the faithful."[14] Therefore, all believers are members of God's people and The Church from basically equal positions. Without a question, each and everyone is chosen, is a believer, and is a brother or a sister.

Next is the concept of God's temple. All who believe in Jesus Christ are freed from sin (Romans 6:18-23). They no longer belong to themselves but to Christ who has freed them (I Corinthians 6:19). Therefore, a believer is a spiritual person who is filled with the Holy Spirit. The Holy Spirit has come upon the Church and each believer, changing the whole Church into a new creation. In this sense, the Church is the temple of God. From within, all believers have become a holy priesthood offering spiritual sacrifices acceptable to God (I Peter 2:4,5). This sacrifice is not a material but spiritual sacrifice of prayer, praise and thanksgiving, and repentance. There is no difference, therefore, between clergy and laypeople in having the indwelling presence of the Holy Spirit, and in being the holy priesthood offering spiritual sacrifice with the help of the Holy Spirit. Lay men and women who form the church are naturally the principal composition of the church and are the community of the church itself. Clergy are also a strategic part of the Church, but only by virtue of membership in the Church community.

Third is the concept of the body of Christ. Paul said that the Church is the body of Christ (Ephesians 1:23). The head is Christ and the body is formed from the believers (I Corinthians 12:27, Colossians 1:18). A believer participates in the body of Christ when he is baptized with the Holy Spirit (I Corinthians 12:13), and experiences supernatural oneness with the body of Christ when he partakes of the bread and the cup in communion (I Corinthians 10:16,17). The Church as the body of Christ refers to the fact that each believer, as an essential part, is important and is equally endowed with special talent and dignity. So, it is imperative that everyone serve with care, love, joy and thanksgiving. Can there be any difference between the clergy and laity in this sense?

A distinctive quality of the body is that it brings all believers into an interdependent relationship. This is so crucial that if a believer is severed from the Church, it is difficult to maintain his or her faith normally.

Faith does not exist by itself, but in the actual men who believe. And these men do not live as separate individuals, isolated believers... they have their faith through the community, which as a believing community proclaims the message to them and provokes the response of faith in them... it can be a relief as well as a burden to realize that despite our total individual responsibility our faith is part of the wider and richer, old and yet young faith of the believing community that is the Church. [5]

Deep dependent relationships among the believers assumes the necessity of mutual cooperation. They cannot exist if they do not help one another. Not only should clergy serve the laity, but also lay members must take the responsibility for the ministry of spiritual service toward one another. For this purpose, the Holy Spirit gives the manifestation of the Spirit to each member individually (I Corinthians 12:11). The manifestation of the Spirit is equal, without exception or distinction. Through the manifestation of the Spirit, each member is combined into the body and shows equal concern for one another (I Corinthians 12:24, 25).

As we have seen through a brief study of these concepts, there is not one basis found in the biblical concept of Church for a higher position of the clergy over the laity. On the contrary, it has demonstrated that the two are equal and have no positional difference. Even so, in reality, lay members of our churches are often treated as if they are lower in class than the clergy. There is a common perception that clergy is the most important part of the Church. Many behave as if the laity are the servants who exist for the leaders. How wrong can we be?

How can lay men and women recover their original status and

fulfill their true role in this environment? If we truly desire to activate the laity and change the character of our churches to build a healthy Church, then we must no longer accept the abnormal and unbiblical act of pushing away the superiority of the clergy status with the right hand while secretly allowing it with the left hand.

The Distorted View of the Word Laity

The word 'laity' is commonly defined as all believers excluding clergy. Why is that? A quick review of Church history can show how the original meaning of the word laity became distorted. Around the third century when the Roman Empire officially recognized it, the Church grew at a tremendous rate, while at the same time, it could not avoid becoming institutionalized. Naturally, professional clergy appeared on the stage to lead these institutions. The issue of what to formally call the general population of believers soon came up. The answer to this dilemma was provided by Bishop Cyprian, who publicly used the word laity to describe them. The titles clergy and laity came to separate those who were professionally working for the Church and those who were not, just as the priests and the people were set apart in the Old Testament period. As a result, the word laity soon deteriorated from its original meaning into a legal usage presumed two tiers of class existence within the Church. It has been commonly used this way for the last 1,500 years or so.

It is abnormal, to say the least, to continue the deteriorated usage of the word laity within the Church when we are all one people and the same children of God. It is important, however, to not only understand the original meaning of the word at our present stage, but it is also essential to comprehend its deterioration over time. Here is the reason why the word is being used even now. Over 99% of the church are lay members. There are many churches in our world but the most visible church is the laity. Though recent media headlines and stories may give a different impression, the world does not watch and observe the clergy in the churches but the laity. They are the ones who will give concrete lessons from their own life situations about the kingdom of God abiding in their lives. After Pentecost, the first church which the people in Jerusalem saw was the laypeople who were singing about the joys of their new life and the change brought about by the teachings of the Apostles.

All the believers were together and had everything in common. Selling their possessions and goods, they gave to anyone as he had need. Everyday they continued to meet together in the temple courts. They broke bread in their homes and ate together with glad and sincere hearts. (Acts 2:44-47, NIV)

At the present moment, the laity appear to have two differing perceptions of the church. A church can either have the courage that David had when he challenged Goliath, or it can be full of fear like King Saul.

The laity can not be independent of the church. They can no longer be spectators who come to church regularly to briefly be inspired by pious rituals and patrons who contribute to the operation of the church. Neither can they be naive servants blindly obeying every command. Lay members are the subjects of the church, not the objects. They are as much a part of the body of Christ as the clergy. They have received the call from the Lord, who is the head, and have received spiritual gifts as it befits each one of them so that they may do their best to function as a part of the body.

The Slumbering Laity

Unfortunately, in many churches, the laity are slumbering. Giants with amazing powers and potential are not functioning. Of course, every church has a group of a few zealous and self-sacrificing laymen. Through the blessings that God has already given to the Korean churches we have seen how precious and beautiful their service is. However, I would like to stress that even these excellent lay members can not perform all the regular service activities that are needed to maintain the functions of a church. Furthermore, a minority of model lay people in the Korean churches have been reduced to the role of passive handmaidens who continually hold on to the hem of the shirts of the clergy. And this is not all. There is more. Passive laymen are sometimes monopolized by a few in the church. Unfortunately, this phenomenon is approved by many as a reasonable practice.

Some leaders contend that the passive state of the laity is not the leaders responsibility but that it is the result of the natural outcome of the actions by the lay members themselves. There is some truth to this thought. It is the corrupt custom of many laymen to produce excuses so as to avoid whenever the leaders diligently desire to teach and train them. They say they don't have time. They reason only theology students or seminarians have enough professional education to evangelize, teach or counsel. They surmise that since their life and work outside in the world is so difficult and busy, they only need to do what they are told to do and keep the back seat of the church warm. Consequently, they easily give up, just as Esau gave up his title of heir, the most fulfilling responsibility that God has given them.

To reflect on the words of Sir Lawrence:

What does the layman really want? He wants a building which looks like a church; a clergyman dressed in the way he approves; a services of the kind he's been used to, and to be left alone. [6]

Just look around and see how many people utter similar words behind the pretext of being just a layperson.

If a church leader caves under such demands by the laity, then it is, in my opinion, the same as that ministry experiencing death. Inevitably, Jesus, the head of the Church, will hold the leaders responsible if the laity have been held back or have become ill. If they have built their house with wood or hay that can be burned, the leaders are liable and not the laity. Therefore, whatever excuses the laymen might come up with are not enough reasons for the leaders to justify the relinquishment of their responsibility. There might have been some shepherds who were eaten by the lions, but there have never been any who were victimized by his sheep. If the laity are in the wrong, then to me it indicates that the leader is at fault. Are the lay members remaining in the church as if they are guests or spectators? Are they slumbering and cannot wake up? Then, if so, it is time to remember the command of the Lord and shudder in fear.

Alienation of the Laity from the Important Work

The general reality of the matter is that in most churches, the lay men and women are not taught from the Bible about who they are, what their callings are, and how they should prepare to serve the Lord. This certainly is a detrimental weakness of the modern church. In 1974 at the World Mission Conference held in Lusanne, Switzerland, the Korean participants submitted a report.

Let me give you my opinion of the words, There is no lack in training. It is probable that the participants were considering training to be in the traditional areas of Morning Prayer meetings, church attendance, and church wide visitation programs, which are strong in Korean churches and are geared toward adults. The importance of these in the spiritual growth cannot be overemphasized. However, I believe, if we are honest before God, in order to accurately point out the weakness of these traditional ministerial programs and the resulting spread of social ill within the Church, then to say, no lack is a careless conclusion. Here I address church leaders. Let's be honest. Do we, the leaders, accept the lay members as active ministry equals by providing a concrete program of spiritual training? [7]

At the Lusanne Conference, a Mr. Madison, a layman, made an unforgettable statement to the leaders who were gathered there. We must not forget that similar words are being spoken around us.

In some ways, the fact that the Protestant Church did not firmly establish the structure of the laity as its principal form appears like destiny. It can be identified as a type of cancerous growth cultivated little by little since the beginning of the Reformation. We should give attention to what Hendrick Kraemer has keenly pointed out. [8]

It (Calvin's Polity of the Church) was the most dynamic of Church orders which issued from the Reformation. His high conception of the excellence, indispensability and authority of the minister, necessitated by the need for a well-led Church, implied however involuntarily a neglect of the real significance and relevance of the laity. [9]

Kraemers criticism is not an overstatement. It is no hidden fact that over the last 400 years, many leaders of the churches that have upheld the theology of Calvinism have professed and declared the priesthood of all believers on the outside, and yet, on the inside, have behaved as if they are like the priests of the Old Testament period. The overemphasis on the importance of the clergy system, which classified clergy and laity as different, has promoted a both dualistic view of spiritual life inside the Church and social life outside the Church. It has also cultivated feelings of inferiority in many lay members because of their perception that they are living a life less holy than the clergy. Additionally, the clergy is full of vanity to think that lay men and women can maintain their spiritual life through sermons only. As a result, many have disregarded the task of raising powerful and active laypeople as partners.

We live in an age where courage and diligence are needed to revive the biblical image of the laity that has been lost. For this purpose, we, the leaders of the Church, must put all our energy into this issue. A church whose lay members are sleeping will decay into nothing but a powerless mob which cannot help the world at all. If the Church is to take responsibility for the coming age of permissiveness, it must realize there is no other way then to awaken the laity from their slumber.

Chapter 4: The Relationship between the Clergy and the Laity

The Position of Clergy as given by the Lord

If laypeople are defined as the principal form of the Church, then how should clergy maintain its relationship with the laity? This is one of the most frustrating problems which has yet to be solved. Historically, the Church has always faced a dilemma concerning this relationship. To be true, it is very difficult to maintain the importance of the clergy without falling into a dualistic separation of clergy and laity. The sensitive relationship between clergy and laity can also become most hurtful. At its worst, it develops into strife between ecclesiastical authority and its opposition. John Stott says,

The spirit of clericalism is to despise the laity, and behave as if they did not exist. The spirit of anticlericalism is to despise the clergy and to behave as if they did exist, or rather, since they do exist, to wish they didn't. [20]

Some say that the ecclesiastical authorities themselves have caused the opposition. Because the clergy often surreptitiously oppress and disregard the laity, they deserve to be rejected or ignored as leaders on the basis of the equality of all believers before God. But though lay members have often been hurt by obnoxious clergy, and if they reject Biblical church order, then their actions are no different than those who favor ecclesiastalism. In human terms, the opposition, the plaintiff, may receive sympathy over the ecclesiasticum, the defendant. But in the highest court, the Bible, if the clergy system itself is opposed, there can be no support of that position. The office of clergy is an office that was solemnly appointed for the Church by Christ himself. "It was He who gave some to be apostles, some to be prophets, and some to be evangelists, and some to be pastors and teachers, to prepare God's people for works of service, so that the body of the Church may be built up" (Ephesians 4:11-12).

When John Calvin discussed the importance of the clergy, he saw the system as an essential key that brings all the believers in the Church together, an element that protects the Church, and a component that is personally overseen by the Lord himself. Therefore, he concludes that opposition to the clerical system is not acceptable.

Whoever, therefore, either is trying to abolish this order of which we speak and this kind of government, or discounts it as not necessary, is striving for the undoing or rather the ruin and destruction of the church. For neither the light and heat of the sun, nor food and drink, are necessary to nourish and sustain the present life as the apostolic and pastoral office is necessary to preserve the church on earth. [21]

We must therefore challenge the dualism which explains the relations between clergy and laity in terms of departmentalization. Of course we should largely restrict the administration of Word and Sacraments to the clergy. It is not lawful for any man to take upon him the office of public preaching, or ministering the sacraments in the congregation, before he lawfully called, and sent to execute the same. But we must be clear that this is a question of order not of doctrine. [22]

Orderliness cannot hold as much authority as doctrine. If the process of a theological seminary education, ordination, followed by a church position, belongs in the category of orderliness, then the possibility of a disorderliness which contradicts such orderliness cannot be completely eliminated.

Those unwholesome meetings and groups that knowingly or unknowingly create misunderstanding still happen around us. Even some young people who used to be a part of evangelical mission organizations in the past are reflecting antagonistic tendencies toward the clerical system. This is tragic. A recent Korean example is an instance where rejecting the position of a clergyman turned into a major effort to disclaim the Church system itself.

Fortunately, there is only a minor number of people who engage in this type of criticism. There is, however, a group that is a greater threat. Whenever the will of the laity is emphasized and an equal position in the ministry is suggested, some immediately see it as a threat to the clergy system. They refute any attempt to minimalize this threat, citing an example of some small lay group that has fallen off from mission organizations. They even use this material to defend their position and authority. To these people, even a Biblically based discussion about the role and the responsibility of the laity is futile. Therefore, it is wise to keep in mind that those who negate the role of the laity as well as those who oppose the ecclesiastical system can fall into the same pit.

Does this mean that the clergy has no authority over the laity? No. Strictly speaking, the clergy has the authority in ministry that the laity do not have. Not all laymen can become pastors. As Martin Luther pointed out, there is a clear separation in the role of the pastor.

Calvin expresses this authority as an uncomfortable authority, because, instead of it being an authority through power, it is an authority with submission. In other words, a pastor is not God. And yet, it is a sacred authority that should not be handled lightly.[23]

The Meaning of the Laying of Hands

Traditionally, the Church officially recognized ecclesiastical authority through the ceremony of the laying on of hands. What does the Bible say about the authority received in this manner? The Bible shows four types of laying on of hands.

The first and primary reason for laying on hands is for commissioning purposes. Moses ordained Joshua as his successor (Numbers 27:23). The Apostles ordained seven believers as deacons through laying on of hands (Acts 6:60). Timothy received laying on of hands at an elders meeting (I Timothy 4:14).

Laying hands on the sick is a second Biblical type (Mark 16:18).

A third is prayer, with the laying of hands for the filling of the Holy Spirit (Acts 8:17).

A fourth reason for the laying of hands was to revive the gifts of the Spirit (I Timothy 16).

I conclude from this that the Biblical ceremony of laying on of hands is not only limited to the commissioning of clergy. So, there does not seem to be an absolute ecclesiastical power in and of itself based on the laying on of hands. And yet, there are few facts with which we need to exercise care. Laying on of hands was commanded by God (Numbers 27:18, 23). It was a public act, not a private occasion (Numbers 27:19). And it was God who chose the individual on whom hands were laid.

In this sense, Calvin saw the laying on of hands as dedicating the commissioned one to God. And he regarded it as a kind of ecclesiastical command when the Apostles continued the tradition. He described the spiritual blessing from the laying of hands as follows: "And surely it is useful for the dignity of the ministry to be commended to the people by this sort of sign, as also to warn the one ordained that he is no longer a law unto himself, but bound in servitude to God and the church." [24]

Therefore, the authority of the laying on of hands comes from publicly acknowledging that one who is sent by Christ to the Church to take care of the sheep. Through this ceremony, the whole church can see the personification of God's calling in that one person. Otherwise, it would prove to be difficult to find another acceptable method of confirming a calling from God to be a pastor. The whole church could see this as an act of confession of faith in the authority of the pastor.

Authority That Comes from Serving and Modeling

Even if a clergyman has been ordained by the laying on of

hands and becomes a leader of a church, his authority is not for controlling, but of dependency on the whole church, including the laity. John Stott depicts this fact by stating that, although the calling of God as a pastor is important, it cannot take a place above the Church, which is the community of believers chosen to belong to God himself. As such, clergy cannot reign over the church, because they belong to the laity to whom they are called to serve.

So if anybody belongs to anybody in the Church, it is not the laity who belongs to the clergy, but the clergy who belongs to the laity. We are theirs, their servants for Jesus' sake. It is, therefore, when writing to a layman rather than to a bishop that we should sign our letters I have the honor to be, sir, your obedient servant![25]

In reality, from my experience, to say that the authority of clergy comes by belonging to the laity could be a stumbling block to many pastors in Korea. Perhaps this is also true wherever in the world we find well structured churches. It is not because this is biblically unsound, but because many of us are so addicted to having authority, that it is difficult to accommodate such a statement with an Amen. We should meditate on the confession of Paul : "For we do not preach ourselves, but Jesus Christ as Lord, and ourselves as your servants for Jesus' sake" (II Corinthians 4:5). What is the main point of this verse? It is that a servant of the Lord is a servant of the laity. When we bow down and submit to this truth, then our authority as clergy and the glory of the laity as the principal makeup of the Church can come alive.

Jesus showed the ultimate servanthood

Jesus said to them, "the kings of the Gentiles lord it over them; and those who exercise authority over them call themselves Benefactors. But you are not to be like that. Instead, the greatest among you should be like the youngest, and the one who rules like the one who serves. For who is greater, the one who is at the table or the one who serves? Is it not the one who is at the table? But I am among you as one who serves" (Luke 22:25-27).

The difference between the authority of the clergy and the world is that it comes from serving. As the Apostles proposed to return to their original intent, the words they used were, "And we will give our attention to prayer and the ministry of the word" (Acts 6:4). The Greek word for the ministry of the word used in this passage is 'diakonia', which means 'to serve'. As we know, 'diakonia' implies serving like a servant. Even the ministry of the word, which granted the authority to the Apostles, is laden with the meaning of serving the laymen. If preaching and teaching are serving others, then what more can we say concerning other works?

Paul himself, when he looks at his three years of pastoral ministry in retrospect at the farewell service with the elders of Ephesus, summarizes genuine service as serving the sheep. "I served the Lord with great humility and with tears, although I was severely tested by the plots of the Jews. You know that I have not hesitated to preach anything that would be helpful to you but have taught you publicly and from house to house. I have declared to both Jews and Greeks that they must turn to God in repentance and have faith in our Lord Jesus" (Acts 20:19-21). Paul refers to himself as a genuine servant through the cross of poverty (Acts 20:33-35 reference). He did not see poverty as a service itself, but, like Jesus, saw it as a means for service. The true service of the clergy is to guide the laity to the proper place in which to fulfill their position. If this is not accomplished, then even hardship due to poverty does not give them right to say they are indeed serving laypeople.

Calvin, with Luther, places the emphasis upon duties, obedience, services, and functions of the ministerial office rather than status, power, and dignity. And these Reformation leaders did not sweep the minister or priest away, but they declared that the vocation of the layman was as deeply religious as that of the priest, in fact, it too was a priestly vocation. [26]

The clergy leader is the one who understands the priesthood of the believers. He works along side the lay members, not in place of them. Therefore, the importance of the clergy comes from helping and guiding the laity to take on the privilege of priesthood, not from representing or replacing others.

One more thing of which we should be mindful is that the position of clergy is a position of setting an example, especially in the areas of servanthood. "Not lording over those entrusted to you, but being examples to the flock" (I Peter 5:3). A demanding attitude is opposite to an attitude of serving. Clergy must be setting examples of service, not demanding, and when it is done right, the whole church will submit (I Peter 5:5). Therefore, the honor of the authority of the laying on of hands only comes when the clergy, who receive the calling, show an example through a ministry of serving. If, however, the position of clergy has degenerated to nothing but a flashy ecclesiasticism of oppressing lay members with feelings of inferiority and inability, then it has become a sin that injures the Church and pollutes the purity of the office of the clergy.

If the relationship between the clergy and the laity are to be properly maintained, the only possible way is to be fully convinced that lay members are the Church. Clergy is a servant appointed by God to serve the Church and do everything possible to point the Church to the right way according to God's will. I believe there is a need in our present churches for the clergy to humble themselves as servants of God. And the laity must humbly submit to the authority of the servants they are under; and so recover their original function.

PART TWO

MINISTRY PHILOSOPHY
- YOUR THEOLOGY OF THE CHURCH
PP65 - PP114

MINISTRY PHILOSOPHY
- YOUR THEOLOGY OF THE CHURCH

MINISTRY STRATEGY
- TRUE DISCIPLESHIP

MINISTRY METHOD
- DISCIPLESHIP TRAINING

MINISTRY FIELD
- THE EXAMPLE OF SARANG

Chapter 5: What is Ministry Philosophy?

It is a surprising fact that many leaders of the Church never really think deeply about the church or what it is. Often the most they can reiterate is some partial knowledge from the systematic theology class they took at the seminary or some information from their denominational rules booklet. Somehow we have all become indolent in our thought life. Yet, if a pastor stops continually asking himself what the church is and what its mission is, then he is forgetting a key Biblical principle. A pastor must have for the church and himself the spiritual priority of constantly reforming and growing. We must not overlook the serious consequences this partial inconsistency has on the entire ministry of a church. It may be more than we can imagine.

A leader who discovers such contradiction in his own ministry must earnestly look deeply into the Word to search out the mission of the Church.[1]

A pastor must always be asking, 'What is the church?' How he sees the church will determine the direction his ministry goes. For example, if he sees church simply as a place of worship, he may prioritize issues related to the building and the order of the worship. If he views church as a place for hurt and abused people to get together for fellowship and healing, it is not difficult to imagine such a ministry taking a completely different direction. So let's stop for a moment and answer the questions: 'What is the church?' and 'Why does it exist?' At the same time, let's try to verify that the answers given are correct.

Rick Warren has spoken words of wisdom about the Church.

Every church is driven by something. There is a guiding force, controlling assumption, a directing conviction behind everything that happens. It may be unspoken. It may be unknown to many. Most likely it's never been officially voted on. But it is there, influencing every aspect of the church's life. What is the driving force behind your church? [2]

The ministry philosophy is the propulsion that moves the church. It is not an overstatement to say that most frustrations and discouragement in ministry come because of the lack of solid philosophy. In other words, uncertainty in leadership as to where the church is going and why wreaks havoc with a congregation. The ministry philosophy of a leader sometimes is hidden behind the methodology. Often times, the success of a ministry is accorded to a methodology and the philosophy or principle hidden behind it is overlooked. A healthy church does not depend exclusively on the methodology. So establishing a ministry philosophy is of the utmost importance.

At SaRang we have special interest in making disciples in order to activate the laity. Making disciples of the church members is not some kind of temporary theological trend or methodology. It must be understood as being based on the Bible, and the fundamental theme that is aligned with the essence and the calling of the church. How we answer what the church is and why it exists will alter our philosophy of ministry, which in turn will determine what the strategy and method of the ministry will be. In this sense, a pastor's philosophy of ministry is none other than a group of convictions gathered from his own doctrine of the church. Let me emphasize once again. Have a philosophy of ministry. To achieve this, study the theory of the church again. Repeatedly ask yourself, 'What is the Church?' until you are so certain of the answer that you will not be confused about the mobilization of the laity.

A Subject That Did Not Receive Attention for a Long Time

The subject of church is something with which we are all familiar, yet at the same time, is much misunderstood. Everyone considers it public knowledge, yet very few take time to seriously examine it. That is why many clergy do not wrestle with the doctrine of the church, and subsequently, many carry on their ministry with limited or incorrect visions.

Neglecting church doctrine is not only a personal issue, but also a problem of church history. A quick glance at church history easily shows that, compared to the other doctrines, the doctrine of the church has rarely received direct or major attention. As we are well aware, issues such as the doctrine of Christianity and the doctrine of trinity became objects of particular interest already in the 4th and 5th century due to the appearance of the cults that threatened the church. And it was possible to consolidate them doctrinally. The doctrine of salvation was the favorite of Protestantism during the reformation in the 16th century and has remained as the foundation of Christian truth. On the other hand, until the beginning of the 20th century, Christianity rarely wrestled with the doctrine of the church. This in fact is publicly mentioned by Plorops at the first conference of WCC in 1948. In his keynote speech, he hit the mark when he prophesied that this present century would be the century of the doctrine of the Church. In the past couple of decades, many significant theses and books have been published on the doctrine of the church. Sad to say, until the 1980s, the subject of the doctrine of the church has also been outside the interest of the Korean churches. With so much time spent living and working in the church, we did not have the attitude of the reformers in asking ourselves as frequently as we should what the church is. Naturally, not having formed a satisfactory philosophy of ministry, ministries were created with old and outdated notions.

A Clearly Defined Philosophy Will Label a Person Possessed

Many clergy agree that in order to turn over the soil of their ministry into a good quality church, activating the laity through discipleship training is about the only solution. However, this cannot be accomplished with vague ideas. Mimicking others who are doing it isn't the way, either. This will only cause one to give up easily because of the hardship or lack of fruit, turning him into a ministry gypsy, looking around again for something new.

The person who can do discipleship training is the one who is completely certain and convinced that his self-discovered philosophy of ministry is a revelation from God, so much so that the strong fire inside of him will not let him stay quiet. At one time, Jeremiah, finding it too hard, wanted to quit proclaiming God's word to his perverse people. He then bemoaned the fact that he could not quench the fire inside him (Jeremiah 20:9). Those who are conducting discipleship training must be this passionate. Borrowing from Jeremiah's words, we should all be able to shout, "If I say I will not do discipleship training, it is like a fire shut up in my bones. I am weary of holding it in, indeed, I cannot."

When one has a philosophy of ministry, fire in his bones, and a clear vision for tomorrow, even if enormous sacrifices are demanded he cannot stop. Discipleship training is almost impossible if a pastor does not have total commitment, to the point of being labeled possessed. It is like a barren land where a seedling can dry up quickly and die. If it doesn't dry up, then it is stepped on. There are those who are dead set against discipleship training. Many are terribly afraid of any change in their predisposed pattern of belief. Not only this, the thought of abusing oneself with discipleship training when it is already impossible to listen to the requests of the congregation due to lack of time from just performing such basic demands as sermon preparation, visitation, and administration, is enough to give one nightmares. From this perspective, feeling so ambivalent, how could discipleship training truly be a priority?

Here's the question, do you really want to mobilize the laity? If so, then you must become as one possessed. Jesus was labeled possessed and so was Paul. You must begin with the feelings that you are in a corner and discipleship training is the only way out. You must have the determination that if you fail to do this, you will leave your ministry.

To accomplish this, the first priority is to formulate your philosophy of ministry. The closer your philosophy is to the essence of the church, the better you are positioned to have a balanced ministry. The door of opportunity opens when you are aligned with the essence of things. Once the philosophy is formulated, strategies develop and, naturally, the methodology of the ministry becomes definite.

So think about this again. What is the church? Why does it exist?

Chapter 6: What is Church?

Definition of Church

The basic definition of church is that it is the people who are called by God, in Christ (I Corinthians 1:1, 2 Ephesians 2:19). It is clearer if the meaning of the word, church is examined more closely. The New Testament contains more than 100 instances of words, parables, and symbols indicating the church. The Greek word, 'eklesia' is the most often used. This word means the gathering of God's people who are called, or, the congregation. More specifically, this word contains the meaning of the process of the congregation coming together and the community of people already gathered in one place.³

God gave birth to his people (John 1:12-13). He made, called, preserved, and saved them. This church of God's people began after the resurrection of Jesus with those who confessed He is Christ and God's own Son. They are new creatures who have been removed from the power of darkness and brought into the kingdom of the Son of God (Colossians 1:13). Therefore, the church is a chosen generation and a holy nation (I Peter 2:9). But because the church is in God the Father, it is not like any other gathering in the world, and because it is in Christ Jesus, it is different from the Jewish synagogue meetings (1 Thessalonians 1:1).

The church, which is God's people called out of the world, can be described as the living, systematic, and public expression of God's sovereignty initiated by Christ's incarnation. If the kingdom of God is the more comprehensive domain of God's sovereignty, then the church is a transitional institution within His reign. The church in a period of transition should earnestly and humbly wait for the kingdom of God so that it will be perfected in the future when the Lord returns. The church has not yet arrived at its final destination but is on its pilgrimage toward the eternal city. The present church, therefore, is a signpost that announces the end, and a billboard that reveals what is to come. When the king comes, the church will inherit the kingdom and this kingdom will be realized throughout the whole universe.[4]

The Calling Is Missing

The definition of the church as God's chosen people is a precious inheritance from the reformers of the doctrine of the church. In some ways, this definition is a perfect definition with nothing more to add or to subtract. But, who would have thought that this perfect definition might ironically be contributing to the handicapping of our present ministries? Let me demonstrate to prove that this is so.

The definition of church as the gathering of the chosen people includes both the invisible church and visible churches. But it is undeniable that the definition, at face value, gives more weight to the invisible church of the 'End Time' than the visible earthly church. Accordingly, the earthly church can appear as if it is already perfect. It gives the feeling of being back home in the Father's house and resting after a long journey. It gives the impression that all else can be forgotten because the rapturous glory in Jesus Christ can be enjoyed freely. But this image of the earthly church is far from the truth. Why? Because the church that is in the world has a specific calling which can even be identified as its reason for existence. That calling is completing the will of God in saving the world. The reason that there are no suggestions or references to this calling may be because it is a good definition of the heavenly church but it is certainly not satisfactory for the earthly church.

Perhaps you think this is jumping around too much. In the past centuries, however, churches that have taught that the earthly church is exclusively God's chosen people have been giving the impression of being intoxicated. Look around with sharpened spiritual eyes. Don't you see many clergy who perceive their ministry to be simply looking after God's chosen people? How many laypeople are there who are half-hearted or indifferent to God's work? They feel relieved that at least they have their salvation and are very satisfied that as lay members they have no special calling. Some clergy do not correct this because they want to parade the authority that comes from being the one who is called.

As a result, how powerless the church is in society. How often it becomes the object of criticism. The majority of laity believe just to earn heaven. They lack a lucid self-conscious desire to lead a spiritual Christian life in order to fulfill their calling. Although they are numerous, they are becoming nothing more than a mob.

We must reflect on why such unsound conditions have prevailed. There are many reasons, but it is necessary to honestly admit that the chief reason is the traditional definition of the church which confused the earthly church with the heavenly church. Any concept or ideology that dulls our consciousness, though it might happen slowly, once it takes place, will steadily bring negative influences to our conduct. The church is God's chosen people. Let's suppose that we continually see the church in this light, on the edge of the doctrine of the church, without ever opening our eyes to view it differently. What would happen to the church?

A denominational supervisor once said, "As I visit around the world, I see that the churches with reformation theology are not growing". Korean churches are no different. We talk a lot, but we are circling around the fence of us. We lack social responsibility. I just cannot come up with any answer even though I have been thinking about the solution. After hearing this, I told him that I thought it might be due to our doctrine of church. Without hesitation he agreed.

The definition of the earthly church, therefore, needs to be reiterated if lay members are to be activated. Being called out of the world is not the only privilege that the earthly church possesses. It also has been sent into the world. If this refers only to the heavenly church, then it has no need to be sent out and has no reason to share the gospel. The church we are serving, however, is a church that is still in the world. We must be able to confess privilege along with calling as our faith. And we must not create a disabled church which only knows the privilege but not the calling. Are you enjoying the privilege of the calling? Then obey the calling to be sent. This is the way the clergy should

76

teach, and the laity should believe and confess, so that the present church can wake up from its muddled sleep.

The New Testament Church is a Local Church

As we discuss the definition of the earthly church, there is another problem we must deal with. What is the true character of the local church? In the New Testament, church is never used to mean just the churches that belong to a certain denomination. In other words, there is no use of the word church to refer to all the churches under the umbrella of the Presbyterian denomination. It is also not used to mean a national church, such as the Korean church. In fact, there is no instance of it being used to mean church in the world. It is only used to mean the universal church or a local church in a region such as Corinth or Thessalonia. Ekklesia refers to the Thessalonian church or to Corinthian church:

Therefore, the local church is not a section or a district of the whole church. Each ekklesia, each congregation, community, Church, however small, however poor, how insignificant, is a full and perfect manifestation of the ekklesia, the congregation, the community, the Church of God.[5]

The local church is not a section of God's church, but it is the church itself, and a definite symbol of its entity. And as it represents God's church, we who are members and are serving in it ought to stand tall. Unfortunately, there are those who are infected by the virus of inferiority. Such a view comes from the germ of comparing one church with another. Once a person is infected, he sees his church as small and shabby like a small crumb off the table. What a wrong point of view. Jesus, who is the head of the church, does not measure his church by size! Why do we always forget the fact that he is not interested in how many are gathering, but who is gathering? Is it because we do not know the true meaning of the local church?

Do you want to mobilize the laity? You must be certain that even the few sheep God has given you are, in fact, God's perfect ekklesia. Take pride in the small local church that you serve, so the world will see God's kingdom coming closer. So when there is a paradigm shift in how you see your ministerial field, then you can dedicate yourself enthusiastically to making one soul into a disciple of Jesus. A pastor who is always longing for a large church will never be able to make disciples.

I am not negating large churches. I am just stating that God's church is not determined by the size. I recently heard a professor at an American seminary speak to the graduates in this way, "I am going to give you one prophecy. No matter how hard you try in your ministry, 80 to 90 percent of you will spend the rest of your life in a small church." Only about 10 percent of you might serve a large church. These are not necessarily encouraging words, but nevertheless they are very close to the truth. A person does not have a large church or a small church just because he desires it. According to the will of God, each is given a church to shepherd. So, you must be certain that, no matter how small or shabby your church might be, it is God's church.

So far, we have examined the weakness in the traditional definition of the church. We have also briefly mentioned the adverse effect this definition has had on laypeople and their sense of calling over a long period of time. What then is the correct definition of the earthly church?

I believe that it can but be defined in this way:

'It is God's people chosen out of the world, and, at the same time, Christ's disciples sent into the world.'

If we are to agree with this definition, then it is necessary to examine more specifically whether the local church indeed understands its calling to be sent out into the world. What indications point to the laity as the called? What is the biblical basis for it, and how do we prove it theologically? These are the important subjects with which we will now deal.

Chapter 7: Challenging the Traditional Doctrine of the Church

Common Criticisms

In the previous pages, I described how even a so-called perfect definition of church can still act contrarily in the ministry field. Let me mention one more thing. The traditional doctrine of church has been so passive concerning missions, that it has weakened the awareness of the earthly church. Consequently, the churches with a reformation theology background are giving the impression that they are taking a passive or apathetic attitude toward the world. How authentic this opinion is, is worth examining.

First, let me introduce several criticisms of the traditional doctrine of the church.

The traditional doctrine of the church comes from the Middle Ages and is no longer suitable for the present age. It poses a problem for the present age Protestant Church to receive the exact criticism the reformers, who lived during the Holy Roman period when the whole world was painted in Christianity, had for the church. When all of the circumstantial elements are considered, however, there is some truth to this criticism.[6]

Here is another criticism.

In the conception of the Reformers and of the majority of seventeenth-century theologians the Great Commission was binding only on the apostles. When they died, Christ's command died with them. It does not extend to the Church which the apostles founded.[7]

This might sound excessively critical. It does not, however, imply that the reformers never mentioned missions in their sermons. In reality, they declared the necessity of salvation for the world many times. Then why is there such a criticism? It is to sharply point out that the reformers doctrine of the church does not fully reflect the absolute calling of the Lord for the earthly church. Later, it will become clear that this criticism is not without a reason.

There is another criticism that we should consider:

The difference between these two worlds is that during the Reformation, the structures of society were for the most part static and fixed, whereas today these structures are fluid and dynamic. The problem is the static way of thinking which is the product of the former age does not suit the age in which we live.[8]

The implication is that while their (Reformers) definition is good as far as it goes, it is inadequate for Christians today, because it says nothing about mission.[9]

Although all Reformational definitions have their point of departure in Scripture, they are not necessarily Scriptural, because Scriptural descriptions of the church arise from the context of mission, whereas Reformational definitions arise from a given situation in society. When the books of the New Testament were written, no notion of a Holy Roman Empire existed. What did exist was the dominating power of pagan Rome. [D]

The identification of a social system as static or kinetic expresses the opinion that the church is either for Christianity or against Christianity in the circumstance in which it exists. The Middle Ages, then, can be said to have been static. In that situation, it was difficult to sense the urgency for the church to proclaim the Gospel to save the world. On the other hand, for the early churches in the New Testament, their existence itself was threatened if they did not spread the Gospel, even with their lives on the line, to advance the kingdom of God. This is obviously a kinetic situation. The church that the New Testament is talking about has this type of kinetic context background. Therefore, though the reformers might have been figures of eminent spirituality, because they were totally submerged in a static condition, there was a limit to their participation in the missions context and their perception of the church through that eye.

Many of the scholars who have brought challenges to the traditional views of the church are from the evangelical camp with backgrounds in Reformed theology. What these scholars are pointing out is not that the doctrine of the church left by the reformers is wrong, but that it contains a serious defect in inspiring the earthly church in its calling to mission. They are expressing their concerns that it is impossible to become a responsible church for the modern society with such a fragile doctrine of the church.

It is very interesting to browse through the commentaries of Luther and Calvin on I Corinthians 12:28 to see how valid the scholar's criticisms are. Here is Calvin on the text:

And in the church God has appointed first of all apostles, second prophets... For the Lord created the Apostles, that they might spread the gospel throughout the whole world, and he did not assign to each of them certain limits or parishes, but would have them, wherever they went, to discharge the office of ambassadors among all nations and languages. In this respect there is a difference between them and pastors, who are, in a manner, tied to their particular churches. For the pastor has not a commission to preach the gospel over the whole world, but to take care of the Church that has been committed to his charge. [1]

Luther expresses an almost identical opinion about the commission:

That the apostles entered strange houses and preached was because they had a command and were for this purpose appointed, called and sent, namely that they should preach everywhere, as Christ had said, 'Go into the world and preach the gospel to every creature.' After that, however, no one again received such a general apostolic command, but every bishop or pastor has his own particular parish. [2]

These two very prominent scholars who were used greatly in the hands of God have interpreted the differences between the

83

apostles and pastors succinctly. But it is surprising that they explain the strict command, 'to make disciples of all nations', which the Apostles received directly from Jesus, as being applicable only to the Apostles. Whatever their intentions were, it is not a mere coincidence that succeeding clergies who inherited the reformers doctrine of the church would be influenced to a rather apathetic attitude toward equipping the laity in the area of missions. I believe it is because they are offered enough justification to think that as long as they are faithful in their churches, they have accomplished their calling. Therefore, it is not an overstatement to criticize the reformers for not having mentioned enough about missions.

The Purity of the Church Was Their Main Concern

Although the Reformers treated the church's responsibility for missions carelessly when they were defining the nature of the church, we cannot fully put the blame on them. They were serving under unique historical circumstances. As we are aware, from 395 AD until the time of the Reformers, the church and the government were so closely affiliated that anyone who seceded from the church could be arrested. It appeared as if the whole world was painted with Christianity. In this kind of environment, mission did not appear to be a pressing problem. Naturally, this doctrine of the church was influenced by the historical circumstances. Hans Kung says:

In any age, the church retains an image of the period and is shaped by the historical circumstances. These words have great meaning. During the first three centuries of the early church, the church and its pagan nations were antagonistic toward each other. Then there was a truce. During the sixteenth century, the two were separated again. Each stage helped to form the image of the church. [B]

During the time of the reformers, Calvin and Luther were very interested in the purity of the church. In other words, they were concerned with the issue of identifying the true church from the false church. It was very important for them to be able to clearly distinguish the difference between the two using the Bible as their resource. As a result, important doctrines of the church were formulated and illustrated by the three famous marks of the true church. They declared that a church that maintained its purity by 1) the proclamation of the word, 2) the administration of the sacraments, and 3) the enforcement of the promotion of the virtue and reproof of the vice, was a true church of Jesus Christ.

We today have received an inheritance that is historical and precious in proportion. They implied that greater distance between the church and the world denoted a truer church. Although Calvin boldly taught that God's sovereignty must be over the whole world, he did not raise his voice to the fact that the church must become the witness of the Gospel to accomplish this work. This is one of the reasons why the reformer's doctrine of the church is criticized as being static. Consequently, over hundreds of years, the church took on the image of being self-centered and narrow-minded, stubbornly and defensively stressing only worship and piety.

If we were to accept the reformer's doctrines of the church as absolutely perfect, and if they were to become our idols, we might obtain unanimity, but at a great cost. We would also be neglecting a core value entrusted to us by the Reformers and the Reformation. I am not saying that their doctrine of the church is all wrong. It is, however, incomplete. Our greatest inheritance from Calvin and Luther is the spirit of Reformation. In order to reform the age that they were living in, they tested, utilized principles, and focused all their energy on using the Bible to find solutions to their problems. We must also live in our own time with that type of mindset.

As Francis Schaeffer warned, we must not confuse the absolute standard for the church recorded in the Bible with the conditional standard that is not mentioned in the Bible. I believe that in any age, the church has the freedom to tackle the demands of the times according to the guidance of the Holy Spirit within the limitations sanctioned by the Bible. If we were to forfeit this freedom and close our eyes to it, then today's church would bring upon itself isolation, or even death." Therefore, if our reformed doctrine of the church does not sufficiently reflect the calling of being sent into the world such that it is not equal to the task of helping the laity realize that calling, then the awkward cloak of the Middle Ages must be cast off. A new cloak must be put on that is essential for this age in which corrupt cultures constantly threaten the church.

In order to accomplish this, we must reexamine the essential apostolic nature of the church which has received illegitimate treatment from the traditional doctrine of the church. The deliberate neglect of the apostolic nature in the theology of the Reformation has negatively contributed to emasculating today's church. The circumstances facing the Twentieth Century church bear a closer resemblance to the situation of the early church than the situation of the church during the Middle Ages. The increase of Christians today does not come near the natural increase in population. The church is surrounded by foreign cultures that are becoming more anti-Christian in nature. Today, the church is facing a civilization which is changing at such a rate that it cannot predict what will happen three years from now. Consequently, we must be open to the apostolic nature of the church and apply it to the modern church. It is urgent for the church of today to equip the laity, who have the most potential for missions, so that they may become witnesses for the gospel like the disciples of the early church were. Rediscovering the Biblical theological meaning of the apostolic nature of the church is the way to solve the problem concerning the laity in the modern church. At the same time, it will become a foundation for developing our doctrine of the church.

Chapter 8: The Apostolic Nature of the Church

The Most Fundamental Nature of the Church

Those who desire to mobilize the laity to their calling through discipleship training must search the doctrine of the church for the basis of their conviction. Without firm Biblical evidence that, in the essence of the church, lay men and women are also called to be sent into the world, just as the Apostles were, they will not be able to convince the laity to go. As the doctrine of the church is reexamined, they will discover that the traditional theology of the Reformation does not have a satisfactory answer. What can be learned there about the essence of the church are holiness, unity and universality. Sometimes the apostolic nature is alluded to, but usually its meaning is reduced and dealt with in sections. [5]

It is easy, therefore, to fall into the trap of thinking that mobilizing the laity is just a personal demand of a pastor. Discipleship training, which mission organizations are successful at, can be imported as a momentary solution. If it is not a part of the essence of the church, there is no need to insist on discipleship training, even if it appears to be a good option.

When I was studying In the United States, at one time I agonized over this precise problem. Then one day in the seminary bookstore, a book opened my eyes and I saw the light. The book was *Church* by Hans Kung, a Catholic theologian, which received favorable appraisal from most Protestants.[15] In Kung's doctrine of the church, the earthly church, as the successor to the Apostles, can confirm that it indeed has a calling to be sent to the world. It can learn that awakening the laity is a command of the Lord. This is because the church in its essence is built on the foundation of the Apostles. Let me explain the apostolic nature of the church more specifically, using Hans Kung as a reference.

The apostolic nature of the church was confirmed by the Council of Nicea in 325 CE as one of the four fundamentals of the church. Since then, much time has elapsed with obvious instances of apostasy in the church. This was done, sometimes, in the name of apostolic succession. By claiming that the papacy is the legal successor to Peter the apostle, the Church of Rome camouflaged its false doctrines as tradition and used the apostolic nature of the church as a necessary and essential prop to justify Catholicism. As a result, the word apostolic has become a term that has naturally been authoritative to the reformers of the church. They took the meaning of the nature of apostolic to be the authority of the papacy. In their fight against the Church of Rome, which insisted that it was apostolic, the reformers themselves did not properly address the apostolic nature of the church, as they should have. As a result, many Protestant scholars have even taken the position that there is no need for apostolic succession. If not adamantly denying, some still went only as far as admitting with Luther that, apostolic nature means truth concerning Christ." They accepted the essence of apostolic to be only the church handing down the teachings of the Apostles.

What Is Apostolic Nature?

What, then, is the correct meaning of apostolic nature? The apostolic nature of the church began when Jesus sent His apostles into the world. He built His body, the church, on this foundation. "As the Father has sent me, I am sending you" (John 20:21). Built on the foundation of the apostles and prophets, with Christ Jesus Himself as the chief cornerstone (Ephesians 2:20).

The Apostles, who were the first witnesses of the resurrected Lord, were personally sent by Jesus to spread the gospel to all the nations. The church was built on the testimony and ministry of these apostles. They were the beginning and the permanent foundation for the church. The church is apostolic in essence. According to Hans Kung, this apostolic nature is the most basic of all the attributes, such as unity, universality and holiness, which describe the essence of the church. He states:

In our search for unity in diversity, catholicity in identity, holiness in sinfulness, the question of a criterion must always be in our minds. How far can the Church be one, holy and catholic? What is true unity, true catholicity, true holiness? The crucial criterion is expressed in the fourth attribute of the Church: the church can only be apostolic Church. What is in question is not any kind of unity, holiness and catholicity, but that which is founded on the apostles and in that sense is apostolic.[B]

The church is holy because it is separated from the world. It is a holy temple of the Holy Spirit. It shows universality by transcending times, cultures and borders to be one. It retains unity through the fact that the head of the church is Jesus Christ alone. If the church, however, is not founded on the testimony of the apostles, then it cannot be called God's church. If it is not built on the teaching of the apostles, then it even loses the meaning of any other essence. The Unification Church calls itself a church. But the reason it should not be recognized is that the Gospel of the Apostles is not their foundation. In this sense, the apostolic nature is the most foundational attribute and it can be the standard to judge all other attributes.

Hans Kung shows great insight in his perception of the apostolic nature of the church. He sees it not merely as one of the many descriptions of the essence of the church but as the most basic of all the attributes. His interpretation reveals how he has removed himself from the traditional Roman Catholic Church and has correctly defined church by basing it on the Bible. If this was not the case, his use of the word, apostolic would not have value for our consideration and it would be nothing more than a false doctrine of the Catholic Church. As long as a church has the testimony and the ministry of the apostles as its foundation, it is without a doubt apostolic. If it is an apostolic church, then it complies with the Bible. There are no sources to confirm the apostolic nature of the church other than the Bible. The authority of the church cannot be replaced by tradition. In this sense, being apostolic and being biblical have identical meaning.

How, then, is the apostolic nature transferred? In other words, what does biblical apostolic succession mean?

Apostolic Succession

Apostleship is unique and cannot be repeated. Only the Twelve who saw Jesus after His resurrection and were personally appointed had the privilege of holding the office of apostle. Paul is the only exception since he was called after Jesus' ascension. Therefore, no one can replace or represent the Apostolate anymore. It is a great fallacy on the part of the Roman Catholic Church to presume that an individual or a systematic succession can recreate apostleship. The apostles, in a narrower sense, do not exist anymore. The only things left are the apostle's teachings and an understanding of their ministry.

Who are the present successors of the apostles? Listen to the words of Hans Kung:

There can only be one basic answer: the Church. The whole Church, not just a few individuals, is the follower of the apostles. We do, after all, confess an apostolic Church. The whole Church is the new people of God, gathered by the apostles through the preaching of the gospel of Jesus Christ. The whole Church is the temple of the spirit, built on the foundation of the apostles. The whole Church is the body of Christ, unified by the ministry of the apostles... This succession must be understood in terms of substance, not just of history; there must be a real inner continuity. This continuity cannot simply be created for the Church by itself, it is something that is granted to it by the Spirit of God and Christ, the Spirit which filled the apostles and their apostolic witness, and moves and encourages the Church to follow them. The Church has the necessary obedience to the apostles and their witness. In this sense apostolic succession is a thing of the spirit. Apostolicity too is a gift and a requirement at the same time. [9]

Since these words are so important, it is worth savoring them again. For the church, the chosen people of God without any discrimination, to be a successor to the Apostles, it cannot promote one person or a special group above others. Clergy and laity, all who belong to the church, have the right to be successors. In this sense, it is correct to say that the whole church is the only successor.

There rises then the problem of where to base this succession. The Pope can appear to maintain his legitimacy through a genealogy from Peter, but the church not only does not keep the record of descendants from the Apostles, it also does not see it as important. All believers are children of God, born in the Spirit. Hans Kung contends that apostolic succession is granted by the Spirit of God. The Holy Spirit who moved the Apostles and caused them to become witnesses, is now in the church leading believers to accept and obey the gospel from the apostles. That is the continuity. As the Apostles were of the Spirit, and we also are of the Spirit, we have the qualifications to be the successors. Are there any lay men or women who would be exempted from this? None, because without the Spirit of God in him, he does not belong to Christ (Romans 8:9).

Following the Apostolic Teaching

Our next consideration is the specific method that a church should employ to be an apostolic successor.

First, the church must follow apostolic teaching. This occurs when a church receives the living testimony of the apostles handed down through the Bible and agrees in faith with it. This implies that the church must follow the faith and the confession

93

of the Apostles. Believers can become one in belief and knowledge in the Son of God because of the succession of the Apostles. The Apostles were the eyewitnesses of the Word Incarnate and His works. They also transmitted the Gospel to us (Ephesians 4: 13, Luke 1: 2). The church can only directly hear the inspired words of Jesus through the testimony of the Apostles. Hans Kung describes it in this way:

> However, a church not only attends to the apostles but the Lord Himself who speaks through their testimony. Therefore, a church must allow Jesus to speak to them personally through the testimony of the Apostles. Those who pay attention to the Apostles are paying attention to the Lord and vice versa. Those who are not paying attention to the Apostles are not paying attention to the Lord. Apostolic succession is therefore a question of a continual and living confrontation of the church and all its members with this apostolic witness; apostolic succession is fulfilled when this witness is heard, respected, believed, confessed and followed.[20]

Therefore, believing and confessing the Apostles testimony which is transmitted by the New Testament records is the only way to achieve unity and fellowship for all the churches in the world. It will not be done through any standard church system or mechanical unity movements.

All Protestant churches agree and practice the tenant that in order for the church to be the Apostle's successor, it must confess and obey their teachings. Churches must teach and proclaim the words of the New Testament as it is, and instruct the laity to receive these words as their spiritual food. We do not restrict, as the Church of Rome, the laity from personally getting near the Word of God. We can thus safely say that churches belonging to Protestantism are all apostolic in nature. Therefore, whether we admit the apostolic nature of the church or not, we are already involved in apostolicity.

Following the Apostolic Ministry

Secondly, a church must follow an apostolic ministry to be an apostolic successor. This means receiving the commandments of Jesus transmitted by the Apostles and obeying them. On this point Hans Kung eloquently declares the following:

Apostolicity is never an unchallenged possession, a secure piece of property which the Church has at its disposal. Apostolicity can never mean power through which the church might rule. It is not a question of others submitting to the church; the Church must itself submit by accepting the authority of the apostles and of the churchs and the apostles Lord... The apostolic Church least of all can be an end in itself. Everything the Church does must be directed towards fulfilling its apostolic mission to mankind. To be a church and to have a mission are not two separate things. To be itself, the church must follow the apostles in continually recognizing and demonstrating that it has been sent out to the world... This makes it clear that apostolicity, like unity, holiness and catholicity, is not a static attribute of the Church. Like them it is an historical dimension, a dimension which has constantly to be fulfilled anew in history. Apostolicity too must continually be achieved afresh, must be a recurring event in a living history which occurs between the Church and the apostles, between the

Church's preaching and the apostle's witness, between the Church's ministry and the apostle's commission... Apostolicity is not something that can simply be stated and proved in theory. The Church must share in this history in order to recognize and understand, to experience and discover what the apostolicity of the church means. As an individual Christian, I must become a true successor of the apostles, I must hear their witness, believe their message, imitate their mission and ministry. I must be, and always become anew, a believing and living member of the apostolic community.[21]

From my perspective, the Korean Church has not properly and theologically resolved the fact that the great commission, or calling to the mission which the Apostles received personally from the Lord, is in fact now the responsibility of the laity, which is the whole church. The climate of the Korean Church is to assume that calling is reserved for only certain kinds of people . Of course, clergy and missionaries, unlike the others, have a special calling in the ministry. It is a grievous error, however, to neglect or abandon equipping the whole church with its apostolic nature, because a few people with a special calling are taking the center stage. How can the laity, who are the principal core of the church, free themselves from the apostolic calling, which is the essence of the church?

Many try to convince people to evangelize using the rationale that the Lord will be happy if we reach our goal of church growth for this year. A portion of the church hears this critically as the personal ambitions of their pastor. They may express irritation or refusal by asking how much more increase in attendance he wants his greed fulfilled. Why does this happen? It is the result of not properly teaching lay people that they are the successors to Peter, who was martyred while obeying the command to proclaim the Gospel to all the nations. It is not wrong to encourage the laity to commit to missions under the slogan of national world evangelism. If, however, they are not given an understanding of the true nature of their calling as the successors of the apostolic ministry, then it would be similar to a man who is told to defend his country without giving him a clear identity of his citizenship.

The Will of God

In order for a church to see the importance of its own apostolic ministry, it must search the Bible and honestly evaluate whether it agrees with God's will for the world. That's the core of the matter. After thoroughly researching the word, will, as it refers to the will of God in the New Testament, Gettlob Schrenk arrived at a meaningful conclusion:

The plural form is almost completely absent from the New Testament - God's will is expressed in the singular because the concept is shaped, not by individual legal directions, but by the conviction that the will of God is a powerful unity.[22]

Why is this so? It is because there is a distinct unity between the will of God and His objective for salvation. In other words, the singular form indicates that His will points only to one objective. That objective is to complete the work of salvation and to save the world through Jesus Christ.

After Jesus had saved the Samaritan woman, He said, "My food is to do the will of Him who sent me and to finish His work" (John 4:34, NIV). The reason He was filled with the joy of the Holy Spirit when the seventy reported back after their mission trip is, in fact, found here (Luke 10:21).

The Apostle Paul strongly suggests in Philippians that the way for the church to render glory to God is to do nothing else but the will of God, which is to save sinners. That at the name of Jesus every knee should bow, in heaven and on earth and under the earth, and every tongue confess that Jesus Christ is Lord, to the glory of God the Father (Philippians 2:10-11, NIV). The church was called to this task. Carl Kromminga has pointed out well the relationship between God's glory and mission work:

> When the doxological motif is isolated from the missionary, the universal expanse of God's saving purpose and the significance of the gift of the Spirit to the church are not given their due. The greater glorification of God's grace and love is obstructed if doxological motif is not complemented by the missionary.[23]

Therefore, a church that aligns itself with God's will, which is to save everyone and to bring them to the knowledge of the truth (I Timothy 2:4), is doing better than anything else it could do.[24]

To a certain extent, the church does not exist to gain salvation. The church already has a new identity. It possesses eternal life. It has crossed over from condemnation to life (John 5:24). The church, therefore, must establish what it will do rather than what it will be. When the great Commission that was given to the Apostles is succeeded and completed by the church, the world will come to an end and the earthly church will be replaced by the New Jerusalem which will come down from heaven. If the church is to proclaim the gospel to all the nations and wait eagerly to inherit the kingdom, which will be given when the King of Kings finally returns, then no other work by the church is as important as spreading the Gospel to the world and sealing it with love. Disregarding the apostolic call to the world is the same as renouncing hope for the return of the King and the coming of the eternal kingdom. And this gospel of the kingdom will be preached in the whole world as a testimony to all nations, and then the end will come (Matthew 24:14). Sometimes, I observe believers abandoning the call to share the gospel, or churches easily forfeiting their spiritual power. I believe that they are being disobedient to God's will and have lost hope in the reality of God's future kingdom.

The Relationship between the Holy Spirit and the Apostolic Nature

The church exists in order to uphold the ministry of the Apostles. It is reinforced in its mission by the work of the Holy Spirit who was given to the church by our Lord. Essentially, the apostolic nature of the church is inseparable from the Holy Spirit. The Holy Spirit calls the chosen to accept and confess the testimony of the Apostles. He helps them to realize that they were called earlier to tell the other sheep that they need salvation and to equip them with power. The world has been encountering a new brand of people. They are clothed with Christ through the Holy Spirit and have the Holy Spirit living among them. These people are the laity of the church who are the community of witnesses. "When the Counselor comes, whom

I will send to you from the Father, the Spirit of truth who goes out from the Father, He will testify about me; but you also must testify, for you have been with me from the beginning" (John 15:26-27, NIV).

The relationship between Jesus, who came to fulfill the will of God, and the Holy Spirit, who came upon Him like oil, illustrates the relationship between the Apostles and the Holy Spirit. It also illustrates the relationship between the church and the Holy Spirit.

As Jesus Himself had been anointed at His baptism with the Holy spirit and power, so His followers were now to be similarly anointed and enabled to carry on His work. This work would be a work of witness-bearing-a theme which is prominent in the apostolic preaching throughout Acts. [25]

As soon as Jesus was baptized and filled with the Holy Spirit, God finally broke the long silence and spoke again. As long as the Holy Spirit who dwelt in Jesus is in the church, there will be no more silence. The book of Acts has also been dubbed the Acts of the Holy Spirit, quite obviously because the early church was not silent.

From the book of Acts, we can discern that the main objective of the arrival of the Holy Spirit was to prepare the disciples to become witnesses for Christ. The Spirit did not come to comfort them, but to shape them into missionaries. For these final days, the Holy Spirit has made the church, in essence, apostolic. Understanding this truth is the key to unlocking the reason why the New Testament Church no longer offers the sacrifices of the Old Testament. Jesus Christ has offered the eternal sacrifice for sin and has made sinners forever righteous. Subsequently, the church has no further need to offer sacrifices for sin (Hebrew 10:12-18). All that is left is to boast about Jesus Christ, who has presented the eternal sacrifice for sinners, and about His cross (I Corinthians 2:2). The Holy Spirit comes to transform the nature of the church so that it can be the right tool to fit His work. As a result, the New Testament Church, from the first moment of its inception, has exhibited the character of a witnessing community. It has become a church that confesses, proclaims, and praises.

The second chapter of Acts describes a dramatic phenomenon that teaches us an important truth. The first thing that happened when the Holy Spirit came was that people began to speak with a new tongue (Verse 4). In other words, He opened the Church's mouth. Why did He open its mouth? Because the earthly church is called to go out into the world and spread the Gospel. On this point, the Holy Spirit did not distinguish between the Apostles and the rest of the disciples. The Holy Spirit came upon all 120 who were in the upper room. They all obeyed the Spirit and opened their mouths (Verses 3,4). Their words were not groanings that disappeared into the thin air. These were loud words that the people of Jerusalem heard and which drew their interest. Although we do not know the specific content of what was said, people have testified that they spoke of God's great works (Verse 11). However, in order to understand what was specifically said about God's great works, the gathering crowd had to wait for Peter to speak. Peter explained that it was Jesus who died on the cross, was resurrected and had become the Lord and the Christ (Verses 14-36).

The speaking with other tongues (by the prompting of the Holy Spirit) dramatically demonstrated the witnessing character of the

Church; Peter's sermon set the pattern through which that witnessing character finds normal and continuing expression.[26]

The Holy Spirit opens the mouth of the church, while Satan closes it. Opening our mouth is obeying God and keeping it closed is obeying Satan (Acts 4:17-20). We can conclude that one of the greatest purposes for the coming of the Holy Spirit on the earthly church is to open the mouths of all believers to proclaim the Gospel to the world.

So far, we have discussed the theological basis for mobilizing the laity in their calling for this age. A church based on the Bible must also be apostolic. In order for it to become apostolic, the whole church, including all laypersons, must believe it is successor to the apostles. It must believe and confess the testimony of the Apostles. At the same time, the whole church must confess and obey the same commandment that the Apostles received to spread the Gospel to the ends of the earth. It is the Holy Spirit who confirmed the apostolic nature of the church beyond a shadow of doubt, and broke the silence of the church by opening its mouth as soon as He came upon the world. Activating the laity, therefore, means teaching them to confess and obey that they are personally called to succeed the apostles in ministry.

The apostolic task is incomplete. It will remain incomplete until the end of time, or until the Gospel is presented to the ends of the earth. Therefore, the church must always remain in the world and confess Christ, witness to others, and serve one another as the apostles did. This is the fundamental and biblical mission that determines the existence of the church.

In Korea, the clergy, must acutely feel the responsibility of not having been able to equip statistically almost 200 million lay people of this country with a clear awareness of the calling to go out into world as the successors of the Apostles. We must now reflect and evaluate who is causing the laity to become sluggish and to slumber with relief that they, as lay persons, have nothing to do with this calling.

Chapter 9: The Reason for the Existence of the Church

I have already discussed the calling of the earthly church as the successor of the Apostles, which is then sent into the world. This could, however, mislead a person into the narrow-minded opinion that the only work for the church on this earth is missions. The church has many other ministries connected to its calling of spreading the Gospel. Without equal emphasis on all ministries, the true church cannot be seen. For this reason, I will now explore in more concrete terms why the church must be in the world.

The usual response to the question "Why does the church exist?" is to glorify God. This is probably the most concise and accurate reply. Yes, it is without doubt that all things will bring glory to God when the church inundates the creation. The drawback, however, of the expression, 'to glorify God', is that it is somewhat abstract. It does not explain how, and with what, the church glorifies God. So, it is necessary now to expound on what the church must do to bring glory to God. As a matter of convenience, I will discuss it in three parts.

To Worship God

First of all, the church exists to worship God. He called the church from this world for His name's sake so that glory will be rightfully rendered to His name (Acts 15: 14). The first priority of the church, therefore, is to worship God. Upon confessing faith, the first thing God's people need to learn is to praise the One who has set them apart. God has given us the privilege of entering into His holy sanctuary to worship Him. Worship is unique in that it is a sacrifice of the total person. The people of God are fashioned together into the body of Christ. Through the headship of Christ, the church became a holy priest, offering itself as a holy sacrifice, acceptable to God (Romans 12:1, I Peter 2:5).

Above all, worship in the Church is based on the character of God. We must know who He is so that proper worship can be given to Him (Psalm 29:2, Revelation 4:8). Worship also must be founded on what God has done for the church. In other words, through worship we celebrate and come to know more of God's work in creation and salvation. The elders around God's throne give glory, honor, and power to God for His work in creation (Revelation 4:11). The angels are worshipping the lamb that was slain (Revelation 5:12). The fact that worship is based on our gratitude for our salvation from eternal death explains why worship in the early New Testament churches expressed gratitude for Christ's presence. This is particularly manifested in the breaking of the bread. Calvin and Luther both wished for the church to retain these spiritual and physical practices because these reformers believed that God accepted this form of worship, done in His Son's name. It was worship that honored His Word and the sacraments.[27]

When discussing worship, however, we must ask what form of worship is considered true worship. Many experts in the areas of worship concede that this deserves more than a simple answer. The church is now in the New era in Christ. Neither the worship format of the Old Testament period nor our tradition bound format may limit or satisfy us.[28] Jesus distinguished the worship in the last days as worship in sprit and truth. I don't think that there are only a few limited ways to worship God in spirit and truth, because I believe that spirit and truth allude to the profound and diverse spirituality of worship.

When you read the four Gospels with the idea of worship in mind it raises many doubts. It is rare to find teaching on worship, even to the point of seeming old. Not only that, it is difficult to find specific instances of worship. The Gospels mention that Jesus and His disciples sometimes visited the Temple and the synagogue. The disciples at the time were following Jesus and confessing that He is the Son of God and the Christ. But there are no references to any kind of communal worship given to Jesus found in the Gospels. Neither does Jesus make any demand of the disciples for some kind of worship to or of Himself.

The epistles do not contain any passages which describe a kind of format for worship. They only indicate that the basic elements of worship are praise, thanksgiving, prayer, and the Word. There seems to be no requirement of a type of worship format with which we might be familiar. Furthermore, it emphasizes that the important worship we must render to God is the spiritual worship of offering our bodies as living sacrifices (Romans 12: 1). More interesting is the fact that Jesus did not give the responsibility of leading worship to the pastor when He explained the reasons for appointing leaders in the church. He gave some to be pastors and teachers to prepare God's people for maturity, works of service and to build up the body of Christ (Ephesians 4:11, 12). If you consider that today the clergy is often regarded as being there only to lead the worship, this is very surprising.

By pointing out these elements I have no desire to demean the importance of worship or to negate the need for formality in worship. I want to emphasize that it is undeniable that one of the reasons the church exists in the world is to give glory to God through worship. From a Korean perspective, I am concerned that freedom in worship in the Korean churches is so very limited. It gives the impression that the church cannot break out of some kind of mold of formality. Many criticize our worship as problematic if there is even a little hint of change. It is my fear that true worship, which is to be in spirit and truth, is being transformed into a form of legalism.

In extreme cases, sharing the Word in a small group meeting is not even considered by some to be worship. Are they contending that Bible study and worship are different? Is that true? In the Colossian church, it was when the believers gathered together to share the Word of God that they were able to truly give praise and thanks to God. They did not have a set time apart to share the Word and then later worship. They did, of course, come together officially on the Sabbath to take the communion. They did not, however, seem to have insisted on one formal type of worship (Colossians 3:16, 17). Thus, it seems there must be no room for a separation between the vertical and horizontal dimensions of worship. Teaching to build up the believers around you and worshipping God Who is above are only two sides of the same coin. Leading others to become disciples of Christ is in itself worshipping God. Therefore, separating worship and the study of the Word is the same as restraining worship through some form of formality.

I would like to point out one more thing. For too many, the job of pastor has almost uncontrollably evolved into leading worship only. A pastor appears to be there only to prepare and lead the Sunday worship. Any meeting with the pastor must start after some form of worship. Even visitation has become centered on worship. Anyone who only attends Sunday service, as long as they are consistent, is still considered faithful. "I have been to the Sunday service" is viewed as fulfillment of all the requirement of spiritual lifestyle. Why is this a problem? It is a problem because having a ministry exclusively to offer worship is unfairly playing a huge role in weakening and putting to sleep. The clergy hastily concludes that the most important role of the laity is to come to the Sunday worship. As long as they aren't absent on Sunday, they are deemed to be spiritually healthy. On the part of the laity, anything that the clergy requires or emphasizes outside the Sunday worship is always taken as too much. This makes the thorough training of the laity an enormous task. How can the church become a place of mobilized laity if these conditions continue over a period of long time?

True believers are not created in a vacuum. They must be shaped. Thoroughly training the laity to become disciples of Christ results in the creation of true worshippers. Ministry that puts exclusivity only on the Sunday worship literally obstructs the creation of true worshippers. In certain instances, it generates the hypocritical idea that worship is not even necessary.

To Save the World

The church exists to save the world. The church is a gathering of believers who are called to witness in the world. Spreading the gospel to the ends of the earth is an important responsibility for the church. Whether it is the clergy or the laity, all are called to this purpose. Every member of the church, all who are in the body, has been given grace to carry out this task.

The greatest ministry to which the laity are called is witness to Jesus Christ, evangelism, which means spreading the good news about Him.[29]

This point has already been thoroughly discussed in the previous section on the apostolic nature. To those of us who want to awaken the laity, however, this principle is so important that I would like to review the doctrine of the priesthood of all believers.

All believers are a royal priesthood (I Peter 2:9). The office of priest has at least four wonderful privileges. First is the privilege of coming directly before God's presence. Christ completely finished the work of intercession through His personal and sacrificial death and opened the veil into the Holy of Holies (Matthew 27:51). As a result, any believer can approach the throne of grace directly by faith. In addition, there is absolutely no need for another human intercessor beside Jesus.

Second, a priest has the privilege of offering a spiritual sacrifice. All believers are under a new covenant and have the responsibility of offering a holy and living sacrifice (I Peter 2:5). The Bible identifies various sacrifices that can be offered to God. Proclaiming the Gospel (Romans 15:16), praise, helping others

(Hebrew 13:15-16), martyrdom (II Timothy 4:6), and praying for the believers (Revelations 8:3) are only some of the spiritual sacrifices. The distinct feature of each of these is that the one who offers it is, himself, the sacrifice. The sacrifices are not only offered in church on a particular day but are done everyday and include everything that has to do with everyday life. There are no distinctions between the sacred and the common.

The third privilege of a priest is to proclaim the Word.

The priesthood of all believers includes not only the witness of actions, of ones whole life spent in living self-sacrifice, but also the specific witness of the word. [30]

Proclaiming the Word has not been entrusted to a few in the church but to all believers who are called the royal priesthood. Why has God called believers into a royal priesthood? It is to proclaim God's wonderful grace (I Peter 2:9).

The fourth priestly privilege is intercession. Priesthood is not just for oneself. It is to encourage the believers to help and serve others both inside and outside the church. A priest is not only involved with the vertical relationship between God and men but with horizontal relationships as well. Praying for others is a responsibility. It involves a spiritual sacrifice of the self. Believers are the priests for the world. With faith we can come to God freely and petition for our brothers and sisters.

The priesthood of all believers consists in the calling of the faithful to witness to God and his will before the world, and to offer up their lives in the service of the world. It is God who creates this priesthood and hence creates fellowship among

110

believers. Each one knows that he appears before God on behalf of others, and knows that others appear before God on his behalf. Each is responsible for his fellow men, called to share in his struggles and in his difficulties, called to bear his sins with him and to stand by him in everything. The priesthood of all believers is a fellowship in which each Christian instead of living for himself, lives before God for others and is in turn supported by others.[31]

Reviewing the privileges of the priesthood of all believers reveals the heavy responsibility of the laity toward the world. Why do we have to go directly to God? It is to intercede for the world. Why do we have to spread the Gospel? It is because it is spiritual worship, holy and acceptable to God.

In reality, we have seen an accelerated development in the hierarchy of today's church, which has caused the word priesthood to be used more for the clergy and less for the laymen. As a result, laypeople are less interested in the priesthood. I believe the churches of today are experiencing an acute problem that can only be solved by bringing a revival to the basic spirit of the priesthood of all believers. If I understand the problem correctly, the laity can help the church to be an apostolic church that fulfills its part only if the whole church, and not just a few, become an ecclesiastical community. We must all come directly before the Lord, to worship, to proclaim the gospel and to help our neighbors. Let's insist that the wonderful office of the priesthood does not belong only to the few who have been called into the pastoral ministry. Such a practice is unacceptable and is an aberration in this New Testament era.

Nurturing Mother

Lastly, the church exists to nurture and to train the believers. This is the central focus of Calvin's doctrine of the church. According to Calvin, the church was given to us by God to fill a need. The church functions to compensate for the flaw in man's character which is so easily molded by laziness and ignorance. Until the children of God, who are in the bosom of the church, reach the goal of faith which is to become mature Christians, the church must provide motherly care. Therefore, it is always disastrous to leave the community of a church because the believer is inherently weak.[32]

As Jesus was leaving the earth, he commanded His followers to teach others to obey all that he has commanded, because that is how disciples are made. The Apostle Paul emphasized the importance of one particular talent as he discussed the qualifications of the overseer. That talent is the ability to teach (I Timothy 3:2). This implies that if the church wants to nurture the believers, then the leader must be able to teach the Word well. According to the Epistles, Jesus, who is the head of the church, gave three things to aid in the ministry of making disciples of the believers. He gave clergy as teachers (Ephesians 4:11), the Bible as the teaching content (II Timothy 3:16-17), and an excellent model as a teaching method (Colossians 1:28-29).

Therefore, if the clergy does not thoroughly teach the laity to become the disciples of Christ, then we can greatly disappoint Jesus who entrusted the church to us and requested to "take care of my sheep". In a way, the content of our ministry has just been to teach to obey . However, we can attest to the fact that the result is not completely satisfactory. All those worship services, all those sermons, and all those Bible studies must be coldly reexamined to see how much change they are bringing to the laity in their sense of calling.

In order to fulfill the role of the church as a mother, we must scrutinize our whole ministry which is immersed in habit. We must firmly decide to correct the wrong and supplement the insufficient. Only then will the church be able to raise up Christ's disciples like a swarm of bees.

Inseparable Relationship

So far we have discussed the reason for the existence of the church in three parts. It is important to remember that these three cannot be separated into independent parts. Each is closely connected, so failure in one area will render the whole inoperable. When these three are balanced in our ministry, neither worship, nor evangelism, nor discipleship can be dealt with carelessly. Thus, we can expect the highest result, giving glory to God.

Realistically, from a historical perspective, the church has always focused on one of them as its reason for existence. This is due to its own incomplete nature. Some theologians talk as if the church only exists for God. Recently, there has been an increase among those who insist that the church exists only for the world. For example, Bavinck says that the church exists only for the glory of God.[39] On the other hand, Kraemer implies that the church exists under the banner of 'The Church is Mission', and presents this as the basic law for the existence of the church. In his view, mission is the essence of the church, not a section of the church.

The church is the community of the sent, just as she is the community of witnesses. She is sent to and into the world. [34]

However, the church must not neglect any of the three mentioned above. God wants to receive glory through the communal worship of believers. He wants to celebrate the return of the lost sheep and He wants His children to grow to the level of maturity set by Christ. It is His will for us not to lose sight of any one of these.

Today's church appears to be losing its equilibrium. It is neglecting its basis for existence. Traditional doctrines of the church have encouraged an over-emphasis on worship, which has resulted in the misconception that the church is not responsible for the rest of the world. Mission has often been assigned as an exclusive right for the elite. The laity have become an incompetent mass whose only request from the church is to provide worship and the fulfillment of personal spiritual needs. Worship has been provided, but it has lacked testimonies. Teaching has been offered but it has ignored the responsibility of training the laity to live according to their calling which is to accomplish the will of God. While absorbed in worldly affairs and debating how to distinguish God's work and earthly work, most lay people are unable to shake off the guilt and fear of being under judgment. Therefore, validated through our apostolic nature and the reason for the existence of the church, we must preserve the doctrine of the church by calling the church into missions. Only then will we be able to blow the trumpet with all our might to awaken the slumbering laity.

PART THREE

MINISTRY STRATEGY
- TRUE DISCIPLESHIP
PP115 - PP170

- **MINISTRY PHILOSOPHY**
  - YOUR THEOLOGY OF THE CHURCH
- **MINISTRY STRATEGY**
  - TRUE DISCIPLESHIP
- **MINISTRY METHOD**
  - DISCIPLESHIP TRAINING
- **MINISTRY FIELD**
  - THE EXAMPLE OF SARANG

Chapter 10: Strategic Merits of Training the Laity

Confusing Terminology

In Korea, these days, the terms, disciple and discipleship training, are being used with much familiarity. At times, they seem even to be abused. Optimistically stated, this demonstrates that many pastors are showing singular interest in discipleship training. They are displaying a strong desire to study it so as to incorporate such training practically into their ministry. Indeed, this positive atmosphere is increasing worldwide. And, the good news is, many ministries are succeeding by using a discipleship training method.

When asked about what discipleship is, however, everybody comes up with different answers. There still seems to be some confusion about this concept. Some people think that it is only a title for a Bible study curriculum. Some even express a critical attitude towards discipleship because of its emphasis on being a disciple. They question what the difference is in using the words 'believer' and 'disciple'. In the theological arena, there is a trend to view discipleship with an extremely ethical motif. The ideologies of Bonhoeffer have had a strong influence on this trend.[1] Some mission organizations are very narrow-minded about discipleship. Others understand it as a product that they manufacture from a mold which is unique to their organization.

The one who commands us to go and make disciples is Jesus. So, we need to correctly understand the proper meaning of the word, disciple. It is not wrong to prominently use this word. But the more we use it, the more we should clearly delineate its meaning and character through the Bible. Do not underestimate the harm that comes from a faulty understanding of even one important concept. It is unfortunate that due to some who teach wrongly many view discipleship training with a critical eye. Some have said, "If this is discipleship training, then I would rather stay home". How did this happen? It is because the leader taught without the proper understanding of what a disciple is.

Truly, churches have closed their eyes to discipleship for a long time. The command to make disciples has been understood to refer only to evangelism. But ever since the founder of the Navigators, Dawson Trotman, saw the light while reading about the 'Great Commission' (Matthew 28:18-20), the discipleship movement brought an awakening in the hearts of church leaders and a sense of purpose during the last half of the 20th century. Trotman's eyes were opened to the truth that Jesus' command to make disciples contains more meaning than just to evangelize, and proclaim the gospel to the ends of the earth. The impact that Trotman has had on Christianity during this century is much larger than we ever imagine.

The Bible does not contain the word, 'discipleship'. Not only that, the definition of 'disciple' is not even explained. Instead, it is full of statements about who can be called a disciple and how he should live his life. So it may seem difficult to explain what discipleship training is. The definition of discipleship training is not as important, however, as knowing the practical side of the character and the life of the disciple. In other words, discipleship training is a lifestyle, a process, and a goal for ministry itself in the church. A pastor who has a burden for awakening the laity to develop them into disciples of Christ must correctly learn with an open Bible what discipleship training is.

Discipleship Training is a Ministry Strategy

Discipleship training can be said to be a biblical foundational strategy that reconstructs the image of the laity into the basic essence of the apostolic nature of the church. It contains strategic directions for how and with what objectives and standards to train the laity who are sent into the world. Discipleship training is the answer to Jesus' self-imposed definition of "this is the kind of follower I want". A pastor could easily and falsely create a disciple that pleases his eyes, or he can train without any standard at all. This, of course, is a great tragedy. We must make disciples of Christ. We must teach them to obey the objectives and standards that Jesus showed us. "All that I have commanded you" (Matthew 28:19) is contained in discipleship training. Therefore, we must not run aimlessly or fight beating the air as we train the laity (I Corinthians 9:26).

Although it is true that the defenders of the ecumenical movement were the first to see the importance of the laity, they did not always follow the strategies outlined in the Bible. They stressed participation and secularization. By participation I mean

119

when the door to ministry is opened wide to anyone within the church. Secularization is when the laity are encouraged to actively and boldly take part in all areas of society, sin excepted, outside the church. In contrast, evangelical mission organizations began with a cry to restore the calling of the laity to missions, and based their strategy for discipleship on what they discovered from the Bible. The ecumenical movement emphasized practical action in its strategy but mission organizations emphasized character formation.

Who was right?

The principle that Jesus seemed to rely on was to create a new person and then put him to work. This is the basic principle of discipleship training. If, however, action or work is put before developing the new person, it is not Christ's way. In other words, if the strategy puts what kind of work to give a person before examining what kind of person this is, then, this is not the strategy that Jesus taught.

What has been the result?

After many years, the lay movement of the ecumenical camp has left the impression of being mere theory, while mission organizations are gathering fruit on a world wide scale. Schrotenboer evaluates it as such:

In some ways, the strategy of making disciples can be said to be a movement to create an elite laity. As Ezra Bounds has commented, the world is searching for a better method while God is looking for a better man. Discipleship contains all the important ingredients in developing the kind of people that God is looking for.

Until now, the churches in the western world, including Korea, have been negligent in making true disciples of Jesus. And now, they are reaping a high cost from their laziness. Secularism, communism, socialism, heretical doctrines, unwholesome Holy Spirit movements, and formalism have seeped into the church. Many churches cannot hold back these waves of the world any longer because they have only the thin walls of a laity who have been trained under their methods of discipleship. In addition, natural increases in world population and overcrowding in the cities have caused the church in some areas to suffer from quantitative obesity, which is increasingly hindering the quality of the laity.[3]

We all know that the basic strategy of communism, like we have seen in North Korea or any other heresy, is to create a few core leading members. Rather than concentrating on a mass of people, they begin by putting all their energy into raising a few so that they will have a pivotal influence to lead the masses. Isn't this the exact strategy we should employ in making disciples of Jesus? When the church has abandoned its work of making disciples, it seems as if Satan snatches the secret and uses it to develop a powerful weapon to attack and destroy the church. As a result, we cannot fathom the harm it has done to the church. We must now return repenting, and learn why Jesus has commanded the church to go and make disciples.

Chapter 11: Jesus and His Disciples

When Jesus began His public ministry, the first thing that he did was to call disciples. Unlike the traditional Jewish leaders, He did not wait for the disciples to seek Him, but He took the initiative and searched for a few men that fit what He wanted. The reason why He chose to have disciples is that He needed people to continue the mission.[4] In a practical sense, they became Jesus' body, so that within and through them, the Gospel ministry would be sustained and declared to everyone. And so, twelve men became the Apostles who were sent (Luke 6:13).

The Twelve were especially chosen among many other disciples (Luke 6:13). Jesus chose them with care. He had spent a whole night in prayer for this task (Luke 6:12).[5] Jesus gave to the Twelve the privilege to always be with Him and learn about Him (Mark 3:14). They had to know Him and become His men before they could do things for Him. They were given to Jesus by the Father (John 17:6). All the words of truth that they had received from Jesus were from God (John 17: 14). Through the Word, they were sanctified (John 17:19). Jesus clearly explained to the disciples the mystery of the kingdom of heaven that He had only told to the crowd in parables (Matthew 13:10b).

He revealed Himself to them as the Messiah and received their confession of faith, while He hid His identity from the public. He was satisfied with their confession and promised that His church would be built upon their confession (Matthew 16:16-20). As His end approached, Jesus completely devoted Himself to the Twelve. Like a famous artist, He avoided the crowds to give the final touch to the painting that was to appear before a public showing. His final touch up was to pray for His disciples (John 13:17).

Even though they were fishermen from Galilee and had come from various backgrounds and experiences, Jesus had keen insight. He was able to look past their ordinary positions to see mighty possibilities. He did not hesitate to instill into these ordinary men a radiant dream of the kingdom of heaven. Although they left a smear of unbelief and betrayal at the scene of the crucifixion, He did not abandon them. After the resurrection, He again shared with these failures a blueprint of the glorious kingdom that would be constructed through them. He could foresee that, although they were unable at the present time, they would soon follow Him (John 13:36). He was confident that they would not only do what He had done, but that they would do even greater things (John 14:12).

Before He ascended, He saw their immaturity and a remnant of unbelief in them and so He executed a very authoritative send-off by proclaiming, "As the Father has sent me, I am sending you" (John 20:21). He also entrusted to them the great commission of making disciples of all nations, baptizing them and teaching them His Words (Matthew 28:18-20). While He was in the world, Jesus did not leave behind any diary or stone monuments to commemorate Himself. The only inheritance that He had left was a handful of ignorant and ordinary disciples who had learned about Him. But He saw value in placing all His life into them. He invested in the production of a handful of disciples.

Chapter 12: The Concept of Disciple in the Four Gospels and the Book of Acts

The places where the word disciple appear in the New Testament are the Four Gospels and the Book of Acts. It is used approximately two hundred fifty times. Examining how each author has used this word will greatly help us to understand the concept of disciple.

Disciple in the Four Gospels

Except for two instances, Matthew always used the names of the Twelve disciples. In Matthew 27:57 and 28:19, we find the word disciple not referring to the Twelve. In some translations, like the Korean Bible, disciple in these two verses appears as a noun. But in the original text it is in the form of a verb, to become a disciple or to make a disciple. Some people claim that because it was not in the form of noun, Matthew used the word disciple in a narrow sense to refer only to the group of Twelve. However, I believe that this opinion is too excessive. Although it is in the form of a verb, the word still contains the root noun, disciple. When Jesus gave the command to make disciples (Matthew 28: 19), He, without a doubt, saw that the disciples would include the Twelve disciples and the many who would become God's people through them. I conclude Matthew is teaching all believers that whether they are pastors or lay persons, they must remain as disciples of Jesus Christ who is the only master.[6]

The Gospel of Mark uses the word in a narrow sense without any exceptions. The author of Mark does not call anyone a disciple other than the Twelve. The book of John uses it in both a narrow and broad sense, as does the book of Matthew. Many people are called disciples other than the Twelve (John 6:66). The author of John shows to all the Jews who believe in Jesus how to become a true disciple. The broad meaning of the word refers to all who abide in His Word (John 8:31).

Luke shows the most innovation in his use of disciple. We can see especially in the Book of Acts that he calls, without hesitation, anyone a disciple if they believe in Jesus. Only two instances (Acts 19:1, 9:25) serve as exceptions. At that time, a great number of believers had not personally observed Jesus but they were given the title of disciple. In the beginning of Acts, new believers are interchangeably referred to as believers and disciples. As the book continues, the former term disappears and the latter is used more frequently (Acts 2:44, 4:32). As the mission trips are taken in earnest, the disciples of Antioch are given a beautiful nickname 'Christians' (11:26). This was an honorable title given only to those who embodied the power of the disciples. Their power was characteristic of their lives.

The Silence of the Epistles

In the Epistles, the reference to disciples suddenly disappears. Why was the use of the word disciple halted in the Epistles? Some say it is because the writers of the Epistles did not want the Hellenistic culture to misunderstand the Christianity to be only a philosophical movement. Others say that the word was used during the earthly ministry of Jesus and no longer described the followers of Christ after His ascension. So, other words displaced the word disciple.[7] It is hard to say whose opinion is correct. Although the expressions are different, the fact that words with the meaning of disciple are used in the Epistles denotes that the teachings in the Bible are united under the inspiration of the Holy Spirit.

Consider also the words whole or mature (I Corinthians 14:20, Ephesians 4:12, Colossians 1:28, I Timothy 3:17). In the original Greek text two or three different words are used, but the meanings they carry are very similar. When Ephesians 4:12 and 13 are observed side by side, one who is mature shares the same vein as disciple.

To prepare God's people (Katartismos, verse 12) was originally used to mean putting a bone back in its place. Accordingly, it implies the act of preparing people with appropriate qualifications. 'Become mature' (teleios, verse 13) follows after and it denotes reaching the goal, or maturity.[8]

Although there is a slight difference in the meanings, the fact that they were used in the verses that carry the same intent shows that there is an accord. From this perspective, it is easy to see that verse 13 explains in detail what it means to prepare

God's people. Paul is using an interesting metaphor for a quick understanding. "Mature in and become mature, attaining to the whole measure of the fullness of Christ" is like being as tall as Jesus and as all encompassing as Jesus. In other words, it is being compared to becoming the adult Jesus. It contains the same nuance as a little child dreaming of becoming like his dad. Therefore, being prepared as God's people means becoming like Jesus. A disciple lives like Jesus.

One who is mature points to two steps in spiritual maturity - which all God's children who have received new life should pursue. The first is maturity that can be achieved in the present. This refers to the perfection of the believer, becoming more like Jesus. This is the mark and the goal of the true believer. He or she daily reviews it and runs toward it. Included in it is a faith that is growing (Hebrews 6:1,2), a character that is maturing, and a life that is victorious (II Timothy 3: 17). It also refers to a maturity that will be obtained only at the Second Coming of Jesus, when we also will be glorified with Him (Philippians 3:12- 14).[9]

Sometimes, there are people who consider being perfect on earth as impossible. They are of the opinion that it is undesirable to burden the church with such a goal. They see discipleship training, which teaches the trainers to be like Jesus and live like Jesus, as an extreme method of ministry. We should keep in mind that this kind of attitude becomes a catalyst in the secularization of the church. When the laity is not given a specific mark or standard of how one should live and who he should become, their spiritual life naturally points down instead up. We should always be cautious of this kind of ideology. Be wary of people who claim that since there is no teaching in the Epistles about making disciples, then discipleship training is unnecessary.

Many think that being a disciple means simply confessing ones belief in Jesus. Yet, the believers of the early church were not called disciples by others just for the sake of being polite. They were called disciples because they completely followed Jesus. I fear that today we might be carelessly misusing the title and blurring the spirit that it meant to convey. Read the Gospels and observe the character and the life of Jesus who commanded others to follow Him. Carefully study the changes that happen to those who are called disciples in the book of Acts. Undoubtedly, you will find unique features not often found among today's believers. Why do they seem so different? They truly are the people of Christ who could be called disciples without shame. I believe there is a reason why Jesus did not tell the disciples to go and make all nations believe in Him, but rather to make them into disciples. He wanted the people of the new kingdom, which He will one day rule over to resemble Him without any exceptions.

Chapter 13: Are All Believers Disciples?

As the local churches exhibit more interest in discipleship training, there are, especially in churches that are carrying out a training program, often some misperceptions of what disciple is. Some regard the training as a measuring stick which distinguishes between those who are and who are not disciples. They compare it to Jacob's staff that separated the spotted sheep and those without spots. Even in my church, the SaRang church, one often hears people who say, "I'm not a disciple yet, because I haven't been trained". Though they know how wrong it is, pastors also subconsciously hold a similar viewpoint. Consequently, they treat some as disciples and some as just one of the crowd. In doing so, it is only natural that one group will act as if they are privileged and the other, oppressed.

The seed of misunderstanding discipleship does not only stem from the training program. It can also be found in the pastor's troubled dilemma. To be honest, what we call discipleship training cannot even be compared to the content and the method that Jesus used to train His disciples. We do not exactly follow some methods of discipleship training Jesus used as recorded in the Bible. We usually apply what we glean from principles taught in the Word to our times. Therefore, there is a possibility that our training could come below the standard, or not even come close to a cheap imitation. Realistically, it is difficult to demand from the trainees that they pay the price for more active and sacrificial training. So, we logically can fall into the dilemma of asking "can we even make disciples in this fashion?" When this kind of guilt settles in, then, sometimes there is the response, there is, yet, no one who can be called a disciple of Christ in our church .

So, whether the misconception happens through the training program or the pastor's dilemma, it cannot be left buried. They are both wrong views. It is contrary to the true nature of the church and it attacks the independence of the laity. In addition, discipleship training must begin with a clear answer to the question of who can actually be called a disciple in the church. The answer must not be known alone by the clergy or the trainees. All members of the congregation must know how to define a disciple. In the previous section, I briefly reviewed the four Gospels and the Epistles on who is called a disciple. It might be helpful to summarize again what was said. Do not forget that the devil's favorite bait to a church that is implementing discipleship training is the divisive debate about who is disciple and who is not. He uses this bait to rip the body of Christ apart.

A disciple of Christ is not a title used to refer to a person who has gone through a discipleship training program in the church. It also is not a name given to those lay leaders who sacrifice more than the others do. It is not a medal reserved for the ones who have entered into a higher spiritual maturity. Neither is it a nickname conferred on the clergy or missionary with a special calling for the ministry. To whom, then, is it alluding? For the answer, it might be most appropriate to borrow Michael Wilkin's opinion. He has carefully dealt with those easily misunderstood problems concerning disciple and discipleship in his famous book, *Following the master*, which he wrote with his heart and soul.[D]

The path of discipleship, which Jesus requires, includes all believers. It cannot be chosen according to whether you are mature or not. It is not for the devoted to submit and the not so inclined to forfeit. Although not all believers are requested to pay the same cost, once they come forward to believe in Jesus, He expects them to walk on the path to becoming His disciples. In Acts, we find that, whether male or female, Jew, Samaritan, or even foreigner, and whether a leader or a lay person in the church, anyone who confesses Jesus as his or her Lord and Savior is called a disciple. This aligns with the Great Commission to make disciples of all nations . Therefore, the path of discipleship must be walked by all who believe in Jesus. We should not forget that it cannot be chosen by programs, degree of devotion, or maturity.

In this manner, all believers are disciples, but there can be degrees of difference in the lives of disciples. According to 'the Great Commission', in order to make disciples, we are to go and witness, baptize, and then teach the Word to obey. If so, then a new believer is as much a disciple as one who is already baptized and striving to live a spiritual life, or as one who is enthusiastically learning and trying hard to reach spiritual maturity. But there is a difference in their spiritual level of maturity. There is no denying that a person who is taught and trained to obey is far ahead as a disciple in lifestyle and knowledge than a person who is baptized but not taught in the Word. Consequently, those who confess Jesus as their Lord do not receive training to become disciples, but they obtain training because they are disciples.

The Twelve Disciples also went through several stages in their development process in following Jesus. There is the beginning stage of believing but intermittent joining (John 2:12, 3:22). The second stage was giving up their worldly vocations and living with Him as servants to share a more intimate relationship (Matthew 4:18-22). But, it should be remembered that they were disciples no matter what stage they were in. All laity within the church, regardless of their spiritual level, if they confess Jesus as their Lord, must not question the fact that they are disciples of Christ. All must be taught unceasingly that the new believer, the devoted believer, and the clergy are all disciples.

Becoming a disciple signifies staying in this world in an incomplete state. It is not possible to be completely like Jesus.⁸ The church, therefore, should constantly emphasize that we, who are called to be disciples, must not stand still, but always be growing and maturing. Discipleship is a method of growing in spiritual life. We are to run unceasingly toward the mark of Jesus who is ahead. Those who refuse to get up and make the effort are in essence throwing their identity as a disciple of Jesus to the pigs. In this sense, discipleship training must be more of a program created for those who wish to be like Jesus and are running toward this goal than a process created to make a special group of quality people within the church. It should also be a training that burdens those who haven't yet achieved a greater level of spiritual maturity to desire to be trained in the Word to become more mature disciples. When this is done, it can prevent futile misconceptions of what discipleship training is and confusion about "Who is a disciple?"

Chapter 14: Personal Trust

Within the concept of discipleship are several important elements which Jesus emphasized throughout His life and His teaching. These elements are: having a personal trust, being a witness, and being a servant. Discipleship can be said to include all three basic elements in one word. There aren't many instances where Jesus personally explained or specifically defined what discipleship is and what is included in it. Instead, He called His disciples and mentored them by living with them. Discipleship, therefore, is living truth actualized in real lives rather than mere terminology.

Because the three elements of discipleship are absolutely related to the character of Jesus, the meaning and the characteristics of discipleship cannot be understood apart from Him. These elements cannot be individually separated and understood independently, but are compound elements that are mutually related. Without personal trust, discipleship cannot exist. Without the element of witnessing, it will forfeit its ultimate objective. And without servanthood, discipleship will lose its appeal.

The Meaning of Trust

Discipleship contains a moral charge to entrust our whole selves to Jesus. A study of the New Testament shows that one cannot be called a disciple unless he knows how to trust. The gospels of Matthew and Mark state that one is not worthy of being a disciple if he does not completely trust the character of Jesus and follow Him (Matthew 10:37b, Matthew 16:24, Mark 8:34b). Luke, narrating the same text, uses the words, 'he cannot be my disciple' to replace the words 'is not worthy' (Luke 14:26, 27, 33). We do not know exactly why the writers of the gospels used different expressions. Perhaps Jesus spoke more than once on a similar topic. He might have used different expressions at different occasions, being thoughtful to teach a clearer message each time He spoke. So it is possible that the writers of the gospels chose those particular expressions that they thought were best. However these expressions came to be written, there is no doubt that the Holy Spirit guided them.

Bultmann, who does textual criticism, tried to compare Matthew's "not worthy" with Luke's "cannot be a disciple" to decide which might be closer to what Jesus would actually have said. He concluded that the gospel of Luke is closer to the word of God.[2] Now, I do not condone Bultmann's argument about which is the genuine message of the Lord in the word of God. We should, however, reaffirm the fact that the characteristic of total trust, that is, giving up everything and taking up ones cross to follow Jesus, is the most basic element of being a disciple of Jesus.

Completely entrusting ourselves to Jesus begins with the calling of the Lord to "follow me" (Matthew 4:19, Mark 1:17,20). This calling communicates the assumption that whoever follows Him must give up everything. In the gospels, when Jesus called a person, there is no instance of someone following Him without giving up everything. One who cannot give up, cannot follow (Luke 18:18-30).

The three verbs in the Mark 8:34, 'come after me', 'deny himself', and 'take up his cross', which convey the meaning of denying oneself by giving up everything, are simple past tenses in Greek. They mean a one time action. Those disciples who want to follow Jesus must decide at once and then put it into action. Denying oneself and taking up a cross to come to Him is not a repeated action. It is a one time event. When this is done, then it is possible to have the continual action of following him. The word 'follow' is a present tense verb which shows continual action. This carries profound truth. It shows that following Jesus is a lifestyle for the disciple which will continue throughout a lifetime. The simple truth taught here, therefore, is that once you have entrusted your life to Jesus, like the farmer who put his hand to the plow to work the soil, do not look back.

Jesus' disciples who are devoting themselves to become witnesses of the gospel for the New Kingdom of Christ in this world (Matthew 10:32-33, Mark 8:38) must estimate the cost that is to be paid. This should not be done carelessly. Jesus did not hide anything from the crowd when He talked about the requirements of following Him. He used the clearest of expressions (Luke 14:25b). It is fitting to estimate the building cost before erecting a tower. Victory is elusive to a king who does not consider the odds of success and failure before going out to a war. Likewise, Jesus says that only those who calculate the cost beforehand are fit to follow Him.

Price That Must Be Paid

A price that must be paid by a disciple of Jesus is war (Matthew 10:34-36). At times, it might not be possible to avoid discord with a close family member (Matthew 10:34-36). This does not imply giving up proper family life. It means that family should not become a hindrance to following Jesus.[B]

Another price that must be paid by a disciple of Jesus is the sacrifice of choice (Matthew 10:37). The demands of the present circumstances are not always in alignment with the will of God. There might come a serious time when you have to choose between Jesus and your family. When John Bunyon was at the crossroad of either forsaking the faith for his family or going to a jail for Jesus, he wrote that giving up his family was like flesh was being torn off the bones. The great martyrs of the Korean Church had to pay this kind of price for the sacrifice of choice. Once again, this terrible choice will come very seldom; in God's mercy to many of us it may never come; but the fact remains that all loyalties must give place to loyalty to God.[M]

A price that must be paid by a disciple of Jesus is taking up the cross (Matthew 10: 38). The desire, the comfort and the dream that he loved till now must be cast off. A disciple cannot do only what he wants to do. He now must do what pleases Jesus. In some cases, he must be ready to overcome many sufferings. Now if we are children, then we are heirs - heirs of God and co-heirs with Christ, indeed if we share in his suffering in order that we may also share in the glory (Romans 8:17). Jesus walked the path of suffering and the cross, so His disciples cannot get sidetracked on a different path. Jesus' suffering is a model to His disciples. 'To this (to suffering) you were called, because Christ suffered for you, leaving you an example, that you should follow in his steps" (I

Peter 2:21). In Christianity there is always some cross, for Christianity is the religion of the Cross.[5] However, it is not a curse to carry the cross. Didn't the great men of God who went before us joyously express that, "at first I carried the cross, but later the cross carried me?"[6]

A price that must be paid by a disciple of Jesus is the adventure of giving up his life (Matthew 10:39). The life of faith in following Him cannot have worldly security as its first priority. A disciple of Christ is called out of the world to serve his God and his neighbor as his teacher did. To reach this goal, he must be able to give up his life. He must believe that true happiness lies in losing his life, because this is the way to find it and enjoy eternal life. However, I consider my life worth nothing to me, if only I may finish the race and complete the task the Lord Jesus has given me - the task of testifying to the gospel of God's grace (Acts 20:24.) This is how we know what love is: Jesus Christ laid down his life for us. And we ought to lay down our lives for our brothers (I John 3:16).

As I mentioned earlier, when we understand that becoming a disciple of Jesus demonstrates total trust in Him by giving up things that obstruct following Him, we often experience confusion. In all honesty, it creates a dilemma in our faith. Because we cannot confidently claim that we completely trust Him, there is a great chasm between Jesus request and our response. Can we still be called disciples? Vincent confessed this confusion in his commentary on Matthew 10:37-39 which seems to demand payment in becoming a disciple.[7]

Although talk of discipleship can bring feelings of confusion and inconsistency, the truth, that being a disciple is a process of becoming like Jesus, cannot be denied. Anxiety, due to our unfinished state, can be created during the process. Suffering may accompany the anxiety because of the present state of incompleteness. This is not at all strange. Becoming a disciple does not mean achieving a complete and flawless life. A person who is happy to be in the process of imitating Jesus even in the face of incompleteness is a disciple who has totally entrusted his life to the Lord.

When we go back to the book of Acts, we can see that the believers of the early church who were called disciples consistently followed Jesus. Yet it is difficult to make a sweeping conclusion as to how they gave up everything and followed Jesus. Were they like the Twelve Disciples who received Jesus' words literally and gave up their families and careers? Except for few cases, they did not do that. Despite this, they were the disciples who totally trusted the Lord. Why? They always believed obeying the will of God was the most important thing, and acted upon it accordingly. How the obedience materialized differed from person to person. It was done according to the leading of the Holy Spirit. However, none gave up the path of discipleship because of the inconsistency or confusion they sometimes experienced. To them, Jesus was their only master, and they were simply like children in their hearts toward Him.

Unique Personal Relationship

The relationship between Jesus and His disciples was personal trust. In other words, the personal element makes it a unique character that cannot be found in the Old Testament period. The relationships between Moses and Joshua, or Elijah and Elisha, were not in terms of teacher and disciple. Rengstorf explains that the reason the teacher and disciple relationship is not found in the Old Testament is because in the Old Testament era, God Himself was the only spiritual teacher and Lord.[8] There was no one who could take the place of God as teacher. Prophets and leaders were only used as mediums to inform the people of God's commands. Consequently, Moses and the prophets could not relay the message based upon their personal authority. To reiterate, they themselves could not become God. No one had qualifications to call others to follow him.

In the New Testament era, Jesus Himself is God and the Word (John 1:1). He was a perfect man. The words that came out of His mouth were the Words of God. God was in Him, and He was in God. Only Jesus, therefore, could become a true teacher who could command others to follow Him on the basis of His personhood. Only He had authority to command others to give up everything. Truly only He is the unique teacher who has authority to demand total obedience. You call me teacher and Lord, and rightly so, for that is what I am (John 13:13). The definition of a disciple in the New Testament is distinctive in that it is a personal unity between the called and the teacher who redefined the disciples whole life. As such, there is no occurrence in the New Testament where the word disciple is used without personal relationship attached to it. The focus is on the character of Jesus who is the teacher. Jesus is the one who called, and Jesus is the one who will provide the method and the content to perfect the relationship between Himself and His disciple.

The unique personal relationship between the two can be seen after Jesus' death on the Cross as the memory of His teachings and the miracles He performed became a strong tie that bound the disciples. When Jesus left, they were bereft of their relationship with Him. This can be seen in Luke where, after the story of Gethsemane, the word disciple is no longer found (Luke 22:47b). When Jesus was arrested, the intimacy between He and the disciples was ruptured. They were no longer suitable to be called disciples. They were in a place where they had to be called together once again after the resurrection.[9] We do not have to agree with this view, but it cannot be denied that during the Passion Week, the personal trust relationship by the disciples fell into danger. It is easy to detect the crumbling of the foundation of their faith in Jesus.

Discipleship training of the laity connotes producing a person who entrusts all of himself in obedience to Jesus in a personal relationship. Partial trust from the disciple is impossible. That relationship is bound to break up sooner or later. (John 6:66) For none of us lives to himself alone and none of us dies to himself alone. If we live, we live to the Lord; and if we die, we die to the Lord. So, whether we live or die, we belong to the Lord (Romans 14:7-8). A good picture of this kind of personal trust can be seen in the story of the widow, Ruth, who followed her mother-in-law, Naomi. Read Ruth's famous line again replacing the word 'you', referring to Naomi, with the word 'Jesus'. You have a definition of true discipleship. "Don't urge me to leave Jesus or to turn back from Jesus. Where Jesus goes I will go, and where Jesus stays I will stay. Jesus' people will be my people and Jesus will be my God. Where Jesus dies I will die, and there I will be buried. May the Lord deal with me, be it ever so severely, if anything but death separates Jesus and me" (Ruth 1:16, 17 Reference). If an old mother-in-law could have been given this kind of commitment, why can we not follow Jesus the Son of God even more passionately?

Unfortunately, so many are called disciples in today's Church who do not exhibit total trust. It is sad to hear people say that only a few are called to totally trust, and it is unfair of the clergy to demand it from all laity. In addition we must remember: not to be a disciple of Jesus means to be a disciple of the power of darkness. And to be a servant of the world and of sin costs incalculably more than to be a disciple of Jesus - the price of it is the loss of the highest happiness in this life and darkness and affliction of soul throughout eternity. How insignificant the price to be paid for rejecting Him is![20]

Most Difficult Crisis Point

Discipleship training is the process of changing a lay person into one who totally trusts. In my experience, nine out of ten who were trained live a life far from total trust. And the lesson on total trust is the most difficult crisis point in discipleship training. When the Holy Spirit works mightily with the Word and power, then there is much travail and tears. It might be slow coming, but this change opens up a glorious world to the repentant. But if this crisis is not overcome, discipleship training faces continual difficulties. It is distressing to see that discipleship training is considered as just plugging through a few Bible studies, and not as undergoing something like the pains of childbirth to totally depend on Christ. Let's reiterate. What is discipleship training? It is the labor to birth obedient disciples who deny everything to follow Jesus. It might not be to total satisfaction, but it is the work of forming a person who would give his best to pay the necessary cost to follow Jesus.

Chapter 15: The Witness of the Gospel

The Ultimate Calling of the Disciple

Strictly speaking, the ultimate work that Jesus commissioned His disciples to do was to become His witnesses. He called people out of the world to testify about Him. So, in the gospel of Luke and the book of Acts, witness or being a witness is inseparably connected with the calling of the disciples. Luke uses the word witness to mean two separate situations. One is used in the case of testimony of the disciples who witnessed Jesus' cross and the resurrection first hand. The other is for those who confess, believe, and testify after hearing the evidence of the Apostles.[21]

Just before His ascension, Jesus commanded the disciples to spread the gospel and preach repentance and forgiveness in His name to all nations starting from Jerusalem. He stated clearly to the disciples that "You are witnesses of these things" (Luke 24:48). He also prophesied that when the Holy Spirit came upon them, "You will be my witnesses" (Acts 1:8). The disciples of the Early Church were made up of those witnesses born through His prophecy (Acts 1:22, 2:32, 3:15, 5:31, 10:41).

Nevertheless, the ministry of witnessing was not always limited to the Apostles. When Jesus said to the disciples that "You are witnesses of these things" in Jerusalem, there were not only the Apostles there. We know that other disciples were also among them (Luke 24:33). The Lord's command was to all who were present in that place. Later the 120 disciples who were in Mark's upper room also became witnesses. Stephen was a witness for Jesus (Acts 22:20). It is necessary to note that Stephen was called to be a witness even though he was not with the apostles to personally observe all that Jesus said and did. Soon afterwards, he became a martyr. The words witness and martyr are both derived from same origin. At that time, to be a witness of Jesus meant to be prepared to lose one's life. Stephen did not become a witness after his martyrdom, but he became a martyr because he was a witness.

To find out how closely related disciple and witness is, we only need to see in the gospels and the book of Acts how often the verb, 'to send (*apostello*, *pempo*)', is used together with the word, 'disciple'. 'To send' was used as often as 215 times, and almost always related to sending out the disciples as witnesses by Jesus. Luke allocates the title of Apostle to the twelve among the disciples, reemphasizing the fact that a 'disciple' is a 'witness' for Jesus. This is because apostle (*apostolos*) contains the meaning of being sent. A disciple is one who is being sent, not one who sends. There is no instance in the Bible where the word apostle is used to denote the one who sends out.[22]

Inner Urgings by the Holy Spirit

It is not difficult to find out how passionate the thousands of men and women called disciples in the Early Church were as witnesses for Jesus. They were not coerced or commanded to be witnesses for Him. It is amazing that there is no occasion where the Apostles charged them to witness. Like the Apostles, most early believers were compelled by an inner urge. "For we cannot help speaking about what we have seen and heard" (Acts 4:20). This is the important basis for explaining the actions of the witnesses of the Early Church who could not be stopped in their passionate and courageous proclamation of Jesus' resurrection.

Then, where did they get the motivation, but to speak? Was it to some kind of leadership pressure to remember and obey the Great Commission of Jesus? We cannot trace any grudging or superficial leadership actions designed just so that new believers could obey the Great Commission.[23] Only the Holy Spirit could have supplied their inner drive. They all belonged to Christ by the power of the Holy Spirit. People with the Holy Spirit possessed an inner witness that aligned with the apostolic nature of church of which they were a significant part. Whenever the Apostles faced a crisis as witnesses of the resurrection, the Holy Spirit repeatedly filled them. This is the drastic measure of God to clearly reaffirm publicly the presence of the Holy Spirit who always works in them to bear witness (Acts 4:8,31, 6:8, 7:55, 13:9).

If witnessing or confession about Jesus happens through the inner urgings of the Holy Spirit, then it is safe to say that this is an ordinary phenomenon expected from all believers universally. The Holy Spirit is a gift given to all who are called by God (Acts 2:39). When the Holy Spirit comes, all receive power, and will become witnesses for Jesus (Acts 1:8). This implies that being a witness is determined by the hand of the Holy Spirit, and not by a person.

We often hear people say that evangelism is a spiritual gift. This is not a completely valid viewpoint. A spiritual gift is a gift that the Holy Spirit in His sovereignty gives to each person according to need for the purpose of serving (I Corinthians 12:11). We should not narrowly interpret the coming of the Holy Spirit on the disciples at Pentecost as a spiritual gift. Certainly there is an element of a spiritual gift, but the coming of the Holy Spirit in that place has greater meaning. If evangelism is narrowly defined as a spiritual gift, then inability to evangelize lies wholly on the Holy Spirit. And it would lead people to think that evangelism is an exclusive tool only for those special people who have the spiritual gift. Insisting that evangelism is a spiritual gift will induce us to commit the error of partially eliminating the basic reason for the coming of the Holy Spirit to the Church, as well as the apostolic nature of the Church that He has created.

There is one passage in the Bible that talks about evangelism as a spiritual gift. Ephesians 4:11 contains the word, evangelist. This could be interpreted as not everyone being able to spread the Gospel, except only those who obtained the qualifications through some kind of spiritual gifting. This verse, however, should not be seen as a proof that evangelism is a spiritual gift. Paul is dealing here with duties of the ministers who will serve the church. The offices of apostle and prophet were appointments and, at the same time, duties (I Corinthians 12:28). The office of evangelist was also a duty. With a duty, an appropriate spiritual gift followed. A person with the duty of evangelism could have a gift of evangelism that others might not have. But, it is not right to apply this generally to all believers. In order to accomplish the duty and the inner urging for evangelism, which anyone who has the Holy Spirit residing in him possesses, it must be distinguished from the special gift of the evangelist. This can be compared to

147

the differences between a faith that leads to salvation, and faith that comes from spiritual gifting for the appointment (I Corinthians 12:9).

Why Is There No Command to Witness?

There is one amazing fact in the New Testament. Why can we not easily find the command to diligently evangelize? The verse we frequently quote, II Timothy 4:2 - "Preach the Word; be prepared in season and out of season" is, strictly speaking, a command given to Timothy, who was a pastor. The New Testament is strangely silent on the subject of evangelism. It is also the same concerning the assembly of the church. Except for one verse, Hebrews 10:25, there is no other place where believers are encouraged to gather together diligently. In reality, evangelism and assembly are vitally important to the life of the church. Voltaire, who ardently attacked Christianity, advised the King that, he should get rid of Sunday if he wants to kill Christianity. If the Church were to neglect or cease those two things it would only be a matter of time before Christianity would disappear from the face of the earth. Why is it, then, that the Bible is so excessively economical in its command to diligently evangelize and to actively assemble? Isn't this in the same vein as pray unceasingly? Again we cannot but be amazed that although the Bible is so scarce in its command, the Early Church was most diligent in evangelizing and gathering together.

The key to understanding this phenomena is in the inner urgings of the Holy Spirit which makes one cannot help but speak about what was seen and heard. To those who belong to the Holy Spirit, witnessing about Jesus is a type of instinctive outcome. Instinctive means it does not wait for the command because it is not necessary. The urge to speak about what was seen and heard overrides the command.[24] If you believe that in the end times the Holy Spirit will come to mold the Church as a community of witnesses and that He will not abandon the Church till the end of times (because this is not a one time occurrence but a continual activity), then all these expressions such as self-evidence, naturalism, or inner urge, or new instinct should not feel awkward. The Holy Spirit is still in the Church making His Church apostolic in nature. Yet, why is it that today's lay persons are not usually experiencing the inner drive to be witnesses? Why is the life of witness that aligns with the very nature of the Church becoming blurry?

The Witness of the Word

There is a problem we could overlook as we consider the relationship between disciple and witness. All that the gospels and the book of Acts mention about evangelism is through word of mouth. The disciples, as witnesses, were to speak about the gospel, not to impress others through their good behavior. Maybe that is why some insist that there is no clear example depicted in the New Testament that the Early Church had any understanding of discipleship from a point of view of the moral act of imitating Christ.[25] This is a very interesting insight. What is the reason that these believers in the Early Church were more intent upon sharing the message of Jesus as the atoning Savior of the world then imitating him as their extraordinary and moral model? Why did they pray "Now, Lord, consider their threats and enable your servants to speak your word with great boldness" (Acts 2:29) as their priority?

As we all know, the Lord heard their prayer and instantly filled them with the Holy Spirit so they may become bold witnesses of the gospel (Acts 4:31). As persecution proliferated in Jerusalem, they were scattered everywhere as witnesses of the gospel (Acts 8:4). As if they were disinterested in the moral point of imitating the perfect character of Jesus, they completely and with single-mindedness devoted themselves to speaking about Jesus' story with their mouth. They were persecuted because of their words, not because of their good deeds. Good deeds rarely bring persecution for the gospel. Strictly speaking, good deeds cannot be counted as a complete witness. Therefore, witness without the spoken words of the gospel cannot save the world. Sometimes, someone might believe that he is becoming a witness for Christ through his good deeds, but if he does not open his mouth, then the Jesus he thinks is in his deeds might not be the same Jesus who died a redemptive death on the cross.

After the death of the 12 Apostles and succeeding apostles, even in the midst of persecution, for hundreds of years the Early Church did not give up witnessing for Christ with their mouths.

There were no missionary societies, no missionary institutions, no organized efforts in the ante-Nicene age; and yet in less than 300 years from the death of St. John the whole population of the Roman empire which then represented the civilized world was nominally christianized... Every congregation was a missionary society, and every Christian believer a missionary, inflamed by the love of Christ to convert his fellow-men... Every Christian told his neighbor, the laborer to his fellow-laborer, the slave to his fellow-slave, the servant to his master and mistress, the story of his conversion, as a mariner tells the story of the rescue from shipwreck.[26]

There are some around us who secretly scorn witnessing for Jesus with words, and contend that in this contemporary age it is more important and more productive to witness through action rather than words. Let's refresh our memories here. Witnessing without words is not the witnessing the Bible talks about. And how can they hear without someone preaching to them? (Romans 10:14) Why can't they hear? Witnessing without words lacks the concrete nature of the gospel of Jesus, even if the deeds are very pure and attractive.

I am not repudiating witnessing through deeds by stating that true witnessing is through words. Deeds are also as important. A serious problem could arise if we were to deny either words or deeds in witnessing. The fact that the disciples in the Early Church considered evangelism with words as overwhelmingly predominant reminds us of the words of the wise that, "even a live dog is better off than a dead lion" (Ecclesiastes 9:4). It is wise to remember that if we emphasize witnessing through deeds only, then we might be putting forward our righteous looking selves rather than Jesus Christ who is the object of 'come and see'.

Training a lay person to become a disciple of Christ refers to making that person into a witness who confesses and testifies of Jesus in all spheres of his or her life. We can diagnose whether discipleship training is healthy or not by observing how much the trainee wants to speak about Jesus. Healthy discipleship training produces witnesses who have difficulty stopping the inner urgings of the Holy Spirit. Discipleship training is assisting Jesus

Christ, who is already present in them, to overflow out of their lives. Not only will they joyfully boast and confess Jesus, but their lives and their characters will also be fully covered by the aroma of Christ. The problem pastors are facing today is that we lead many lay persons whose deeds reek because their mouths have been shut up. Have you seen anyone who witnesses about Jesus with his or her mouth but does not try to imitate Jesus in doing good deeds?

Chapter 16: A Servant Who Serves

The Example of Jesus

In the New Testament, the disciples of Jesus as servants and the act of serving are closely related. Two expressions are used. One is a noun, servant (doulos); and the other is a verb, to serve (diakoneo). These two words are used as a set and appear often in the Bible (Matthew 20:27-28, Mark 10:44-45, Luke 12:37). The word servant refers to the identity of a person and how he should act in Christ as a disciple. To serve emphasizes ability rather than identity and teaches how to conduct a life of a disciple with Christ as his master.[27]

A disciple of Jesus must become a servant who serves. It is not accidental but inevitable. No one can be exempt because it is essential. Why is that? Our example of servanthood is Jesus. Jesus came into this world taking on the nature of a servant (Philippians 2:7-8). He lived in this world as a servant. "But I am among you as one who serves" (Luke 22:27b). His whole life was a process of sacrificial devotion, of giving Himself to the world that He loved. On His last Passover at the Last Supper, He acted out a living lesson of serving by personally washing the feet of the disciples, whose necks were stiff with pride, to show that a true disciple is one who serves. "Now that I, your Lord and Teacher, have washed your feet, you also should wash one another's feet. I have set you an example that you should do as I have done for you" (John 13:14-15). When He gave up His life on the cross as an atonement lamb, He finally confirmed the true figure of a servant. "For even the Son of Man did not come to be served, but to serve, and to give his life as a ransom for many" (Mark 10:45).

A disciple who personally trusts and follows Jesus cannot help but take the example shown by his teacher. If he is hesitant about becoming a servant, then he is foolishly thinking that the servant is greater than the master. Jesus foresaw such danger for His disciples, and warned in advance: "I tell you the truth, no servant is greater than his master, nor is a messenger greater than the one who sent him. Now that you know these things, you will be blessed if you do them" (John 13:16-17). Blessing for a disciple is to know that he is a servant, and that he is not greater than the master, and to act accordingly. Honor comes to a disciple who does not forget that he is only an unworthy servant no matter how much he serves. "So you also, when you have done everything you were told to do, should say, We are unworthy servants; we have only done our duty" (Luke 17:10). To such a humble servant, the master finally bestows praise and honor. "Well done, good and faithful servant! You have been faithful with a few things. I will put you in charge of many things. Come and share your masters happiness!" (Matthew 25:21).

Joining in Jesus' servanthood means that a disciple as a servant is prepared for persecution. To Jesus, there was no difference between being a servant and dying on the cross. A disciple's mission cannot be undertaken without readiness to loose his life. Jesus sent His disciples into a corrupt world ruled by human rulers. A servant, therefore, must drink from the same cup as his master (Matthew 20:23), and be prepared to face calamities as his master did (John 18:33). In this sense, Bonhoeffer was not excessive in his view to say that when Christ calls one to become a disciple, He is calling them to their death.[28]

From a servant's point of view, therefore, giving up ones life is to live, and saving ones life is to die (Matthew 16:24-25).

The aim of Jesus and his disciples is not to set up human orders in this world. Their concern is with the kingdom of God and the age of glory. But the way to this goal leads through suffering and death. This determines at once the attitude of all whom God calls to His kingdom. The point of suffering is to be found in the service accomplished. This makes it sacrificial.[29]

In other words, servant and suffering have inseparable functional relations. Servanthood is a complete, not partial, commissioning of the character and life of a disciple in following Jesus, and is to be carried out continually, not occasionally. Experiencing suffering as a servant is the same as a letter guaranteeing discipleship (John 15:19).

The Inevitable Demand and the Evidence of a Confession

Because of the contents of the gospel that were given to them to preach to the world, the disciples could not escape servanthood. The object of their proclamation was Jesus Christ

(Mark 1:1). God's love is poured out on Jesus and that love is spreading and working through Jesus' sacrificial death. He opened springs of righteousness at the cross that the whole world could drink from. 'This is how God showed his love among us: He sent his one and only Son into the world that we might live through him" (I John 4:9).

To Jesus, 'love' was will and action. This is because in God's law of love, it was always expressed through action. That love becomes visible and flows into the hearts through the sacrifice of a servant. There is a deep truth in the fact that the word, 'agafao' which denotes 'agape love', was almost always used only in the passages concerning Jesus. Jesus, as a servant, never showed or spoke hypocritical love absent sacrifice. A disciple of Jesus Christ, therefore, must become a servant to be a witness. And through his words and actions he must show Jesus Christ, who suffered with love. Without this, it is impossible to become a witness for Jesus. The life of a disciple must be thoroughly constrained by the Gospel he is proclaiming. A disciple must love his neighbor as himself while sharing the Gospel (Matthew 22:39). Love must be given away (Matthew 5:42), while serving gladly (Mark 10:42-45, Luke 22:24-27). In this way, there will be no contradiction in the witness of Jesus.

There is a reason why Jesus loved. As disciples, we also must have the same reason. Jesus came to find lost sheep. In the parable of the Good Samaritan, Jesus taught the disciples three points about His mission (Luke 10:33b). To whom should they take their agape love? To the almost unconscious traveler who was mugged by robbers-what is the reason for loving him? To save his life. How should that love be shown to him? By serving him with readiness to give up even their own lives.

The Apostle John declared the servanthood of discipleship in this direct manner: "This is how we know what love is: Jesus Christ laid down his life for us. And we ought to lay down our lives for our brothers" (I John 3:16).

But His self-sacrifice is not just a revelation of love to be admired; it is an example to copy. We ought (i.e. should be willing) to lay down our lives for the brethren, or our profession to love them is an empty boast. We ought to do this, as a definite Christian obligation, because we belong to Christ, just as we ought to follow His example in all things and walk even as he walked (I John 2:6).[30]

Volunteering Servant

We should not forget here that servanthood in discipleship is a volunteer position. A disciple is not a slave brought in by force. He has become a servant of Christ with joy. In the Old Testament, there were slaves who loved their masters and volunteered to serve them for life. Their ears were pierced to show their joyful willingness to serve him with love (Exodus 21:5-6). A disciple of Christ is a servant whose ears are pierced. He does not serve unwillingly.

As I have said so far, to be a disciple of Christ means to become a servant. It implies an oath to be obedient and devoted to the Lord and to follow His examples. Not only that, it denotes serving in this world to the point of giving up ones life. A disciple of Jesus knows that the message he shares is a binding promise that he is indeed a servant and that he is to serve with love. And it becomes a law in his life, that he cannot deny his discipleship to Christ. He has willingly chained himself to the law of love through his confession. But he does not consider this a heavy burden; rather, he is full of joy and thanksgiving for the blessing.

Discipleship training in the church is teaching what the character and life of a servant of love, who is imitating Christ, should resemble. It is not to explain the job of the servant but it is to help him to practice the life of a servant. Here, a leader must recognize that Jesus did not just talk about his life as a servant, but he showed it through his actions. The power of love was in His actions not His words. This is the fundamental principle of perfect divinity and humanity. Without lowering Himself to taking on the form of a servant, the victory on the cross would not have followed. Words alone would not bring any changes. As a person does not change by putting on a beautiful garment, a servant of love is not produced through mere beautiful words. What truth should we learn from this? It is that the leader must teach by showing himself a servant. As such, Paul always lived his life as a model. "Follow my example, as I follow the example of Christ" (I Corinthians 11:1).

I am afraid that we give a lot of lip service to being a servant of love after the example of Christ, but on the inside we secretly condemn it. There are many who would like to be first and be served in the church. The clergy especially is not immune to that. What is the reason for becoming so stiff-necked and stubborn once a person becomes an elder? I think many disregard God's truth that the greater you are, the lower you should become. And many forget that the authority in the church comes from serving, not from being served. It should be normal for one, who has been a believer for a long time, who boasts much faith, and who seems to pray up a storm from early morning on, to be more like Christ as a servant who serves. But the reality is otherwise. When the principle of the world has replaced the principle of the kingdom of God, then the church reeks of human guile. It is natural to expect a depraved world when evangelism is stopped and the voices of those who have abandoned their attempt to become disciples of Jesus rise. What is discipleship training? It is about healing such chronic ills. It is a ministry of the Holy Spirit that brings the clergy and the laity to a lower place.

We have discussed three basic elements of discipleship. The world will see Jesus in a person who trusts, who is a witness, and who is a servant in his character and life. The zenith of discipleship training is that Christ will be reflected in our lives. In other words, the world needs to see in the change and the maturity that took place a little Jesus. Is this not the most pressing ministry for the laity who must daily live and work in the world with so many unbelievers?

Chapter 17 : The Nature of the Church Will Change

If there is a strong desire in today's church to recoup the apostolic nature of the church and discipleship, which is the identity of the laity, then it is inevitable that there will be a radical reformation of the basics. Various shields that many churches already put up tell how urgent the need for radical reform is. This is certainly a problem before a revival. If we were to desire church growth before the church is reformed in its nature, then the church will more than likely face danger in its life and spirituality. How would the church be reformed if we were to practice the philosophy of ministry of making disciples of the laity? I am very sure we would see a few changes in the basics.

We Will Be Able to Renew the Image of the Church

Previously, I stated that the Church is a community of chosen people who were called by God for worship, growth and witness. Today's churches are abusing these definitions of Church. There is a tendency to fall into a self-satisfactory mode stemming from a strong sense of privilege as a community of called and chosen. Many are under illusion that they are already the Bride lifted up into the air. Insisting on the privileges while being oblivious to the appointed task are the chronic dispositions of the Jewish religion that was prevalent in Jesus' time. If the earthly Church is a people of God called out of the world, then it also is a disciple of Christ sent to the world. With privilege there is a responsibility. Why isn't this fact taken seriously? When Jesus summoned the disciples to 'follow me', he gave it as a prerequisite to a secondary command, 'as the Father sent me to the world, I also send you'.

The image of a gathering church also contains the image of a dispersing church. Being called and being sent out are not two different ideas. There are two sides of one truth. When a church rediscovers its apostolic nature, it will clearly show this dual nature. As this happens, that church will not stay fixed on the idea of getting together as an only goal. In fact, gathering together will be seen as means to accomplish the ultimate goal of the church. God can receive glory just through the mere existence of the church, because He has purchased it through His blood. However, He is more joyous when the church becomes the body of Christ giving glory to God. The church has to become a school where the people of God can receive spiritual training. It has to become a workplace where God's laborers work, a barracks where the soldiers of the cross are equipped for war, and a refuge where the tired and oppressed come and rest. It has to become a lighthouse of last hope for those who are in the midst of the storms in life. It must be a lamp of life to individuals, and a power plant that can light the society spiritually through them. I believe that a church with this image can be produced through discipleship training.

The Self-image of the Laity Can Be Correctly Defined

Reforming the nature of the church depends much on how the lay people see themselves. Who they think they are and what their response is to that perception will determine the nature of that church. If the lay people think of themselves as objects of the church, then they will be satisfied with the protection under the umbrella of the clergy. They will be like a lethargic child whose response is always passive. This is unsuitable to a church posting the flag of the victorious Lord Jesus Christ. Unfortunately, many churches are producing laity who see such a sickly self-image as being proper. The principle of discipleship is a Biblical strategy to change the lay persons way of thinking. What an amazing change would come over today's churches if people who confess Jesus as their savior were to identify themselves as the disciples of the book of Acts! This might not be as hard as you think.

Nevertheless, it is heartbreaking to see many churches looking for reforms in the nature of the church in other places. It cannot be done through changes in programs. It will not come by renovating its facility. A pastor in America was obsessed with the idea that the church had no hope unless its facility was changed. One day, he suddenly put the pulpit in the middle of the sanctuary like in a boxing ring. He had the congregation worship around the pulpit. He was hoping that this action would change the cold attitude and passivity of his members. However, before a month was gone, church attendance shrank down to half. This might be an extreme example, but it is no different than a woman who expected her marriage to improve by rearranging the bedroom furniture. We must not commit such childishness. Change the self-image of the laity based on the principles of discipleship. Then the nature of the church will change beyond belief. If you find this unbelievable, then visit other churches which have succeeded through discipleship training until you are convinced.

Converting Guardianship to Training Ministry

A pastor is without doubt a shepherd. The words shepherding or ministry came from the fact that Jesus said, 'take care of my sheep'. I wonder, however, if our definition of the word is too narrow. Is taking care of sheep just confined to feeding and protecting, a type of overseeing work? I don't think so. The idea of taking care of sheep contains a very positive meaning: 'teaching them to obey' (Matthew 28:20). In the word, obey is the active ministry of continually leading the believer through a change in character to be more like Christ and to practice God's will in his life. We use the word, training in place of teaching them to obey. A ministry that sets training as a prerequisite has a specific goal. Training without a goal does not make any sense. What is that goal? It is bearing fruit. It is producing many lambs so that God, Who is our master, will be happy.

The best ministry, therefore, is making sheep strong enough through training to self-produce. Guardianship ministry will weaken the laity. They want to be spoon-fed and will only think of themselves. Instead of planning big things, they will collide and argue with one another about little things. Because their perspective is so narrow, they will not be able to escape the

163

boundary of an 'only us' attitude. A ministry focused on protecting cannot help but further harden such a makeup of a church. What can the Lord do with such a church? Discipleship training can eradicate such ills. Through training, lay people can be transformed into strong and productive entities.

The Whole Church Can Resuscitate Cooperative Relationships

Discipleship training that upholds cooperative ministry among the laity to serve one another will develop into various kinds of living organic relationships. Church members become one in love and caring for each other's spiritual life. Most church members will cease to see themselves as independent entities but recognize themselves as existing to help others. They will heal many ills caused by various barren groups within the church. Discipleship training will cultivate the laity to be functional people who are essential members in the church for all cooperative ministry. It will also create various conditions where this cooperative ministry can bear fruit, whether inside or outside the church. As a result, mutual relationships between the believers will develop through a special spiritual relationship the Bible talks about (Colossians 3:16, I John 1:3-4). This is koinonia, experienced by sharing the Word in the Holy Spirit and serving one another with love. This relationship is totally different from the human closeness that could happen through certain circumstances in the church, as when a project must be finished.

Do discipleship training. You will observe within two to three years a change in the nature of the church from a mere organizational form to a genuine organic function of cooperative ministries.

A Clergy Centered Structure Will Evolve into a Lay Centered System

Some theologians lament Luther proclaimed the priesthood of all believers: nearly 500 years later church forms still deny it.[31] Many churches conduct church life on the inside as if only the clergy are priests, while at the same time saying outside that there is no difference between the clergy and the laity. When clergy desire exclusivity and authority, it erodes ground for the laity to stand as priests. Changing such a chronic state of the church might prove to be as difficult as the Reformation in the Middle Ages. But if we have a correct understanding of what a lay centered church is, then I think it might not be as dismal as it sounds.

I have already pointed out previously that I am in no way condemning the clergy system. A lay centered church is where the clergy serves the laity in discovering their rightful place as the main subject of the church and in fulfilling their position according to ability. In order for this to happen, the clergy must seek the lower place. This does not have to be taken as the notion of a greater or lesser position. When the laity find their rightful place, then the position of the clergy will be equally modified. Discipleship training can change the abnormal nature of a church where the laity seem to exist for one clergyman into a healthy body where the clergy exists for the lay members. When this succeeds, I believe both the clergy and the laity will survive.

Lay Leadership in Ministries Will Increase

The greatest anguish for any pastor is the feeling of isolation that without him there is none other who can work.

Consequently, he will carry a burden beyond his ability and face the danger of loosing passion due to burnout. Often without his awareness, he will become victim to a mentality of peace-at-any-price. Just as Moses at one time thought he could judge all the complaints and problems of the people by himself and did not try to find leaders who could share the burden, many pastors are unwilling to find and train the members of the church to be partners in ministry to share the burden.

The ministry that I refer to here is not like that of being an usher or the head of the evangelism department. I mean a pastoring type of ministry that nurtures others through the Word and prayer. It's about sharing the gospel with neighbors and spiritually healing those who are sick and hurt. I refer to encouraging trained lay people to share in Jesus' ministry of preaching, teaching and healing. Which church will harvest more, the church where only the pastor is working, or the church that has 50 other lay leaders working together? There is no other way to create lay leaders than through discipleship training. If you are a pastor, do not hesitate. Start quickly. The sooner the clergy and the lay leaders work together, the better it is. I remember seeing a title of an article in a magazine, introducing a church in Los Angeles. It was a church with 900 active pastors. How enviable that they can boast in such a manner when there is only one ordained clergyman in that church!

Sustaining Church Growth Can Be Expected

When the number of lay leader increases and church members are being nurtured continually through discipleship training, the strength that comes from such activity can be the generating power to a church revival. Wherever the lay person spends time seven days a week could become a mission field. All conversation could be a path to sharing the gospel. Everything he does could be used as an opportunity for saving lives, either directly or indirectly. From this, the possibility of a revival and continuing church evangelism can be expected. We should not define church revival as a result of some kind of project. Growth or revival should be viewed as an issue of the nature of the church. Desirable growth comes naturally and continuously. When discipleship training is in place, the church will grow without any further forced means. How could it not be full of sheep when they are constantly giving birth to more lambs?

Let me say a little more about church growth since this is of major interest to all pastors. It is strange that so many think that using the method of discipleship training for church growth is unreasonable. Of course, there are various ways to church growth. To insist that discipleship training is the only method is showing ignorance to the wisdom of the Holy Spirit and the diversity of grace. But it is also an immense misunderstanding to see a huge gap between discipleship training and church growth. In one word, when discipleship training is anchored to the very heart of the church, then healthy growth can be expected. Growing is not a problem to a healthy child, and the same can be applied to church growth. Go ahead. Carry out discipleship training. Your church will turn into a healthy growing church.

There is one truth that you must understand. Discipleship training should not be used only as a method for the growth. This will deteriorate your discipleship training before long. Discipleship training does not offer anything that will satisfy a pastor who wants instant church growth. But it does present many gifts to satisfy one who desires a continuing natural growth of the church. It will first of all transform the sermon of the pastor into a message that people can hear. While conducting the training the pastor will be personally blessed and, at the same time, will realize what the spiritual needs of the members are. He will learn their language. How can the sermons not change? Furthermore, a pastor will develop a new paradigm for leadership. A traditional leadership where one asks what can be done for the laity will be transformed into a leadership that asks what can be done with the laity. Discipleship training requires many things from the lay person. It burdens the trainees with challenges such as: read more Bible, pray unceasingly, go out witnessing, be a good husband, and be committed. This will make some pastors uneasy and worry that some people might leave the church. It is more likely , however, that the opposite will happen.

Roger Finke, who has analyzed and diagnosed the growth and decline of American churches for the last 200 years, reached a very encouraging conclusion. He says the main reason why the mainline denominations have declined at such a rapid rate from the latter half of the sixties is due to clergy trying to please the laity and demand too little from them. On the other hand, evangelical churches shone in their growth because the clergy demanded much from the laity. Based on this analysis, he presents three strengths of a growing church.

First, strong organizations are strict. The stricter, the stronger. Second, a strong organization that loses its strictness will also lose its strength. Third, strictness tends to deteriorate into leniency. [32]

Discipleship training has the tendency to make a church strict. It gives the strong impression that it burdens the laity. The fact of the matter is that these challenging training programs have actually been real building blocks in church growth. This is proven in the Korean churches that are experiencing continual growth through discipleship training. I say it once again. Do you want a healthy church that has natural and continual growth? Go forward with discipleship training. Before long, you will observe right before your eyes, what Isaiah saw in the vision: "The least of you will become a thousand, the smallest a mighty nation. I am the Lord; in its time I will do this swiftly" (Isaiah 60:22).

PART FOUR

MINISTRY METHOD
- DISCIPLESHIP TRAINING
PP171 - PP260

MINISTRY PHILOSOPHY
- YOUR THEOLOGY OF THE CHURCH

MINISTRY STRATEGY
- TRUE DISCIPLESHIP

MINISTRY METHOD
- DISCIPLESHIP TRAINING

MINISTRY FIELD
- THE EXAMPLE OF SARANG

Chapter 18: The Purpose of Discipleship Training

If we recognize that discipleship is a Biblical principle which can be adapted to the demands of new eras, and it is an important pastoral ministry strategy for changing church structure and reforming its image, then we need next to find a practical way to apply it to a pastoral environment. What can we do to help develop a lay person into a well grounded disciple of Jesus? Discipleship training is a practical pastoral ministry method that answers this question.

A Tragic Misconception

In order to do discipleship training correctly we need first to remove a few misconceptions that are often heard. There is no guarantee that a pastor or church leader can persist with discipleship training well to the end if he does not have a clear answer to the common misconceptions about it.

To be honest, discipleship training has been greatly

misunderstood as a result of leaders who claim that they are training disciples, without properly knowing what developing a disciple is all about.

It is also true that critical statements made by discipleship training leaders who failed to defend themselves also became the cause of various misconceptions about discipleship training.

In addition, many people make statements on the basis of some abstract image or notion, without doing any serious research. Whatever route it took to become a misunderstanding, it cannot be seen as a good thing.

The primary misconception is that discipleship training is Bible study. The Korean church and many others I have witnessed around the world experience a kind of depression which I believe is brought about by discipleship training that only teaches Bible study.

Until now discipleship training played a big part in the growth of the Korean church. However discipleship training is the cause for the recent Korean church's growth halting at the present level and showing stagnation. Discipleship training is, as the definition of the term states, training for making disciples. The result of discipleship training is that Korean church congregations became people who like to hear and speak well. But if there are positive effects of this training then on the opposite side the fact cannot be denied that there is an increase of believers who are content with mere learning itself. [1]

It is true that there have been many reasons for the rise of such serious misunderstandings. There are churches doing poor discipleship training. In an extreme case, there was some

174

discipleship training too pitiful even to be called Bible study. In cases like that, we have little to say to statements about discipleship training being nothing more than another outdated method of Bible study.

One must be able to distinguish, however, between having such a misunderstanding and making a definitive declaration. In very clear terms discipleship training is not Bible study!

Bible study is no more than a step of discipleship training. I do not believe, for example, that discipleship training brought a slump to the Korean church. There is not a single concrete proof that can link discipleship training to today's stagnation. It might be more convincing, rather, to question the responsibility of leaders aloof to discipleship training and the majority of laity who acted like the faithful while evading what they viewed as burdensome training.

The second misconception is viewing discipleship training as a course for making competent lay technicians, skillful at evangelism and teaching. If the purpose of discipleship training is to make competent lay evangelists who teach the Word well and are dedicated to serving others then this training will not last long.

Discipleship training that counts its profits will be difficult to maintain its purity. Of course, eventually the purpose of making disciples includes forming a competent person who is a witness of Jesus in the world, and serves others in the church.

We should not forget, however, that to make such narrow interpretations, to limit being a disciple to only a functional aspect, is dangerous. The focus of discipleship training has to be on learning what it is to be like Jesus and to follow him.

Certain questions must remain in a lay person's thoughts all day long. Is my character, in faith, aiming for the level of maturity according to the standard that Jesus showed? Have I received the accountability of missions and society as my calling?

It is an insult to discipleship if we recognize someone who has strong faith but his character has not changed to be a true disciple of Jesus. If we look at someone who lives a double life, separating church and daily life, and identify him as a disciple of Jesus simply for the reason that he completed a formal course of discipleship training, then it unfortunately promotes the secularization of the church.

If after completing discipleship training there are many laity who are earnest in evangelism and are competent leaders of cell groups, but are skillful at avoiding practicing social justice and helping their neighbors in need, then we have to humbly admit that we have gone far astray from the essence of discipleship training.

So, do not do discipleship training by pushing numbers on a calculator. In some ways honest discipleship training often does not have an exact profit or loss. True discipleship training cannot be stopped even with a loss. We must frankly admit this fact in order to avoid any unnecessary misunderstandings.

There is one fact I especially want to point out here. For the past half century in many evangelical churches there was a strong tendency to understand discipleship training in the framework of nationwide or worldwide evangelization. Thus, it is true that discipleship training became known as a means for training evangelists and for church growth.

Consequently, many Christians who loudly proclaimed the gospel maintained a passive or cynical attitude toward social accountability. So what happened? Unhappily in Korea the church

176

experienced the tragedy of becoming divided into a radical conservative and a radical liberal camp. The former emphasized eternal life, the latter emphasized present life. Ultimately both sides have made the mistake of losing the other.

In addition, since the roots of discipleship training lie in an evangelicalism which has a strong tendency toward conservatism, we have to bear in mind that if we are not careful, there is a great possibility of developing a passive position about a lay person's social accountability.

Genuine discipleship training considers it important to clearly teach laity not to separate the sacred and secular in our daily life and calling as a high priest. We must simply give all of our life as a living sacrifice, pleasing to God.

For this purpose in 1974 at the Rosan Worldwide Evangelization International Convention this declaration was made about Christian social accountability:

> Gospel evangelization and politics, social participation is every Christians obligation. Social welfare is at the same time a result of sharing the gospel and a bridge to sharing the Gospel so these two are companions. Gospel is the root thus sharing the gospel and social accountability are all its fruit.[2]

Thus one must be able to see that regarding discipleship training as simply a course for rearing evangelists, or a ministry for leading cell groups is another misunderstanding.

A third misconception is that discipleship training is possible only with laity from middle class status and up - those with a high standard of living. It is strange to me that so many pastors have this misconception. It might be a very convincing way of defending oneself for not doing discipleship training, but in fact one must know this is very convoluted and incorrect thinking. Rather than giving a long explanation here, however, it will be more helpful to remove the misunderstanding by sharing a small incident.

About ten years ago I had the opportunity to give a lecture at a seminary in Seoul. The audience was made up of young pastors attending the seminary from its denomination. Of course, the theme of the invitation was 'Discipleship Training and Pastoral Ministry'.

After the lecture there was a time for questions.

A pastor in his early thirties abruptly stood up and stated, "After listening to your lecture, it looks like discipleship training can be done if targeted for areas like KangNam, Seoul, where the Christians are college graduates and have a high standard of living. Not long ago I founded a church in the Inchon slum neighborhood. I don't think discipleship training has the slightest chance for survival in this church, and I would like to hear your opinion."

It was a very meaningful question. I could not change, however, the fact that his thinking was wrong. Jesus never said to make disciples only of people with a high standard of living. Before answering the young pastor's question, I asked him a question. I said, 'Thank you for asking a good question. But before answering your question, may I ask you a question? If I were the pastor ministering in your church do you think I would do discipleship training? Or do you think I wouldn't?"

The young pastor brought his hand up to his head and for a slight second seemed embarrassed and said, "If it were Pastor Oak then you would", and sat down.

The key to discipleship training hangs with what kind of a person the leader is and not with what kind of people are the laity. Even now there are pastors in farm churches and poor village churches who are doing discipleship training well with creative methods.

Besides those mentioned above, there still remain all kinds of misunderstandings. To name a few: Discipleship training creates fanatics who throw away their family and business. 'It makes the church into an academy.' 'It takes away a lay person's identity.' 'It is weak in prayer and spiritual training.' 'It makes the pastor ill.'

A misunderstanding, however, is always just a misunderstanding. Do you want to develop disciples? Let's begin by removing the misunderstandings first.

Why Call It Training?

I don't know exactly when forming disciples was coined with the term discipleship training, but I believe there is a purpose in the term training. Traditional churches have used the term education rather than the term training. Perhaps that is why for a while there was strong negative reaction against the term training itself. Now it looks like the vocabulary has settled in to be familiar and accepted in all churches. Under such circumstances it is good to know the reason we use the term training.

Perhaps the phrase discipleship training is tinged somewhat by a lack of confidence in the traditional educational methods of established churches. The phrase implies a strong assumption that were in need of more constructive and concrete educational methods. The traditional systematic and formality filled educational environments do not show any more success in conveying knowledge. I have come to the conclusion that Sunday school style education has met its limitations.

Perhaps the term training emerged as a reaction to the education that seemed to be failing at established churches. Whether one agrees with this opinion or not, I don't think it is a big problem.

According to Hee Seung Lee's Korean Dictionary, the definition of training is 'A practical action applied in order to reach a definite purpose or standard. It is considered to be a part of an act of studying'. According to this definition there should be a few practical characteristics to define making disciples as training.

First, discipleship training has to have a goal. Second, a specific training method has to be determined. And third, there needs to be a chosen recipient fit for training. Lastly, one has to have strong expectations for the actual results which come through the training.

Let me say again, when we begin discipleship training, we must carefully consider the purpose, target, specific training method and actual results in order to have proper training.

The term training itself is so forceful that sometimes we are reluctant to use it. Yet to obey and follow the solemn command of Jesus to make disciples, there is not a more suitable term.

Training can be another side of discipleship. Discipleship without training is like waiting to run the marathon without ever training for it. Spiritual training is continually making open time and space for God. Solitude needs training, worship needs training, and serving others requires training, too. All these require that we prepare the time and place to acknowledge and respond to the merciful presence of God with us.[3]

The Purpose of Discipleship Training

Once more I want to be cautious and clear on the purpose of discipleship training, since it is the subject of discussion here even though it has been examined a lot.

What is the ultimate goal of discipleship training? To state it succinctly, it is to help a believer want to be like Jesus and live like Jesus did. It is establishing the believer's self-identity to becoming Christ-like in character and daily way of life.

The disciple we need to develop is a disciple of Jesus. He or she is not a disciple of the Apostle Paul or a disciple of the senior pastor. Jesus Christ is the purpose, the standard, and the theme of the training. From this viewpoint if one takes Jesus out from discipleship training then there is nothing left.

To become a disciple of Jesus means to serve Jesus as my King, and my Lord, to follow him, and obey him. Included here are both my character and my ministry.

Discipleship training first needs to develop a person's character to be like Jesus. The trainee has to become Jesusfied just like the founding 1st century church Christians received the nickname, 'little christs'. The importance of the character and personal devotion of a disciple lies right here. More than anything else discipleship training has to become a work to change the person. The person of God has to become a thoroughly equipped person and live a thoroughly equipped life through the influence of the Word and the Spirit (2 Timothy 3:17).

From this standpoint one can say that discipleship training is a kind of a spiritual struggle in which the pastor leading it and the laity receiving the training participate together.

In this world where we live clothed with a physical body no one can become like Christ completely. We all are on the road together. We have not yet reached a state of perfection free of flaws or blemishes. We are in the state of being broken and melted in the hands of the Spirit, and remolded into the likeness of Jesus.

For this reason discipleship training itself is a labor of being born again, a closet of repentance and confession, a hanging onto the grace of God at the hills of Gethsemane. After realizing this fact, one cannot make the mistake of thinking that discipleship training is a program which can be mastered in a few courses.

Next, discipleship training is a work that calls and bequeaths one with the ministry of Jesus. Jesus taught, spread His love, and healed in this world. For this work he gave his life completely as a witness to the truth, and sacrificed himself as a servant of love.

Thus, discipleship training has to be a process of developing a person into a witness of the gospel, a teacher of the truth, and to sacrifice as a healer in love. One must receive Jesus' vision as his own vision. Whatever your occupation, whatever circumstances you may live in, you must do your best as one called to bring glory to the name of God, and for God's will to be done wherever you may be. This is discipleship training.

The Pastoral Ministry Method Closest to Biblical Principle

I am distressed when I see many leaders regard discipleship training, which is so important, as someone else's task in the church. The Lord gave the minister in the church to be both a pastor and a teacher at the same time, because, as the Apostle Paul teaches, it is to prepare God's people for works of service so the body of Christ may be built up (Ephesians 4:11-12). To prepare

God's people is to see faith grow (Hebrews 6:2), character mature, and to raise them up to live a victorious life everyday. In other words, it is a ministry to teach and train people to be filled with Christ.

The works of service give an opportunity to dedicate oneself to the ministry Jesus commanded the church to carry out. The church will grow in quality and quantity all around if such training is done correctly. Through this miracle, God's kingdom will come.

The definite rule of pastoral ministry is to take nothing away from these three Biblical principles and do not change their order. It is so sad that while doing pastoral ministry we often take out whatever we want and rearrange the order. It is not just a few pastors who have given up the task of preparing God's people. Let's be honest; don't we most often assign a person to start a job rather than first investing in preparing that person?

This is clearly defying the Word. The Lord's command is to direct a person to works of service after going through some level of preparation. But we make the excuse that it is an urgent matter and choose a less difficult shortcut.

As a result, what happens to the church? From a Korean perspective I ask, 'Who is to blame for the suffocation of the life of pastoral ministry?' and 'what is the cause for the bitter roots growing inside the church?' In my opinion, it is the foolishness of we pastors who give a member work to do before first preparing him. In some ways we've thrown ourselves into the pit dug up with our own hands.

A day mustn't go by without returning to the Word. A healthy pastoral ministry can be expected only by faithfully following the Biblical principles. The reason I call so loudly for discipleship training is because this is the closest approach to the Biblical principle of a pastoral ministry method.

As I said before, if the final purpose of discipleship training is for a lay person to choose the character and the life of Jesus Christ to be his own, then the practical benefits we can expect here are multiple! The most important one is the fact that we will acquire many lay leaders. The truth is, as heirs to the apostle who sent out the whole church to the world, the possibility for ministry can be wide open.

From this point of view it is not a big error to say that discipleship training is the method of pastoral ministry that is nearest to the Biblical principle and purpose. When we undermine this truth, I believe we clearly commit sin before God.

Chapter 19: Who will Direct Discipleship Training?

It is the Responsibility of the Pastor

It's not just once or twice that we hear about the importance of discipleship training. For some years now the challenge has reached most churches. Yet, the sobering fact is that those pastors who are the ones that most need to stand up and get going with discipleship training can't make the final decision. The sobering reality is that how lay members develop is completely up to the leader's philosophy of pastoral ministry.

The image of a lay person is rightly the reflection in a mirror of the senior pastor's pastoral ministry. The senior pastor, therefore, has to direct discipleship training. It should not be entrusted to someone else. Isn't it difficult to call a child my own if someone else gave him birth?

A pastor who does his best only for his own self-progress but makes no effort to train the laity needs to examine his heart and evaluate for whom he is standing in his present position. I believe the effectiveness of the local church's pastor should be evaluated primarily by the power of the gospel witnessed in the character and life of the members.

If the parents are healthy but the children are always weak, then this poses a serious problem. Healthy parents give birth to healthy children. Effective parenting yields well balanced and healthy children.

The pastor's spirituality, ability, and character should not be buried within himself but should be the kernel of wheat that dies on the soil of the members and testifies by bearing much fruit. Then the pastor and the laity together can become a healthy church.

A pastor is a person who dies for the sheep. "The good shepherd lays down his life for the sheep" (John 10:11). He is someone who lays down his flesh and blood for the sheep to eat. Like the mother spider who dies after carrying her young on her back, letting them eat through her, until she is only a shell, a pastor must give himself until he is empty in order for the laity to live well as servants and witnesses.

There is a side to discipleship training that puts emphasis on the sacrifice of the pastor. A pastor should not avoid this or be afraid of it. The Lord entrusted his church to us for this work. In other words, do not entrust discipleship training to someone else. To give up the 'yolk' of pastoral ministry is the same as giving up ones happiness.

Become a Disciple First

When we decide to begin discipleship training, there is always a problem that entangles us. It may seem like we know everything about it, but once we're about to start, we can't quite get the feel of it. A leader can manage a task with a whole lot more efficiency if he has the sense and feeling of being able to see the whole picture.

The same applies to discipleship training. If one starts to lose his way from the beginning because he isn't sure, its obvious that it won't last long. So it is very important to be able to grasp a sense for it.

There are many men and women pastors who are responsible for discipleship training at SaRang church. Something I often hear from them is, "Pastor Oak, for the first and second year I was unsure and had no idea. But now I think I'm beginning to have a feeling for what discipleship training is about".

That doesn't mean they were incorrectly making disciples for those few years. It means that they were extremely tense and could not have confidence in their work because they couldn't quite get a feel for it. How can one have the sense of it from the beginning? Let me share one or two suggestions.

The first recommendation I have is for the pastor himself to receive the practical training of becoming a disciple himself. A disciple makes a disciple. One cannot develop someone else into a disciple without first going through the process of becoming a disciple. Karl Barth made a statement that cut through the core of Jesus' commandment to go and make disciples of all peoples. He said, "Peter, go and make someone like yourself".[4]

Peter was already a disciple of Jesus who was molded in the hands of Jesus. Thus Jesus could make the command, 'make someone like yourself'. Paul also makes a statement with the same meaning, "Follow my example, as I follow the example of Christ." (I Corinthians 11:1)

There are many opportunities today for a pastor to participate in discipleship training if he makes up his mind. The Leaders Training Center affiliated with SaRang church operates programs several times during the year for pastors ministering in rural cities. It's not totally satisfying because it uses 12 short weeks to train. But it is receiving positive reaction. One pastor came every week by plane in order to participate.

How about this method? This was an actual experience told by a pastor who was ecstatic about discipleship training.

It was about ten years ago that he came to the seminar and caught a vision for discipleship training. Once he decided to start, however, he just felt desolate. So he decided to start discipleship training on a trial basis with two young couples he had evangelized and brought to the church not long before. They were careful to keep it a secret from the others in the church. With the wife of the pastor coming also, three couples began to meet. The advantage was that these people were new believers, so he led it without feeling a big burden. It was a good opportunity for the pastor to test the possibility of discipleship training and check up on his own gifts and spirituality.

A year later that pastor became a discipleship training fanatic. He could not suppress his emotions because the trainee's apparent changes and bearing of fruits were far beyond his expectations. He confessed that he had many regrets for not knowing about this good thing before, if for nothing more than that the grace and blessings he himself received were so abundant. Naturally, he became convinced that he could make disciples and had a passion that he'd go crazy if he didn't. Doesn't that sound like a great method?

The necessity of a Philosophy of Pastoral Ministry

The next problem to contemplate is that a pastor must not accept discipleship training out of a desire to imitate.

Imitation lacking conviction is the same as a lifeless statue. Imitation pastoral ministry has a short life span. A pastor has to reexamine his philosophy of pastoral ministry and strategy when starting discipleship training. His view of the church is an essential factor in laying the foundation for discipleship training.

Let's say that a pastor has a theological opinion that he alone is a person with a calling. Can he make disciples? And will he be able to feel the need for discipleship training if he looks at a lay person and thinks of him not as the subject of church but an object? It will be very difficult. He might give it a try because others are doing it, but he will not have the desire to lay down his life for the work of awakening the layman.

Only the leader who sees the congregation at worship as heirs of the apostles sent out to the world will be able to put his hand to this work of discipleship training. How can he send them out to the world empty-handed? How can he send them out without first being armed to fight the world? From this point of view, ones philosophy of pastoral ministry is an indicator of definite success or failure with discipleship training.

The Importance of a Teaching Ministry

There is one more thing one must know before starting discipleship training. That is the great importance of the pastor of a teaching ministry. It's easy to see that during His ministry in the world, Jesus preached to the multitude, taught disciples, and to the individual he gave counseling.

We pastors are called to be the servants of Jesus. Thus the most ideal method is to do pastoral ministry like Jesus did.

Jesus disciples were always present among the multitude when Jesus preached. He did not, however, train his disciples only with public preaching, but taught them separately. It was more important for their benefit to teach them than to preach at them. The four Gospels use the term rabbi, i.e. teacher over fifty times in referring to Jesus. He was the most excellent educator - a genius teacher who knew better than anyone the effectiveness of teaching face to face.

Teaching is the most important skill for the person called to be a pastor. The Bible says God gave the church pastors and teachers. Looking at this not as two separate functions but one person with two jobs can be said to be a correct understanding of the meaning of the original text. The leadership function is that of a pastor and a teacher at the same time (Ephesians 4:11).[5]

These words make the role of a pastor clear. A pastor is someone who ministers to the needs of the believers while at the same time a teacher who trains them. That is why Paul said an overseer must be able to teach (I Timothy 3:2). Calvin said that God designed the church for the purpose of education and explained it this way:

Despite the fact that God has the power to bring his people to perfection in a second, one can know that he desired them to be nurtured little by little to reach sainthood under the education of the church.[6]

In spite of the hardship we are all suffering together, in actuality the typical pastor is unable to devote himself to the work of teaching. He places all importance on preaching alone.

The problem of finding what is different between preaching and teaching is still left unsolved. Looking at the case of Jesus, sometimes these two are distinguishable, but at other times they are not. The Reformers also did not consider the two to be completely different.

A great sermon is indeed great teaching. And a great teaching contains the preacher's characteristic in it. Preaching and teaching both are for the ministry of spreading the Word of God. It is Jesus Christ we have to teach and Jesus Christ we have to preach to the believers. The contents are the same for both.[7]

Speaking clearly from experience in pastoral ministry, however, the fact is that preaching cannot completely fulfill the function of teaching. The sermons preached today are a big difference from the sermons of the Reformation. A sermon can play a great role in inspiring the audience and calling upon their reactions, but it is really inadequate to change a person fundamentally and fill him with the sense of a calling. In spite of its impact, we are still only preaching and not teaching. So, how can the church not suffer ill?

A recent survey gathered data from pastors of traditional American churches that are continually declining without any growth. It explored how these pastors prioritized their ministry activities. It showed the pastor's top priority was preaching, and the least important was teaching. The specific ranking went in this order: preaching, pastoral care (counseling, visiting, etc.), organization, administration, and teaching. Ranking actual time spent in various ministry activities, with the most time spent starting at top, it was administration, pastoral care, preaching, organization, and teaching.[8]

This data confirms how much current pastors consider the ministry of teaching to be trivial. I regret that there isn't any precise data on the Korean church, but generally I don't think in this case that there is a great difference from America. The development of an actual curriculum for adult education which deals with the whole character must become an immediate priority in the church.

Discipleship training can become an innovative method of pastoral ministry to cure this sickness. Yet it will take a pastor who puts the work of teaching as the top priority. Only then can we expect to see effective disciples in the church.

Chapter 20: How Will We Start?

Once the pastor decides that he himself is ready, from then on it is time to start the specific work of planting the particular seed of discipleship training on the soil called church. We know well when in spring a farmer goes out to the field to plant seeds, how much devotion he pours out, he cultivates the soil. He provides irrigation and fertilizer. No matter how superior in quality the seed is, if it is thrown on thorn bushes or on rocky ground it cannot bear fruit.

In order to obtain good results in discipleship training, the basic ground preparation has to be done wisely. Sometimes there are leaders who cannot start it up again after terminating midway through it because the work is done carelessly. This is very unfortunate. So let's consider a few fundamental things to help do this work well.

Share Your Philosophy

A pastor who wants to train disciples must have a certain purpose or goal for why he must do this. He must have a clear understanding as to where his ministry must go. He should have a distinct vision about what can be expected from the success of this ministry.

A clear philosophy is bound to become a visible vision. Thus, in some cases the philosophy is the vision and the vision is the philosophy. A dream seen while asleep at night disappears the minute one wakes up, but a vision seen during the brightness of day does not disappear.

The vision for discipleship training must be received from God by faith with eyes wide open to how it will become a reality. To try discipleship training without such a clear and organized philosophy will in some ways be the same as preparing to fail.

A leader has to share something he has seen and has assurance about. The greatest act of a human being in this world is to clearly tell others what he has seen after he's witnessed it. '

A discipleship philosophy of pastoral ministry is something a leader holds tenaciously because he has seen it with his eyes. He is passionate and cannot keep silent. It is natural for people to say what is in their mind. So whenever people see or think about their pastor, they should have the strong image that he is passionate about discipleship training.

Such an image shows that a church, when it is continually being strongly challenged by the leader, is unable to reject the vision. But, the moment such a challenge is weak or ceases, the vision or the dream will begin to disappear.

To effectively share his vision of discipleship training, the terminology and the contents need to be clear - aiming for the future, visible, challenging, and at the same time realistic. If the wording is complicated it will lose its effectiveness in transmission. It has to be expressed so that the trainee can always look forward to it. The leader must plant the expectation that when one is well trained in discipleship he will be able to become a competent and happy Christian. Then he should draw for the trainee a lovely picture of the future of the church.

The picture Moses showed his people day and night while wandering the desolate desert for forty years was the land of promise flowing with milk and honey. This had a visual effect, which led those who heard it to imagine an ecstatic paradise.

A pastor who is speaking about discipleship training also needs to draw such a picture. I don't mean to make it sound like riding on a cloud. It needs to be realistic enough to show that it is possible, and plant self-assurance that anyone can definitely succeed. Perhaps some may feel that sharing the vision of discipleship training is very difficult. One must be confident, however, that the door is always open for the person who gets on his knees and seeks the Spirit's wisdom.

The approach the pastor can use most often to share his philosophy and vision is during the fixed times of preaching and prayer. There are plenty of passages in the New Testament one can use to share the vision of discipleship training. There is one thing, however, to be cautious about. Preach so that the congregation will be able to listen positively and in good spirits.

Remember listeners can easily becoming tense because the image of discipleship training is quite forceful. The sharper the edge of the sword, the deeper it should be kept in a sturdy sheath. It is meaningless to brandish it thoughtlessly. It is not at all difficult to talk about the blessedness of discipleship training after wrapping it with the sheath of the gospel and grace.

If, while listening to the pastor's statement, the congregation can become excited with eager anticipation, then that sermon is successful. It is essential, also, to develop various ideas to utilize prayer to its fullest. The pastor should set discipleship training as his top priority in prayer and pray about it during all meetings without ever leaving it out. Sometimes that prayer should be immersed in the very tears of the pastor. Make discipleship training a prayer request wherever the congregation is gathered. A prayer request that is made without rest or ceasing will seize a person's heart and become his desire.

If the cultivation of discipleship training commences this way, people will begin to agree with the pastor's philosophy and vision. At first it will only be a small number who respond, but the existence of this group will bring great encouragement to the leader. They can become the pastor's shields. They can blow the horn which proclaims the vision louder. The speed of change in the atmosphere of the church may gradually become faster as the people who devote themselves to discipleship training increase.

When such a team is found the pastor should meet with them often, he should share with them his thoughts and vision, pray with them, and clothe them completely in the garment of discipleship training.

The pastor has to observe when exactly the best time to begin discipleship training is. He has to be cautious not to make the mistake of picking either unripe or overripe fruit. Let's pray that God will give us the spiritual insight to discern when the best time is.

Choosing the Target

When the atmosphere is ready and the decision is made to start discipleship training, the first thing for a pastor to do is to choose the target. It is good to keep in mind that future discipleship training will succeed or fail depending on the people accepted at the first discipleship training. Therefore, selection should be made very carefully.

Follow the principles of Jesus. The first principle Jesus applied while making disciples was the principle of 'selection'. Robert Coleman gives this principle a clear explanation:

Jesus began his ministry by calling a few to be his disciples (John 1:35-51). For him, people were the method to lead the world to God. His interest was not in a program to lead the multitude. Rather it was with the few disciples whom the multitude would follow. The people he called were all ordinary people, each with a diverse background.

Jesus, however, saw in these simple people a leader's potential to lead the world to the kingdom of God. They had a desire to learn and had the simple faith to wait for the Messiah and His kingdom. They wanted to be used in the hands of the Lord. Jesus could put into his hands anyone who wanted to be used and remold them into a giant who can move the world.[D]

First, let's consider the call of the established church: An established church has a ministry setting where the history goes back many years and where many pastors ministered. If the congregation is a little over a hundred people then in general there are several elders and deacons serving. Such a church is usually made up of members whose age is comparatively older. I would say that over half of Korean churches fall into this category, and it appears that the same is true in most other countries.

In a majority of cases, the soil of such an established church is unsuitable and inadequate to plant a seed of discipleship training. Looking at examples of discipleship training in established churches I've seen so far, most of them have entered a radical phase of 'do' or 'die'. If successful, the church will have exorbitant blessings. If unsuccessful, the church meets a tragic end. That is how very complicated and complex the situation often is.

I've already explained earlier the importance of a pastor starting out by sharing his philosophy and vision. Because it is so important, I want to emphasize it one more time. One should be careful not to hurry discipleship training in an established church. It is a foolish act to press on by edict or command before the atmosphere is well ripened. I would say that to begin discipleship training in an established church is the same as altering the direction of a traditional pastoral ministry 180 degrees.

There are several reasons for such a conclusion. After beginning discipleship training it is expected that the pastor give most of his time to those few people. The rest of the congregation will then criticize and complain that the pastor is playing favorites.

And, of course, pastoral administration and home visits in which the pastor had put in much of his time and priorities earlier will gradually be pushed to the back of the line. If this happens, there may be elders and deacons who will consider such an event to be a failure on the part of the pastor.

Especially when people who are changed through discipleship training begin to appear, an unexpected tension may exist between them and the general congregation. This may become a major cause for the pastor's concern.

Looking at these few realities, it is clear that trying discipleship training in an established church is definitely not a simple task. It may become a huge burden for the pastor himself. It is important, therefore, to handle it very carefully from the beginning.

On the other hand, in an established church one does not have to worry about whom to accept as trainees in the first discipleship training. One should select elders and deacons without a question. Don't make an issue of their age. Their educational background is not a problem either. One cannot go another step further if these leaders do not first become disciples who share the pastor's philosophy and vision.

So, if a pastor fails to draw this group of leaders into discipleship training, he has to either wait until they are convinced, or give up. Discipleship training should never be used negatively as the cause of arguments and fights in the church, or to ultimately divide the church, the Lord's body.

It is not an easy task to suddenly draw people of leadership positions into discipleship training in the established church. It is more difficult for people whose ways of thinking are already fixed in the church's traditions and long customs. So it would be most helpful to utilize ministry and prayer centers to fellowship comfortably and have personal relationships with the elders. Make opportunities to share the philosophy of pastoral ministry often and naturally.

Pastoral ministry is, for the sake of argument, a ministry grounded in personal relationships. It's easy to make time for natural conversations in a prayer center with a quiet environment. It isn't difficult to have deep spiritual fellowship with each other there through the Word and prayer. If a pastor uses such an opportunity to convey his thoughts little by little then the negative or passive reaction which comes from lack of understanding by the listeners can be greatly lessened.

We can find around us examples where the church foundation was reformed and revived surprisingly will as a result of the success of the discipleship training of elders. You will be able to learn a lot by visiting such a setting.

When the elders are changed through discipleship training and this influence affects the rest of the church, then there will be an immediate rise in the number of people who desire discipleship training. From that point on, the selection of the target trainees should be very progressive and methodical. As empty husks of grain are lessened, the effectiveness of the training will be maximized.

To be focused does not mean to be secretive in selection. There must be an official door always open for anyone who wants to apply. It may be wise, however to keep the criteria for application a bit restricted in order to minimize the aftermath of people who later drop out.

There are a variety of plans for choosing people with good potential. In order to find out which method is the most effective, you can go and ask the churches in your vicinity who are excited about discipleship training. There isn't a specific formula that specifies only one way. So, it is a good idea to examine various models.

I want to say one more thing about selection. We might think that it is good if everyone who takes discipleship training has great faith, obeys well, and has a good personality. In reality it is difficult to experience change with these kinds of people.

With such, the waves of change are so minimal that it is hard to feel it.

Yet, if one wants to anticipate a radical change like Zacchaeus becoming a new person, then it is good to accept one or two people who are considered to be spiritually hopeless. The atmosphere of the class will become immediately different after such people experience change.

Grace is contagious. When the meanest person is blessed first the grace epidemic spreads extremely fast. It can be a great adventure for the leader to accept such problematic people, and a catalyst to depend more on God. I recommend that you try it once. If one really wants to have exciting discipleship training, don't be afraid. Venture into it.

For newly founded churches with few human resources, in the majority of cases, the reality is there isn't a problem of worrying about target selection. At best it is the few people who are the initial founding members.

However, the pastor should not let such an opportunity slip away. To think that one will start after the church has grown a little is taboo. It is right to plan with all adults as the first target for training. It is one's free choice whether to begin with separate mens' or the womens' discipleship classes. The only limitation is that the size of the group should be 5-12 people.

It is true that in planting a church, the purpose of the first discipleship training is to raise up a few lay leaders. But of greater significance is the fact that the pastor has decided discipleship training to be the church's foundational pastoral ministry method. It will not only build up the structure for the continuity of the ministry but it will also be an important factor in determining the constitution of the church.

In reality, a discipleship class that begins this way has a weak point. The majority of those trained do not have great expectations. It may seem idealistic for all adult members to be trained, but among them there are always some who are incompatible with the training, and some who feel forced into it. So, it is true we face many problems in trying to train a high percentage of the members.

In the case of the first womens' discipleship class at SaRang church, it began with 6 people, but only one remained till the end to become a lay leader in the church. The rest gave up after a while or moved to another church. Ultimately the target for training changed so often that there was nothing else to do but to start all over again from the beginning.

No matter how difficult the training may be in the initial period, however, the pastor should never stop or resign. He will get self-confidence after about three years of pressing on. The joy of seeing a few disciples as a result of all the suffering and toil makes it all worth while. From this he will be able to build the next level of human resources from which to select people with better qualifications.

The Principle of Concentration

Once the target group is selected and the training starts in earnest, a pastor will definitely not succeed if he isn't resolved to follow the principle of 'concentration' according to Jesus' role model.

It's necessary to examine first why Jesus especially taught the twelve, or the three, in order to understand what the principle of concentration is.

Jesus chose twelve people separately from among his followers when he reached about two and a half years into his public ministry. These twelve disciples were in need of more opportunities to remain close to their teacher. They had to learn and be inspired so as to become little christs who would become a reflection of Jesus and keep his teachings imprinted in their minds (Mark 3:13-15). It seems clear that in order to concentrate on a higher degree of training, Jesus had to restrict the number appropriately.

Perhaps this is the most difficult part for pastors. We are often tempted to teach many people at one setting whenever possible. The reason for this is simple. Our logic is that by teaching one more person we can reap that much more in results. This can be mathematically or economically reasonable, but it doesn't apply to character education when dealing with people.

God blessed Adam and Eve to be fruitful and multiply but did not permit Adam and Eve to reproduce many young all at once like other animals. To nurture babies is to mold their character, so it isn't normal to have 7 or 8 babies in one pregnancy and raise them like human beings. Of course, we can always come up with exceptions, but in general this is how God designed us as human beings.

Another human truth is our experience that we ultimately lose all when we try to hold onto many at once. The degree of concentration is bound to drop the more we are greedy for numbers. Even Jesus did not do it this way. So what kind of power do we have to gather hundreds of people at once and train them to be disciples of Jesus?

The majority of pastors who give up midway through

discipleship training usually are those who neglect the principle of concentration, try irregular ways, and fail. This calamity results from their lack of awareness as to what true discipleship training is.

Making disciples can succeed only when the pastor can pour most of his time and energy into the few. This is precisely the great principle Jesus taught us. Can we be wiser than Jesus? For those people who think so, they can ignore this principle.

There is something else to keep in mind about the principle of concentration. This applies both to the pastor and the trainees. First the pastor has to resolutely get rid of anything that interferes with his own concentration. If you decide every Tuesday morning is the time of your meeting, then keep that time even if it appears the sky will fall in. If you change the time or postpone the meeting because of a wedding, a son's 1st birthday, or a denominational convention, then this training is lacking concentration. If such an incident happens more than twice, then the trainees lose their dedication, and their confidence in their leader drops.

Therefore, from the beginning the leader has to make the resolution to die, if necessary, before God and his trainees. I once heard an inspiring testimony of a pastor who committed to discipleship training in an established church. He had a kidney problem and was hospitalized. Yet he continued with discipleship training even while in the hospital. In the hands of such leaders, who begin with the resolution that they are willing to give their lives for the trainees, how can we not develop great people with a sense of calling?

The trainees must be solidly prepared so they too can concentrate. One church after selecting the trainees had them participate in a solemn pledge. They had to sign a commitment (this was no joke) that stated during discipleship training they'd neither get sick nor die. And wives who had the possibility of getting pregnant during that period were not accepted from the beginning. As a result, there wasn't a single person absent with sickness for over a year. Such an event can be anticipated with a leader who has a clear knowledge about the significance of concentration.

The Significance of the First Discipleship Class

Whether it is in an established church or a newly planted church, the first discipleship class has a very significant meaning in various ways. Since there is no guarantee that the first discipleship class will succeed in a church plant, one should expect some trial and error. But if the first discipleship class in an established church fails, then one can expect great frustration. Not only will the leader be stunned, but it can also be like throwing cold water on all expectations for discipleship training.

It is necessary, therefore, to pour out all of one's energy and resolve that the first discipleship class will definitely not fail. When the first discipleship class goes well, the good news spreads within the church immediately. Let's say that this class is made up of elders. When they are changed, their families begin to get excited. The elder's prayers during worship will become different. Like one body, church elders will gather to serve in whatever way they can, from cleaning basement bathrooms to praying with grieving families. The church council or board that had been divided and rumored to always have conflicts becomes one in love, and begins to show the example of servants serving the church.

If this happens, how will the congregation look at discipleship training? Won't they think that they, too, must receive discipleship training? Won't there be requests like, "Next time please accept my husband?" Won't the congregation have confidence in the work of their pastor and their eyes twinkle with the anticipation of discipleship training? Don't forget, therefore, that the first discipleship class holds the key to a decisive power that influences the rest of the training ministry to follow.

Chapter 21: Teaching Tools

Jesus' Three Training Tools

What tools should be used for training in discipleship? What are the specific contents?

The three fundamental tools Jesus used for his teachings are: 1) the Word of God, 2) Jesus' own role model, and 3) the disciple's experience. The Word of God became the specific educational material content. Jesus himself, as the living Word of Truth in the flesh, became a role model for the disciples to follow. The disciple's experience was an exercise to practically apply what they learned.

The model disciple we hold up is a mature character becoming like Jesus Christ. It means new lives completely distinguishable from the world can reappear in our communities. For this reason we must give the most significance to the character building element of the training content. The three training tools Jesus used are truth of character, the role model of character, and the experience of character. These were fundamentally different from the dead Law which the Jewish Rabbis taught.

When we use the Bible in discipleship training, Scriptures should always be handled as the living truth so we meet the living Jesus Christ directly. The leader should be open as a role model for the trainee to see with his eyes and objectively ascertain truth. And, the truth that is seen and learned should become individually experienced in each person's daily way of life through obedience.

The Word of God

The most important tool Jesus used for training was the Word of God. The Word of God, which Jesus taught, had two origins. They were the Old Testament and His own teachings. He was God's final revelation (Hebrews 1:2). Only in Him was the Word of Life (John 8:31).

So, whoever wanted to be a true disciple of Jesus had to remain in his Word (John 8:31). At the same time He came as the fulfillment of the prophets so that not the smallest letter, nor the least stroke of a pen, will by any means disappear from the Law (Matthew 5:17,18). After His resurrection He explained the Law and the Prophets many times to His disciples to lift them out of their disbelief and failure (Luke 24:27, 44-47).

For Jesus, the Bible was in private or public a textbook for teaching the eternal Word of God. In the four gospels there are at least 66 times when Jesus cites the Old Testament while conversing with His disciples. While conversing with other people He refers to the Old Testament 90 times.

The Role Model of the Leader

The second tool Jesus used in training was role model. Jesus was not the kind of a teacher who presented the Word simply as theories to the disciples. He lived exactly what he taught. Jesus himself was the perfect role model and an object lesson. So what the disciples needed to ultimately learn was their teacher himself.

The great source of the power in the teachings of Jesus lay in the harmony of his teachings with his way of life.

Here Jesus' method was more than a continuation of preaching. This was like an object lesson. This was the key to his influential teaching. He did not ask a person to do something unless he showed the example in his own life first and by doing this he showed that it could be done and proved its relation to his life's calling... All of his words and actions were actually his individual teachings and since the disciples paid attention to it while being there they were learning realistically every moment they had their, eyes open. "

Jesus lived daily with His disciples in order to train them by His role model. The highlight of His training program was living with them. The disciples were able to see and understand all the substance of the truth they learned through his vivid character by being daily with Jesus.

From this point of view Jesus put His whole self on display as an open training content. Far from some rule or method, Jesus made living together itself to be knowing and learning. He was always an object of attention for His disciples. Thus, for their benefit He had to spend more time with them.

When we hear such an account we are stunned and challenged till breathless. We are filled with anxiety and frustration, since we can't escape from the thought that we should quit right away. How many leaders are there in this world who can open themselves up as a perfect role model like Jesus?

The burden that the leader must be the role model, however, cannot be avoided. One cannot expect to make disciples unless the leader becomes a living, walking truth in the eyes of the trainees.

To speak directly, just like we who are training others follow Christ (1 Corinthians 11:1), we have to be prepared for them to follow us.

We are on exhibit (Philippians 3:17b, 1 Thessalonians 2:8, 2 Timothy 1:13). They will act according to what they hear and see from us (Philippians 4:9). Through this kind of leadership when the opportunity arises, we can share our daily way of life with those who are always with us.

We must accept the truth in our own way of life. We cannot avoid accountability in character. We show the way to the people we train and such an example should come out of a deep fellowship with the Spirit. This is the Lord's method and any other method definitely will not be enough to train other people. [12]

Though we cannot copy the exact style of training by living together as Jesus did, we should unquestionably follow the principle it shows in our discipleship training. We are imperfect. Yet as leaders, we need to demonstrate through our imperfections how willing we are to follow Jesus with our blood, sweat, and tears.

The trainees do not ask for a perfect example. They all know that we are all human. They only want a leader who is willing to be personally vulnerable. If the leader doesn't open up at all, or leaves no crack open for them to see what he is thinking, or how his family life is, they will turn away and close their hearts. It is important to develop a disciple of Jesus under such a leader.

So we must open up our way of life. The writer of the book of Hebrews counsels that a teacher should not teach only with his lips but with his actions. This comes with the strong hint that if it doesn't have a guarantee of actions then the faith itself that they are teaching isn't worthy of learning.

"Remember your leaders, who spoke the word of God to you. Consider the outcome of their way of life and imitate their faith" (Hebrews 13:7).

Be a role model. This holds the key. By it you decide the success or the failure of discipleship training.

The Disciple's Experience

Jesus had another tool of training that He did not neglect. That was to provide opportunities in a ministry setting for the disciples to experience first hand. "Open your eyes and look at the fields" (John 4:35). His finger was always pointing at this world's work places. There were many suffering people wandering about like sheep without a shepherd. There was a Samaritan woman thirsting for living water. There was Jairus whose daughter was dying in an attic.

Learning from experience came by drawing close to His daily way of life and listening carefully. Jesus wanted his disciples to know the reality and to understand correctly the life of suffering.

After preaching to the multitude with many kinds of parables, He explained them to His disciples, and how did the main theme of these parables came out of common everyday life? When the disciples searched carefully with eyes of wisdom, they could see that Jesus taught truth that was not found anywhere else but in the setting of everyday life. For this reason Jesus took His disciples everywhere He went.

This was not strange at all. They needed to go and see more of the world. They had to wrestle with actual problems. They had to hear many people's stories. To understand the world and humanity well meant that the content of training had to become that much more realistic and down to earth.

"(Jesus) saw the multitude and had compassion for them" (Matthew 9:36). How was such a pastor's heart possible for Jesus? He knew the world deeply. The disciples who followed Jesus had to have the same heart. To do that they had to meet many real people and see and hear for themselves how heavy was the cross these people were carrying on their shoulders.

Sometimes our discipleship programs interfere with a genuine discipleship. What I mean here is we are so engrossed in our programs that we can alienate ourselves from our actual life. Jesus did not call his disciples to him so that they would forsake their life but rather to teach them the rule of living together with him in their daily life. That is right. True discipleship is living together with Christ. [5]

The disciples also needed to personally experience the power of the gospel through an exercise program.

"They went out and preached that people should repent. They drove out many demons and anointed many sick people with oil and healed them" (Mark 6:12- 13). They returned after practical exercise and reported to Jesus everything they had done (Mark 6:30).

There is no doubt from their report back to Jesus that they learned and experienced much through this exercise. The Lord could not hide his great joy after hearing their report (Luke 10:21).

Discipleship training is not only done in a room. It should be on the scene training applied to daily life through practical exercise. Neighbors with many problems can become very valuable training materials for us.

To share the gospel with them and to pray for them in earnest can be the same as igniting flames under the charcoal of truth in our hearts. To raise the quality of training is to try this spiritual experiment. Bring whatever you see and hear in the world in front of the Word of God. Then return and apply at the scene of action the answer found there.

When discipleship training approaches midterm it is good to do exercises more frequently if possible. There is nothing in the training content which doesn't need application. Evangelism, prayer life, service etc., all things need to be experienced again in the world and evaluated again to become a living truth. One should never forget that discipleship training isolated from the world is not the training Jesus showed.

It is necessary for the leader to examine often whether the discipleship training he or she leads has the three primary elements Jesus used overall: The Word, Jesus role model, and experience. If one among them is handled carelessly or missing then it should be supplemented immediately without hesitation.

A leader who firmly maintains this kind of careful attitude until the end meets the qualifications to do discipleship training.

Chapter 22: Good Teaching Material

Although it is the living Word of God that we are studying, if there aren't suitable teaching materials, then one cannot teach effectively. It has already been demonstrated through many trials that it is difficult to reap desirable results by teaching only with the Bible. So it is necessary to have a systematic and well-balanced curriculum, or set of materials, in order to effectively do discipleship training.

There are plenty of teaching materials with the title discipleship training on the market today. Some are excellent materials with abundant inspirational content. I have found that especially the teaching materials translated by evangelical mission organizations have superior characteristics and advantages.

To teach the members in the church with these materials, however, poses limitations, as was mentioned before. This is due to the fact that there are many differences in approach between a mission organization and a church environment.

A church ministers to a diverse and complex congregation

made up of different living standards, education, and age. According to the denomination with which each church is affiliated, it has slightly different theological colors. And, more importantly the senior pastors leading local churches want to train members according to the vision and philosophy of pastoral ministry in which they have confidence. If there is teaching material that reflects these points then it will definitely be a big help.

For us to reap the results we anticipate, teaching material that can be used effectively in a church should at least have systematically balanced the following few factors. Remember, this is very much my own subjective judgment, but it is an opinion based on experience that such training won't go terribly wrong.

Is the Gospel Alive?

First the gospel has to be alive. On this point I can say that we are very indebted to evangelical mission organizations. The strongest point in their teaching material is the power of the gospel. That is why their celebration of new lives being born continues without ceasing. An added blessing is that the excitement of salvation is not easily cooled down.

Looking at many of the materials used by the traditional churches until now, it is clear that the gospel is not alive for most of them. They are excellent in doctrine, which can be said to be the skeletal structure of the gospel, but they lack the passion and excitement in the abundant life which pours from the gospel. Perhaps that is why the majority of church members do not know the gospel well. They have been taught by materials which lack the joy and excitement which comes from understanding the Gospel's passion for the salvation of lost people. Even more grievous than this is the fact that many pastors are not even spreading the gospel of salvation.

It might sound strange, but they often consider gospel preaching to be the most difficult. I've talked with many who confess that they feel somewhat awkward. It is true that many pastors have a vague anxiety that the congregation will not listen well if a pastor says, 'Gospel', they will answer by saying 'We already know', or 'Not again'.

Thus discipleship training material has to initially be able to teach the gospel. It must have the inspiration to lead anyone to come before the cross and praise God who gave salvation, no matter how long or short their life in faith has been.

There are many people in a church who need salvation more than we know. People who will live completely changed Christian lives, if only they will meet the power of the gospel, are now lethargically spending their days in church because they have not felt it. It is such a sad thing when a church is unable to get rid of its stagnation because it cannot start the fire. It will revive at once if the flames of the gospel burn in the hearts of the members.

There is no reason, however, why we should just sit here and sigh. If we start right now to awaken the members through teaching material which reveals a powerful gospel, then we will experience amazing blessings in just a short while.

Are the Contents Well Balanced and Systematic?

A second qualification for good teaching material is that the material content should be systematically well arranged.

216

Systematic content is important because, if we are not careful, the material can contain one sided content.

For example, making disciples is not simply making people passionate for evangelism. If too much relative importance is placed on the calling to evangelism, then this material cannot be said to be good material. Teaching material that is only concerned with having personal devotions is also not favorable. If it teaches much about obedience and dedication but is careless about mature faith and character, then this, too, is definitely going the wrong way.

The Bible doesn't hesitate to use an extreme expression to refer to a disciple of Jesus as a 'perfect person'. What is being perfect? It refers to a state where nothing is missing. So, as we examine our teaching material, it is important to look for what might be missing in order to develop well balanced disciples of Jesus.

Is the Application of the Word Emphasized?

The third qualification of good material is that it should emphasize the application of the Word. I once heard that to study the Bible and not apply it is like a woman's miscarriage. It is an appropriate expression.

The church has been teaching the Bible for many years in its own earnest way. But many churches have stopped with transmitting knowledge and have not been able to teach how to apply that Word in the family or society. Jesus said, "Go teach to obey." That is making disciple , but it is true that we have often been educating without seriously contemplating what 'to obey' is meant by.

This has been gradually changing recently. Still, the Bible study materials in traditional churches show they are weak in application of the Word. On the other hand, it is often true that a strong point of mission organization teaching materials is that they have a very effective application of the Word.

To build up a lay member of the church into a disciple of Jesus, one has to use material that will solidly plant the fundamental rule that the Christian life should be learned exactly as it is lived out. There is a need for a material that takes one through the struggle of real life learning while at the same time having the power to illuminate each individual's life by the Word in step by step detail.

It has to have the strength to prevent both the leader and the trainee from hiding their hypocrisy and lies before the Word. The Word unleashed pierces through the defensive walls. The material must provide an opportunity to share the joy that comes from the new life as a result of obedience. And, teaching material that is strong in application is the best method for a leader to see close up the changing and maturing appearance of the trainees.

The Significance of Doctrine

A fourth element of good training material is to maintain the structure of doctrine. Mission organizations have the tendency whenever possible to avoid doctrinally sensitive content in their teaching materials. This is understandable considering their challenge to do nondenominational ministry.

It is worthwhile, however, for us to at least consider another side to this issue. Why do mission organizations have a tendency to be anti-doctrine? It is often a reaction against the traditional church being too conscious of and rigid in its doctrine.

Historically, evangelical mission organizations have their roots in the 17th century piety movement.[4] At a time when the German church was losing its life by being attached only to dead doctrine, the piety movement followers claimed they needed to find a gospel that emphasized salvation and spiritual experience again. During this time they became deeply anti-doctrine.

(The Lutheran church) kept the doctrinal purity and was devoted to preventing the believers from leaving the church. There was absolutely no appeal for emotion. There was no invitation for decision making and did not teach servanthood or a devout way of life at all. They only wanted the believers to know the doctrine, attend the worship service and listen to the doctrinal sermon, and participate in the communion... There was no teaching about inner life and inspiring faith experience.[5]

The church, however, is not a mission organization. A church is usually affiliated with a certain denomination so it is bound to have a doctrine that agrees with the denomination's theological background. Doctrine is not always different in every denomination. There is general doctrine that all churches confess together. Although there may be slight differences in opinion, there is a core doctrine which they all recognize. Discipleship training material can avoid doctrine that may bring dispute but it is beneficial to reflect sufficiently the important doctrine that is the basis of Christianity.

As an example, the doctrine of predestination arouses a great difference of opinion between the church following Calvin's theology and the church upholding Armenian theology. But that doesn't mean we should keep quiet, or give an ambiguous explanation while studying the grace of God calling us out of the world as His own.

It is better to have a content that sets up the framework of one or the other of the two views. In this way the leader using that material can modify and teach it according to his perspective. It is necessary for the leader doing discipleship training in the church to teach without hesitation the doctrinal content about which he is certain. If the study material has flexibility, then it can be much more useful than a material that does not.

Be a Reflection of Your Philosophy of Pastoral Ministry

The fifth element qualifying training material is that the study material be able to reflect the leader's philosophy of pastoral ministry. I've already discussed what a philosophy of pastoral ministry is and why it is important. Then is it enough for the pastor alone to know it? No, it is not.

I have found that one of the important purposes of discipleship training is to raise up lay leaders who will sit in the same boat as their local church pastors. The pastor, therefore, has the responsibility to teach and instill his philosophy in them. We can work together when our thinking and purpose are the same.

How can the church work together with those whose point of view is not the same? What can be asked of those believers whose self-identity as a church member is not correctly known? If the pastor's philosophy of pastoral ministry is derived from ecclesiology, then for certain, lay members should know this and be convicted of it. The important privilege of a church is to plant a clear ecclesiology in its members which the mission organizations cannot do.

To be honest, my philosophy of pastoral ministry was not reflected well in discipleship training during the initial period at SaRang church. My ideas came through very indirectly to permeate the conscience of the members. At the time we were using study material published by the Navigators. There was nothing about ecclesiology in its content to teach. Now, however, we teach it thoroughly in our ministry-training course. I've come to realize more as days go by how important it is to equip the members with the pastor's ecclesiology and philosophy of pastoral ministry.

Is it an Inductive Method?

A sixth element of effective training materials is that it uses an inductive method. I'll explore more details of the inductive method in Chapter 24. As a teaching method, it is essential for the cell or small group structure. Since discipleship training is the most effective in the small group environment, the materials should be appropriate for this setting if we expect desirable results. In a small group, everyone enjoys the freedom of holding each person's ideology, concept, emotion, attitude, and values in common

The Holy Spirit makes the truth realized through the leader while at the same time He makes it known through each person being trained. Such a personal realization is most effective when it is guided by the inductive method which asks a proper question, observes the Word, helps interpret it, solicits feedback, and finally applies the truth. This method has been effectively tested through numerous studies and experiments.

I recommend study material that faithfully follows this method far above that which does not.

At one time college students were surveyed about the inductive method study material. Out of the 592 students who answered, 77.3% said 'very good' to the method. Such a response reveals a lot about the serious weakness of traditional Bible study materials.

Here we need to think about the theological background of why the inductive Bible study became an object of attention. First, this method has something in common with a lay person's theology and mentality. Lay theology gives high points to the fact that to teach the Bible is not only possible by pastors who complete a theological education, but a lay person can also understand the Word and share it with other believers.

Inductive material leaves half of every study page blank. This is the same as declaring that anyone who has the anointing of the Holy Spirit can realize the truth on his own. (I John 2:20, 27).

It can be extremely challenging for a trainee to use the various inductive questions about a Bible passage to look for answers himself. It is a challenge to correctly understand the meaning, and to write out a correct answer. So, naturally one has to personally come face to face with the Bible. One has to personally knock on the door of the Bible.

Through an inductive Bible study, the trainee becomes a person who tries hard, and who finds the truth on his own, rather than like a parrot that repeats someone elses interpretation and answers.

After a concerted effort, when he is given the opportunity to share that discovery and see other believers blessed through him, he is soaked in the rain of grace once again. Finally he will become someone who cannot hide the excitement as he hears the inner voice: 'you can become a great Bible teacher'.

The induction method is rooted in the theological background of contemplation. In the early 20th century, neo-fundamentalist theology, which was very influential in the study of theology, emphasized the personal experience of meeting God through the Bible. I do not intend to dispute that theology in itself. It is not necessary to have a formal discussion about the Bible as revelation itself, or as revealed understanding in a personal existential encounter. I merely want to point out the fact that the 'Experience of personal encounter' which that theology stresses has played a part in opening the eyes of traditional churches which have been teaching the Bible in a dry doctrinal way.

Today the education in the church does not put a significance to meeting God personally. It stresses a teaching or having a third person teach their experience of meeting with God rather than concentrating in an education that allows for the trainees to personally meet God. [6]

This kind of a criticism became an alarm bell to shake up and awaken many leaders of churches who have until now considered Bible teaching as a kind of ritualism and literalism.

Truthfully, one cannot anticipate change in character without a meeting with God through the Word. I do not agree with neo-fundamentalist theology, but it is very important for us to correctly understand and apply their emphasis here. The popular inductive study materials among us were developed through such trials.

Until now the image has been fixed, pastor as speaker, layman as listener. Consequently we've come to the state of anxiously asking whether the church is not suffocating the Word. When we do discipleship training with an inductive study method, it will be a great contribution to preventing such a disaster in the church.

The Discipleship Training Study Material - Awakening the Laity

I took a trial period of more than ten years at SaRang church before completing the material we are using today. This material supplements what we felt were weaknesses in material published by mission organizations, and has the primary objective to properly train the lay members in the church.

In other words, it allows the gospel, doctrine, and way of life to be a well-balanced trio and to hold in common the pastor's philosophy. Its purpose is to create a nucleus of dedicated and designated people who can share the ministry with pastor.

SaRang uses the inductive approach suitable for the small group setting. This material is divided into two parts: discipleship training, and ministry training. It is designed to have a trainee complete the course in 2 years, but it can be extended to 3 years according to need.

The Discipleship Training course lays out the foundation of the truth of salvation one more time. It is made up of three sections: the fundamentals of discipleship training, salvation truth, and the life of faith and character. This enables the trainee to aim for the character of faith and holy life, inspired by the wonder of salvation, guided by the example of Jesus.

Ministry Training is a course for those who have determined

through discipleship training a desire to work together as leaders. In addition it puts focuses on changing the trainee's thoughts into the study habits and practices necessary as a leader.

Trainees can learn clearly about the pastor's philosophy and what the role and function of members themselves are. Consequently they will accept the pastor's paradigm of church as their own. To do this they study the four sections of the keys to new life: Holy Spirit (Romans 8); church and member's self identity; small group and leadership; and Old and New Testament themes and content.

Attached to the Ministry Training course is a guidebook for the leader. It may not be totally satisfactory but it was prepared to ease even the smallest distress felt while using the material for the first time. It can be a useful tool depending on how a leader uses it.

Teaching material is merely a guide. It cannot contain every complete element or every bit of detailed information. Keep in mind that how the leader uses it will determine whether or not he will reap success beyond expectations. At SaRang Church there are countless people who have felt a kind of Copernican great earthquake in their lives through the use of this material. It is my sincere desire that all churches will experience the same.

Chapter 23: The Small Group Setting

The Willowcreek Church situated in Chicago almost 15 years after its founding had become like a giant dinosaur swaying back and forth. It was then that small groups were introduced in earnest, and leadership began to set up the internal structure of the church. Founding Pastor, Bill Hybels, who has led the church from the beginning, said that he most regrets not having led the church from the start with this type of small group approach method."

As a matter of fact, many church leaders still do not understand well the necessity and the special, amazing function of small groups. Until recently, most churches operated under the assumption that in order to have education in the faith it is essential to have a teacher, student, and a study material. If the purpose of the education is to simply convey knowledge such an idea is not so wrong.

In the case of discipleship training, however, where the focus is on character building, we already know from many examples how ironic this idea is.

Restoring the Original Structure of the Church

A cell, or small group structure refers to an educational environment where a mutual relationship of character can develop between the people gathered there. For that reason the group should be able to meet within boundaries where an individual will not stumble. Jesus pioneered this kind of small group. During the three years of his ministry, through His experience and the results of time spent with His disciples, He powerfully demonstrated the possibilities of this structure.

Jesus does not explain why He chose the small group structure. And He never commanded the church to follow some form of small group organization. Nevertheless, the 1st century church followed Jesus precedent and formed a unique congregation made up of numerous small groups.

The best example is the first Jerusalem church. They all met together as a church often but the actual fellowship between the believers, tasting the joy of new life, was in small groups meeting at homes (Acts 2:42, 46). We don't know exactly how many small groups were scattered over Jerusalem but it isn't difficult to imagine how important their role was.

The Corinthian church was not a one building church like today's church. It is a well-known fact that the church was made up of 20-30 home churches.[8] Churches after the New Testament period followed the same model and spread like yeast in all directions.

They were achieving fellowship unit through high mobility structure like home church or activity centers. They met privately as well as to gather publicly. They made this small fellowship unit in every level of society, everyone of all levels who met with

them heard the message of deliverance that gave freedom from
sin and enabled them to see the influence of that message. They
had great flexibility but no existence of disorder.[9]

How the New Testament church grew from a cell based
structure to the complex bureaucracies of the Middle Ages, the
multifaceted ecclesiologies spawned by the Reformation, and the
worldwide variety it represents today is the subject of another
book.

Entering the 20th century, small group movements began to
spread like an epidemic. In actual fact, however, they were a
greater object of interest in general society than in the church.
Mental hospitals, prisons, social organizations, and educational
guilds began to gradually and conspicuously utilize the small
groups unit structure to cure and counsel mental disorders, in
social activities, and in research.

According to Paul Hares research, from the years 1899-1958,
hundreds of academic research theses were written about small
groups.[20] Especially before and after World War II, with the
knowledge that a small group structure was very effective in
production, a research team was formed called The Test Tube
Group.

The group documented that not only is a small group structure
useful in increasing production, but it also gives new meaning to
human relationships. As a result, it changes an individual's
character.

On the other hand, small groups were more of an interest to
some, not for their utilitarian purposes, but because of a silent
faith that small groups could, to an extent, fill up the strong
emotional hunger hidden inside modern man.

People are famished for deep human relationships everywhere. They need relationships that bring security and belonging in the abruptly changing and growing world. Small groups can fill a man's deep craving for love and recognition impossible to attain in an assembly of hundreds and thousands of people.[21]

Modern man, who cannot survive loneliness and tries to obtain security and a sense of belonging from anywhere, became the motive for a great interest in small groups. We cannot deny that the modern church will naturally be slightly or significantly influenced by this trend. It is somewhat foolish, however, to try proving that the reason the church opened up its eyes to the significance of small groups came completely from external environmental stimulation. Even if such an influence cannot be excluded at all, a more direct root cause is Biblical. It is apparent that many people, as they agonized over the granite-like expanded organization of the church, could not turn away from the small group mentality overflowing in the Bible.

"Today the church needs 'home churches' like the New Testament period. We need small groups."[22] Almost anyone can see that in order for the church to recover the function of the body of Christ it has to return to the constitution of the 1st century church or it will not happen.

The greater purpose of discipleship training is not only to produce lay leaders but also to return the church constitution to an organic personal group that places greater emphasis on forming personal relationships. That is why small groups have so much significance.

Amazing Elements of Healing

Small groups play an important role in bringing new changes in peoples attitudes, value system, and character. This can be said to be a kind of a healing element. When the children of God share a deep spiritual fellowship centering on the Word in a small group, the Holy Spirit works to bring healing on them. The ministry of healing is entirely up to the Word and the Holy Spirit but we know that the Holy Spirit does not wholly use supernatural means.

A small group is a natural channel that the Holy Spirit uses. The reason things happen in small groups that we cannot expect at great revival crusades is the source of a healing element contained in the function of a small group. We emphasize small groups because compared to other forms, we can see how dramatically they provide an effective tool for the Holy Spirit's work.

Yalom identifies eleven elements of healing found in nonchristian healing small groups.[23] It is difficult to accommodate all these elements of healing to small groups in general, because his research group members were abnormal patients.

It is difficult, however, to deny that spiritual changes happening in small groups doing discipleship training, or other similar meetings, have something in common with what is discovered in healing groups. It will be helpful here to introduce a few important elements of healing discovered by Yalom to understand the relative importance of a small group educational environment in discipleship training.

We are All in the Same Boat

First, let's discuss the element of universality. Each person participating in a small group has a problem they alone know. It can be a secret, which they can't just tell anyone. Naturally, they will often think that they alone possess this problem and are agonizing over it. In some cases they have a deep sense of guilt and the belief that they never receive forgiveness. Most of the believers taking discipleship training have this kind of a secretive problem and suffer with insecurity and an inferiority complex.

A characteristic of the small group is that it is easier to open oneself up there than in other group forms.

For the initial period the participants keep up their own defenses. After two or three months, however, they find security in the group and begin to trust others with whom they always meet together. Afterwards they begin to open themselves up without hesitation.

Until such an event occurs in a small group, the first 2 or 3 months are difficult. If quite a bit of time passes and still there are no hearts opening up, then that group may be diagnosed as being sick. A person who opens himself up usually shares his hidden problems or worries. Then those who hear him realize that the problems they have hidden are not theirs alone. "Now I see that this is not just my problem." Such sympathy will not only change the mood of the group, but will also bind the mutual personal relationships with deep love and compassion.

Of course, to open oneself up is not to empty out anything. When each person evaluates himself in the mirror of the Word of God, he discovers that the Holy Spirit directs us to confess or give testimony. The Holy Spirit uses the Word as a key to open up the heart. So each person's statement contains truth and earnestness. It has the power to draw in another person. It is precisely in this area that a discipleship training group is different in character from other healing groups.

Everyone will come to realize that they are all pilgrims continuously aiming for the goal they can see far away. In an atmosphere of talking about themselves in the light of the Word, they realize that there is not one person perfect before the Word of God. Then they will approach the Word and understand and love one another with a lighter and cheerful heart. We are all in the same boat.

You are All My Teachers

The second important element of healing groups is interpersonal learning. This is often considered the most important element in healing groups. In a discipleship training group one can discover that this element is essential in remolding the trainee's character. Many psychologists assert that ones individual personality is mostly a product of personal relationships with other people. Based on our experience with small groups, this opinion has a very high credibility.

When opening up oneself becomes possible in a group, it is like a small society where each person rediscovers and reforms himself within that meeting. One learns more precisely about himself through other people.

Other people can help us analyze what our own words and actions mean to other people. We can learn what is lacking in ourselves by comparing it openly to other people. At the same time we can easily discover our strengths. We can also determine our spiritual gifts through these relationships with others.

And, perhaps most significantly, we can realize the relative importance of our own role in sharing that gift with others. There is nothing more effective than discovering that we are a very important person to others in bringing big changes to their attitude and character. What an amazing truth! The Holy Spirit uses other people to mold our character into the direction that he wants. People do learn from other people.

It is well known from small groups that the development of character is partially received from the personal mutual relationships. Forming a new character or amending it does not, however, only happen in small groups. The fact is it is experienced continually through the whole of church life. However, its possibility is much higher in a small group.

I Want to Try it Too

The third important element Yalom identified is imitation. We've already discussed that a role model is one of the important training contents of discipleship training. This refers mostly to the act of becoming like the leader. In a small group, however, role modeling is not limited only to the leader. By doing discipleship training, it will amaze you that there are as many cases of imitating other trainees in the group as the leader.

The average lay person does not think it a big deal that a pastor is more mature in the life of faith or in Biblical knowledge. If something is regarded as obvious, then it cannot bring much inspiration. Rather, people are very sensitive to the changes happening in other people within the group. It is easy to see strong intention in the speech and actions of trainees to follow a peer's good points when he is considered to be ahead. In a small group where it is easy to see one another close up, each person is a role model and can become the subject of imitation by others.

I Really Wanted to See It

The fourth element is cohesiveness of the group. There is a kind of loyalty that comes when the trainees in the same group share their hearts in love and accept each other as important people. This happens more as one recognizes that the small group with which one is associated is extremely important. The stronger the attachment and sense of importance, the more a person will become dependent on the leadership and decisions received from there. When group attachment is strong, then that meeting is more productive. Morale is high. It is effective in its operation. The atmosphere is bright and happy and the attendance is very good.

The progress of group attachment in discipleship class is the same as the key to determining the success or failure of discipleship training. A discipleship training which has to force attendance every time it meets will already find it difficult to anticipate great results.

It is good to keep in mind that group attachment does not happen with the Holy Spirit uniting and the power of the Word transforming, without the effort of the people. How much concern and love is the leader expressing? Is each individual considered with the same importance as the rest of the group? Is the groups purpose being correctly instilled? Is the purpose of the small group well communicated and implemented? As mentioned earlier, examining various other healing points will play a great role in raising the level of group attachment in the people being trained in discipleship.

What a Relief After Confession

One last thing I want to mention is the healing element called catharsis. People in general speak their thoughts, but are reluctant to speak their feelings. The exchange of feelings, however, is possible in an appropriate setting. Small groups have the big advantage of creating a safe atmosphere for anyone attending to express what they are feeling without difficulty.

In the case of Jesus we find a similar example. In general, He did not express his emotions very much. However, the three years of personal relationships he maintained with his disciples met its climax as he went up the Mount of Gethsemane. At that time the Lord expressed his emotions honestly, to an amazing degree.

He took Peter and the two sons of Zebedee along with him, and he began to be sorrowful and troubled. Then he said to them, "My soul is overwhelmed with sorrow to the point of death. Stay here and keep watch with me" (Matthew 26:37-38).

The fact that Jesus as a perfect man with human nature, disclosed his heart and opened up without hesitation at the gathering of his three disciples whom he loved is helpful in understanding the function of small groups.

Comparatively, when a small number of brothers are gathered and their hearts connected in love, each expresses their feelings honestly, and often discloses hidden worries. For those people who keep their problems inside because they do not have anyone with whom to share, it is natural to find an outlet in small groups.

From this point of view, discipleship training, like small groups, acts like a sponge in soaking up each others emotions. To confess to a person becomes confession to God. To praise and pray together, the mutual communication of speaking and hearing without fault finding, quickly recovers security and peace in the heart.

In discipleship training, while healing, the Holy Spirit works without crisscrossing the human beings mental state, which he created. It is very significant for church leaders in charge of the ministry of healing to know that.

Until now we've reviewed the function and the healing element contained in small groups. The reason discipleship training looks to a small group environment is not only because a leader can only effectively handle a certain number of people. Discipleship training anticipates the spiritual changes which happen in sitting around together and reflecting each heart in the mirror of the Word.

In other words, extreme importance is placed on the personal mutual relationships through which the Holy Spirit works. The most fitting environment for this kind of a purpose is in small groups.

The purpose of emphasizing small groups in discipleship training is first to fill the spiritual needs of those participating. Going a step further, the purpose also lies in satisfying the needs of the whole church.

It is a challenge to prevent the process of reforming the whole church into small groups from being a stumbling block. To make it possible for many believers to discover their function and role as part of the organization is also a responsibility. This challenge and responsibility lies with the lay leaders who were trained in discipleship class.

For this work they must first have been constituted in the small group way of life. They have to be changed first. They will be molded into a suitable vessel, through such experience, to serve others in meeting their spiritual needs. In other words they have to be trained until they are able to share the Word of God with other brothers, counsel them in their problems, and show an example as a witness and a servant.

So, one cannot expect the desirable effect unless lay leaders with qualifications are all assigned to adult small groups in the church. From this point of view the discipleship training small group is the most suitable way to utilize both characteristics of training and healing concurrently.

Chapter 24: Understanding the Inductive Method

Inductive Bible Study is already quite well known. Even now as it is rapidly being assimilated into more churches, it does not appear to have the fresh new feelings it had in the past. This is a very encouraging development.

The majority of discipleship training study materials available use this method, so you can naturally understand what an inductive approach is simply by using such materials.

Study material, however, is only a guide. It does not contain everything needed to inductively study the Bible. To compare it to a drawing, the study material is just a sketch. The leader and the trainees using the material have to complete the picture together. For this reason the leader needs to know the theory of the inductive method, be well experienced, and be able to expertly lead it.

First Become an Expert

An inductive method may be somewhat different in application than a personal devotional time and study of the Word, but as a team together in a small group, its principle and process is almost identical.

Here is the most important thing. The leader must practice this method diligently using his personal devotional time meditating on the Word. Just like eating three meals a day, he should not rest from diligently going before the counsel of the Word with a pen and a notebook. And so when he first is greatly blessed by using it, he will have confidence in this methods excellence and understand the necessary skill to train others in discipleship.

To develop the skills to lead an inductive Bible study well, there is nothing better than to go and practice. Go visit discipleship training classes led by competent leaders.

Even if they show a bit of irritation, put on thick skin, go frequently, and observe and learn until your eyes are open. Ask questions such as, "What will I do in this situation?", "How is that pastor different from me?", "What are some things I need to learn?", and "What is my weakest point?".

Keep asking questions of yourself. Continue to observe and learn. Practice what you learn without hesitation. Then, not long after, you will be able to see tremendous progress.

You may have a certain weakness by nature. For example, you're very impatient and unable to listen to others well. You're very talkative so that you cannot stop once you begin to speak. You're weak in logic so that you often lose the main point and wander.

Your face is so inexpressive that you're burdensome to others. If you find out these weaknesses, then you need to kneel before

God and pray until your cushion becomes worn out. It will not be easily cured until you experience the Holy Spirit's special hand of healing.

Be frank, therefore, about these kinds of weaknesses to the trainees and always ask for their prayers in an attitude of humility.

Understand These Special Features

The inductive method, when compared to the deductive method, has several effective characteristics. The leader needs to understand these special features properly. If you don't, then you will not be able to use them effectively.

First, every participant is both a teacher and a student. It is not a relationship where the pastor speaks and the others listen. Its purpose is for everyone to share what they think and have discovered. In many cases this characteristic is not properly understood and later ends up in failure.

Second, unlike the deductive method which follows the logic of proof, the inductive method follows the logic of discovery. In the deductive method the leader decides first a certain truth for discussion. Then to prove it, he has to explain or interpret. Others are led to understand through the explanation and persuaded.

By contrast, the inductive method is when each person discovers something in the Word and by sharing it they determine the truth. The leader cannot monopolize this discovery.

The leader is not more than a discoverer himself. The role of the leader here is to encourage and motivate everyone to discover for himself.

Third, communication is not one sided but has a compound aspect. Communication is a conversation where there is give and take so the leader cannot monopolize the conversation. If a leader or any other person within the group monopolizes the conversation here then it shatters the possibility of meaningful communication.

Fourth, the inductive method is concerned with changing character rather than conveying knowledge. In other words it focuses on maturing and becoming like Christ in the God given new life. For this reason, compared to the deductive method, it may have the shortcoming of unstructured or non academic content. The fact is, however, that it is in the inductive method that such shortcomings operate as strengths.

When structural or academic material is used, it takes away the freedom for a learner to discover on his own. When personal faith is going the right way, systematic theories can always be supplemented by other reading, or through a seminar. Let's not forget that our problem does not come from a lack of knowledge but because our character is not right.

The fifth essential characteristic of the inductive method is that it is concerned with the application of the Word. With the deductive method, many times it is possible just to listen, agree, and then leave. But the inductive method doesn't allow completion this way. When someone, after sharing it and testing it with other members, discovers and realizes the truth, the inductive method asks for a specific decision to then apply the truth. No one in the group escapes from it.

Approach the Word This Way

Using the inductive method, here's how to approach the Word. The first step is observation. Observation is an attitude where one intentionally tries to find something of meaning in the Bible context. The majority of church members are not well trained in Biblical observation. For a long time the church was dependent on the deductive method in teaching the Bible. So, as a result, its after effect is that many people have become accustomed to opening and shutting the Bible with their eyes closed.

People who are accustomed to just hearing the sermon after reading the context close the Bible unconsciously. Then they wait to hear what the preacher has to say. Naturally such people give up the opportunity to observe the Bible on their own. As a result no one knows to what degree the church is spiritually damaged.

The inductive method in essence forces us to see the Bible afresh every time we open the Bible. It guides us to observe the Word like a lover reading and rereading a love letter. You can search the text using the questions who, what, when, where, how, and why to understand the whole context. Then examine the detailed content as if looking through a zoom lens. Pay attention to the words being repeated a few times. Search for the content being emphasized. Look for relevant or conflicting content. Then you will see truth you would normally be unable to find.

The second step is interpretation. Interpretation is wrestling with any hidden meaning in what we observe in the whole context. A Bible study that changes life must continue on to reach a correct understanding of the content. You must concentrate in order to know the meaning.

We accept the Bible record of revelation in the ancient times as the Word given to us living in the present, so we next need to study to overcome any linguistic or academic barriers. To accomplish this, it will be good to recommend helpful reference books to the trainees. There is one thing, however, we must know. The fact is that a lay person normally needs the pastors help to insure an accurate lingual interpretation. We must not let them say; "I can understand everything without you" (2 Peter 3:16).

Step three is response. Response is stating what you feel after you realize the meaning. This is the step of internalizing the Word as ones own. It is here that the Bible as the voice of the living God begins to work within us. The deeper the inspiration, the more positive the response will be.

Jesus explained the Old Testament in detail to the two disciples he met on the road to Emmaus. What happened to them? "Were not our hearts burning within us while he talked with us on the road and opened the Scriptures to us?" (Luke 24:32). They felt burning emotion. So what was their reaction? They urged Jesus to come into the village and stay with them. This was obviously a very positive reaction.

The inductive method always has room to anticipate this kind of response. A leader who keeps this fact in mind will guide and encourage the trainees to express their deepest realizations well, and without pretension.

Application is the fourth step. When the Word inspires us then certainly we must allow it to continue on to the next step. That step is obedience to the Word.

We can be so moved and inspired by the Word that it is impossible to stop the tears. But if we don't make an opportunity or room for that Word to change our life and character, then that inspiration cannot be said to be the Holy Spirit's blessing. Application is creating the opportunity and room for the burning inspiration of the Word to work freely within us.

There are many people who think that making a statement like, "From now on I'll love my Christian brothers and sisters" is an application. This is nothing more than merely revealing a general thought. Application has to be specific. It must be accompanied by an actual plan. If there is something to be confessed then there must be a decision to fix it. Application must even go as far as designing a series of inspections to make sure that our obedience is carried out correctly. When that happens, we can stand in a position of becoming more like Christ.

A leader must lead the trainees well so the application is not done deceptively simply because they were compelled to do it. Let's be sure of one thing, however. A leader cannot substitute a response or application for the trainees. Depending on the situation, the leader may substitute observation and interpretation. The leader must guide each trainee, however, so he can truthfully respond and design a personal application before God.

A Question is a Very Useful Tool

To the leader directing an inductive Bible study, there is nothing more useful than a suitable question. It is necessary, therefore, for the leader to train himself in the skill of asking the correct questions. Depending on what the question is and when it is used, the direction and atmosphere of the study is greatly affected.

To become a competent leader, you must always prepare effective questions to open up the hearts of everyone in the discipleship class. Have interest in each person and help them share the truth and emotional changes the Scriptures have brought to them.

Using questions in Bible Study is not a new skill. In the Gospels Jesus asked more than a hundred questions. Someone said that Jesus did not come to answer questions but to ask questions.[24] Jesus gave a hint of the kind of answer he wanted, and frequently used guiding questions to help a person being asked to come to a conclusion on their own.

When a trainee is asked a question, he will come to a sincere attitude of waiting for the Holy Spirits leading as he thinks about an answer. At the same time, the leader moderates himself from speaking in general. Everyone is intent on hearing the answer and this is effective in helping the trainee to concentrate. Not only that, but it forms an atmosphere of participating together in the conversation.

Someone made a brilliant remark about the effectiveness of a suitable question.

Asking the right question is like rolling a stone. Even though you're sitting quietly on top of the hill the stone will roll down and make other stones roll down with it.[25]

Asking the right question can function like a rolling stone to bring everyone into the conversation.

The meaning has to be clear if we want our questions to be well thought ones. They should also be interrelated with the core issue in the text, and be able to stimulate the discussion. The content of a question should not be complicated. It also cannot be weak in its relevance to the study content. It cannot be uninteresting and stale either. For these reasons it is good for the leader to prepare appropriate questions in advance.

It is not necessary, however, to avoid effective and instant questions that the Holy Spirit gives during the time of discussion. Often better questions are found during this time than the ones prepared.

The leader has to be careful while asking questions not to create an atmosphere like that of giving an oral test. He should be able to elicit answers with a soft voice, and lighten the tension with a sense of humor. He should not request an answer in haste, or quickly turn the question around to someone else. He has to express sincere interest in the person answering and listen intently. And even if an answer is not satisfactory, if the leader shows a positive reaction, it will very quickly help to raise their morale.

If he is a competent leader, then he will not try to give an answer to everything, as if he were an encyclopedia. He has to aid the learner to answer on his own. It is better for the leader to avoid immediately answering a trainee's question if possible. Rather, answer a question with a question, and lead them to come to a right answer by themselves.

A discipleship-training leader has to avoid closed questions that may be answered with a simple 'yes' or a 'no'. This has the danger of discontinuing a conversation. A good question is an open question that leaves a person's mind open. Such a question usually begins with why, what, and how etc. He should avoid clumsy questions with obvious answers.

It Can Stimulate These Advantages

We need to remember that if we utilize the inductive method

well then we can obtain many benefits: First, it makes the trainee recognize the authority of the Scriptures on his own. Even for a person who trivialized the authority of the Scriptures secretly, once he opens the Bible, and begins to write answers on the blank spaces of the study material, he will discover that he is recognizing the authority of the Scriptures. A while later he will be overpowered by the absolute authority of God's Word.

Another advantage is that it plants self-confidence in the trainee to study the Bible by himself. Inductive material is designed to help a person look up a passage in the Bible, write out the context and his understanding, and apply a decision from his heart.

In other words it doesn't make one feel that Bible study is difficult. This plants self-confidence that he can understand the Scriptures on his own.

An amazing power of the inductive method is for a person studying the Word to quickly receive it without hesitation. When one meditates on the Word inductively one is bound to record what he discovers and realizes. No one doubts a truth he himself discovers. He will believe the Scriptures right away, even if it's something he did not believe previously. Scriptures that are this easily received can bring great changes in him.

For someone who has learned the Scriptures for many years by the deductive method, it is really not surprising when he starts to study it inductively and changes to a completely different person in a month.

When one keeps in mind these kinds of advantages of the inductive method, he will be able to train in a more creative way.

Chapter 25: Leadership Necessary in Discipleship Training

Leadership that Brings Change

To be honest, whether discipleship training is healthy and successful or not is entirely up to the pastor leading it. If it goes well, it is his responsibility, if it goes poorly, it is his responsibility. There is no need to blame the trainees. Don't blame the method either. One has to recognize that all the responsibility, 100% of it is on the shoulders of the leader. Remember, uneducated fishermen of Galilee became men who overturned the universe when Jesus took a hold of them.

How can we dare imitate Jesus? We have to recognize one thing as a truth. If a leader is excellent, then, even if the vessel is of lesser quality, it will not be greatly affected.

So, did you fail discipleship training? There is only one reason. You met an incompetent leader. If someone who is well equipped begins discipleship training, whether the setting is in a country or the slums, it will not be a problem. In my country today there are numerous examples found in various places to prove that this statement is not an exaggeration.

With this in mind, we can say that a course not to be omitted is a serious study of leadership. I read an article by Layton Ford in a magazine called *World Evangelization* where he writes about Jesus' model of leadership that brings change. I got the assurance from it that a pastor needs to develop this kind of leadership to do discipleship training. So, I am introducing its content here briefly.[26]

Jesus is a perfect model of 'leadership as change agent' for us. The first characteristic of his change agent leadership is to become a Son of God. Its symbol is an open ear. It was important for Jesus before he began to do anything - before preaching, teaching and healing-to receive baptism from heaven and hear the voice of God the Father saying, "You are my son, whom I love; with you I am well pleased." Why? Leadership comes from learning a secure self-identity.

Wrong leadership originates from insecurity about the self. Everyone has a weakness and feels insecurity from it. The beginning of healthy leadership is to come out of this insecurity and learn to have assurance of being secure. How is this possible? It is possible by hearing. In other words it is possible when we have the understanding that God is pleased with us. Such a secure recognition of the self allows us to listen intently to the voice internally and externally.

The second characteristic of Jesus' 'leadership as change agent' is the power to change what we see into action. Its symbol is an open eye.

Vision begins from seeing. Right after being baptized, Jesus 'saw' Simon and his brother Andrew throwing the net and told them to follow him. Afterwards he saw James and his brother John.

Jesus was a pioneer who had eyes that saw eternity in ordinary daily life. He said in the Gospel of John that he was only doing the work he 'saw' the Father doing. Thus for Jesus, vision was seeing what the Father was doing. If there is no seeing then there cannot be leadership that brings change.

The third characteristic is the power to contain truth in storytelling. Its symbol is open lips. Jesus conveyed his vision with stories. When the Word became flesh, the Word that materialized in the story was like a time bomb that exploded God's power to bring change to people's thoughts and hearts.

The fourth characteristic is entrusting or transferring the authority. Its symbol is the open hand. Not only did Jesus have concern for saving the lost sheep, but he was also interested in transfiguring them into shepherds. The secret to his successful ministry is that he regarded the people around him to be valuable. And so he commissioned his disciples with his authority. An open hand means to entrust the authority in ones own hand to those called by God.

As leaders, we have to ask ourselves whether we have an open ear, an open eye, open lips, and an open hand. In discipleship training the leader has to be prepared to be the first to hear, see, say, and give. Then he can expect the miracle of change to happen in someone else's character and life.

Like a Parent, Like a Coach

There are other criteria besides what I discussed earlier a leader has to meet in order to use small groups in developing disciples. These criteria can also can be easily found in Jesus and the Apostle Paul.

First, the leader has to have an attitude of a parent who loves and nurtures his children. "Therefore brothers, in all our distress and persecution we were encouraged about you because of your faith. For now we really live, since you are standing firm in the Lord" (I Thessalonians 3:7-8).

The leader should never stop encouraging even though a trainee did not meet the leader's expectations. It is important for him to feel that he is being loved. Don't ever show favoritism.

Give a clear 'yes' or 'no'. One of the most damaging things to a person being trained is when a leader shows an ambiguous attitude. Not only that, a good leader must respect each person's value and always keep that in mind so that his personal fellowship will not be severed.

One thing that seems easy, but is difficult to do in discipleship training, is being honest. One should not be afraid to say, "I don't know." The more the leader opens up in honesty the more affection trainees will feel towards him.

A good leader must train with the heart of a parent. He should not have an attitude of a general commanding a force. That doesn't mean it is good to just let them be. It is good to maintain an appropriate tension between a leader and the trainees.

The degree of this tension is dependent on the selection of a form of communication.[27] In a persuasion style the leaders authority becomes bigger and the groups freedom withers. In a discussion style something totally opposite occurs. These two types are very useful depending on the situation.

In general, however, most leaders select the conversational style in discipleship class. Just like a parent and a child sit together affectionately and converse, the discipleship class must maintain a sufficient tension without making it feel stressful. Let love overflow in your speech and expression. This love is the most mysterious power that changes a person.

Generally a leader's role in small groups can be compared to a coach. Coach is a sports term. The function of a coach, however, has many similarities to a leader in discipleship training. It is a well-known fact that the progress of a soccer team, or a baseball team, depends a lot on the quality of the coaching team.

A coach's glory is that he is a person who finds, advances and trains other peoples ability... A Christian coach has to be someone who is more interested in developing someone else rather than lifting his authority.[28]

The reason we say that a discipleship training leader is like a coach is not only because he finds lay people and trains them to serve. That is also true, but something else similar is the style in which he leads the Bible study. A coach sets up a strategy to win a game. He doesn't show himself when the athletes run on the field. The athletes act as they receive his signals. The winning or losing of a game depends greatly on the coach's leadership and strategy.

A leader teaching the Bible in discipleship class is someone who has a similar role. He can cram the Bible just like a coach who studies hard before the game. If possible, however, he hopes that the trainees will participate firsthand. He wisely thinks it important to help them understand and apply the truth on their own. This resembles the role of a coach who sends the athletes out in the field while the coach sits on the bench and gives signals.

Nevertheless, the whole flow of that time depends on him. The leader's role determines how successful the study is. In essence he is in the position of leading the whole but by looking from the sideline. It is as if he is coaching the team of those studying.

Good leadership depends on the motivational skill to allow the trainees to run excitedly. When one is actually being chased by discipleship training, however, there are many times that one forgets this important principle and tastes the bitterness of trying to pull it all along by himself.

Chapter 26: The Importance of the First session

Items of Inspection Before Training

After a long preparation and careful selection of target members, once the time arrives for the pastor to begin discipleship training in earnest, there is something else waiting to be done promptly. The pastor or leader must individually meet the target members, review the items necessary for the training, and tell them in advance what they need to prepare. In an established church if the target is elders, or other core members that the pastor knows very well, then the items of inspection may be a little different from the general membership. Depending on the situation it will be necessary for the pastor to make the right judgment and take care of it.

The first item is to visit the potential trainee at home beforehand. It is best if this home visit is done about two weeks before the discipleship training opening worship. Don't forget to pray for them before the individual interview. Pray for each member of the family by speaking their names. We know from many experiences that there is a big difference between meeting someone whom we've prayed for and meeting someone whom we haven't prayed for.

Examine the trainee's spiritual state and background first. If the church structure is small, then the people are so familiar that, perhaps, there isn't a need to meet separately to do the work. However, even though some may be very familiar, it is best to give them the opportunity to examine themselves as they go into training.

Carefully review together how long they have had faith, whether they have ever been involved in a pseudo religious sect or cult, if there is assurance of salvation, how are they maintaining daily devotional life, how deep is the understanding of the basics of the Bible, and what are the spiritual problems, etc. These are all vital items that should not be left out. And it is good to know if there are any family difficulties or suffering.

If these data are well arranged in a file, it will be very helpful in understanding how to deal with the person during training. And, one can always add additional new information to the file as training progresses.

Second, while visiting them at home tell them the rules and regulations of discipleship training. Explain that they need to spend two or three hours a day to review and do homework. Obtain their promise to do so.

Tell them the general content of the homework in advance. Explain, and have them agree with the fact, that if they're absent more than three times then they may not continue. Ask them if they can open their home as a meeting place when their turn comes to do so. Don't forget to bless that family with the Word and prayer before leaving. It will be best if the Scripture shared here during the one year of training encourages them not to give up when the desire comes to do so.

When the individual home visits and inspection is done, put a big sign in front of the church and prepare for the discipleship training opening worship. The pastor mustn't let this discipleship-training look like another educational program. The pastor has to make it so important that the congregation will feel the significance without a detailed explanation that the pastor begins this effort with his life on the line and that it is one of the most important ministries in the church.

For this purpose it is necessary to specially manage the entrance service and the completion service a year or two later. For a long time, at the SaRang church the congratulating services of admission and completion have been the most passionate and well attended services.

The First Session

At the first session, just meeting together itself is so exciting that it overflows with grace. The pastor should try to leave a good impression. It is normally not burdensome for the pastor, but keep in mind that meeting each week in a limited space with ten or so people can be very stressful for the lay person. If the mood is peaceful then it is a good sign.

Choose a secretary and a treasurer at the first session to help out the pastor. Select someone who the pastor thought was appropriately qualified while doing individual home visiting. It can be better for a pastor to choose if all consent to the choice and explanation.

When the membership goes over 10 people, I recommend that

a committee of three or four people be formed according to the locality, then set up a person in charge of each. This will be very helpful when there is a need to make an urgent call or a need to examine each other spiritually. Write down the names of two people who will support them in prayer. They have to be accountable to pray for that person for the duration of the training.

At the SaRang church much information and many assignments are given out during the first session. For example, the monthly dues are decided on. A hymnal, a Bible, study material, Quiet Time binder and memory cards, colored pencils, and even a handkerchief are all given out. Someone may ask, Why give a handkerchief? It is because the handkerchief has a symbolic meaning. It carries an implication that the training will be one of many tears. There will never be training where there is only laughter from the beginning to the end. The pastor then explains in detail the assignments to prepare for the next meeting. Everyone, perhaps, feels overwhelmed at first, so one needs to consider the circumstances and the abilities of the trainees. For training to be training it is better if the assignments are a bit difficult. If the burden is too heavy, however, then it can have a reverse effect. If the ministry of discipleship training is already well settled in the church, it will be most effective to begin discipleship training without reviewing everyones circumstances in the first session.

For the church just starting out, however, the pace has to be well matched to the level of familiarity among the trainees. To obtain good results, though it is difficult, should be interesting, and feel worthwhile.

One important goal is for the trainee to experience the Holy

Spirit's working through home assignments. The pastor should seriously consider this challenge and handle it with wisdom and prayer.

The pastor should also caution all the members about how to open up their home. There are many cases when homemakers show a great deal of insecurity or sensitivity in this regard. A member with a very well to do home may secretly wait for others to visit so they can anticipate the reaction. But for a member with a less well to do home, having visitors can be a burden. They may feel awkward because their house is small and unimpressive to others.

So, we need to be careful not to make someone else stumble. A few months after the training begins, when, after visiting each other's homes, everyone sees and understands the circumstances of each person, they will realize that correcting their thoughts early makes a great contribution to going up the next level in their personal faith character.

A discipleship class will progress into a relationship of loving each other. When each realizes that everything seen and experienced becomes the fertilizer to grow as a disciple of Jesus, boasting will disappear. Shyness will melt. Only the one body of love averaged out in Jesus will remain.

When preparing your home for a meeting, put away anything that can be distracting. Perhaps, take the phone off the hook during the time of study. Try to make sure there won't be any sudden, unexpected visitors. Another important matter is the meal times. For some the class may be over lunch, for others over dinner. Naturally, it is expected that the home providing the meeting place prepares the meal.

I've come to know from experience that meal times can often

become the devil's temptation. The homeowner is so busy preparing the meal that he or she can't receive proper training. When the whole house is filled with the aroma of food, the mood is also not right for training. A wealthy home may completely overload the table with food. Others, who are impressed or shamed by this, are discouraged and fall into temptation.

It is necessary, therefore, to set up a mutually agreed upon rule right from the start. There are many methods. You may choose to agree on one standard dish, or give each person a number and have a few members each bring a dish. However it is done, make sure the quality of the spiritual training will not fall short because of a problem of what to eat or drink.

At SaRang church, whoever is late or absent has to pay a fine. If someone is absent more than three times then he or she is considered for automatic dismissal from the training. Trainees absolutely may not borrow or lend each other money. If such a situation is discovered then they are asked to leave the group immediately.

Members are also strongly cautioned to avoid conflict between husbands and wives because of the training. Sometimes we see husbands or wives who are so engrossed in their homework that they study well into the night, and don't join their spouses for bed. As a result, one spouse may threaten to quit discipleship training, or they fall into some other dilemma.

We have also seen situations where children and family are ignored. To bring harmony with the family and training, or business and training, then there is no other royal road. Each one has to become two times or three times more diligent. Repeat this point many times during the early stages of training.

It may also be good for the pastor to make a few predictions before the first session finishes. He may predict, for example, that at first they will feel the homework is burdensome and fall into the temptation of wanting to quit. They may be tested with family difficulties not to persevere. There will be times when they will be hurt by one of the other members of the group. They can carry a big emotional burden or scar which will prevent them from living out what they learned. For reasons unknown, there may be times when they don't want to see the pastor anymore. When predictions like these are made beforehand and when a similar incident actually occurs, they won't be so confused. It is necessary to tell the group these things because these are actual events that often happen.

We have no need to fear if we know Satan's schemes. Emphasize that we all must admit that we are human, complete with flaws, and that compassion for each other must come before discipleship.

Before parting after each meeting, take each other's hands, look at each other, and confess, "We are a body. We need to help each other. I need your help. Please help me. I love you." Many will get up from their seats saturated in deep emotion.

Is there anything else as enjoyable to a pastor as discipleship training? Discipleship training is truly a pastoral delight with rich rewards for the whole church!

Chapter 27: The Necessity of a Training Ground for Discipleship

To what extent is it possible to disciple the laity within the local church? This was a question that sprang up in the latter half of the 1970s as SaRang Community Church began its ministry. At that time, no one could give any definitive answer. Not one church could be found in which discipleship training had succeeded to change the church structure in any notable way. Although there were one or two churches that were known for conducting discipleship training ministries through small group Bible studies, it was difficult to view these as ministries with their roots planted firmly in a discipleship training philosophy. Thus, it was only with a great deal of uncertainty that our discipleship training ministry could be advanced. Despite my personal conviction of the possibilities for discipleship training, in truth, no one could guarantee its success. As is the case with most frontier endeavors, many obstacles stood in the way of establishing a specific ministry for the training of disciples. To put it bluntly, the general church climate was hostile to the introduction of such a ministry.

Why the Need?

Why is it essential to have a training ground for discipleship? We could spend time speculating, but what good are models when the presence of a tangible ministry would do more to convince us of the possibilities of that ministry than just mere talk. If we only spoke of discipleship training in theory and could not show its fruits in any real way, then it would be over-ambitious to expect people to respond with any degree of interest. If discipleship training is indeed consistent with the intrinsic nature of the church, and if it is the most appropriate method of ministry based on biblical principles, then it is only by establishing a healthy environment for such a ministry that ministry workers can share in the work of awakening the laity. There is yet a further role that the ministry of discipleship training can play - it can open up a new vision for the mainline or mission driven church.

In order to be effective, a particular ministry must be able to satisfy several indispensable conditions.

First, it must be a church with a thorough philosophy under which pastors can conduct the ministry of discipleship training. Unless a leader is totally excited and enthusiastic about discipleship training, other people will not be convinced about the power of that ministry. Churches that are unconvinced themselves and test it out for a little while on a trial basis will certainly have no power to convince anyone else.

Secondly, discipleship training must have been established in the church for at least seven years, so that it has become central to the entire ministry. Only then can we examine the changes taking place in the whole church specifically through discipleship training, and only then can we see the ways in which a church with such a ministry differs from that of other churches.

There is one more condition that a church must satisfy. There must be evidence to show that it is a healthily growing church. The adult attendance for Sunday services should be at least over 500 people for a church located in a near or urban area. Naturally, circumstances would be different for rural churches.

Until the middle of the 1980s, no such church could be found in Korea. In 1986, SaRang Community Church opened its ministry to other churches for training. At that time, many pastors in Korea and abroad responded beyond expectations. This was, I believe, because an opportunity arose to promote and reinforce the discipleship training ministry, which would not otherwise have been possible. Since then, SaRang Community Church opened its ministry of discipleship training to thousands of leaders 45 times and again, serving to plant in them a vision for discipleship training.

Serving in this role over a long period of time, it has become evident that the opening up of the discipleship training ministry was indeed a special cross which we chose to bear. It was difficult not to feel its weight. Not only was this a difficult task, but also it was certainly not one which we could carry out carelessly.

It may be said that SaRang Community Church has now lost its capacity to serve effectively as a training ground for discipleship. In order to truly be the such, a ministry which purports to provide training ground for discipleship must be able to provide an atmosphere of unity to visitors. It must be able to encourage them and instill a sense of confidence that they, too, are capable of participating in such a ministry. SaRang Community Church, however, has grown too large over the years to effectively serve that role. It may be meaningful to prove that even through a ministry such as discipleship training, it is possible to build a large church. There is, however, the fear that visiting ministry workers participating in the training programs may feel a little more than overwhelmed their outward calm amounting to the same kind of resignation as when struck with the awe of a mountain that cannot be climbed.

We should not, however, lose sight of the fact that, whichever church we visit, the things that should interest us, the things we need to look out for and identify, should not be just the external appearance. We must be able to discern the things that are hidden behind the external appearance, that are not easily visible to the eye. Everybody knows that when a doctor examines a patient, he or she is not interested in how big or how good-looking the patient is. We must also adopt this same attitude when observing a church and its ministry. We must be able to read from the church environment the pastor's philosophy. We must be able to perceive the spirit with which the church community is governed. We must be able to check what events are occurring. And we must be able to identify reasons for the health of the church, and where its source of growth lies. Only then can we be certain of what we should take with us back to our own respective ministries. If we were to borrow a common spiritual expression, we would say that we must be able to hear God's voice, see His vision, and then return to our places having seen and having heard. If visiting pastors could look at SaRang Community Church with this same sense of discrimination, then they would see that it still possesses sufficient qualities to render services essential for discipleship training.

Examples of Effective Ministries

In contrast to when SaRang Community Church first opened its ministry, there are now many wonderful and healthy discipleship training grounds all over Korea. For the past 10 years or so, God has blessed ministry workers in a powerful way. Now it is not in the least bit difficult to find abundant evidence of the sweat and tears that they shed day and night in order to awaken the laity. Not only in Korea's big cities, but even in the smaller provincial cities, there are many churches that can now boast discipleship training ministries. Furthermore, even in Japan, where they said for the past century that revival was impossible, you can now find many churches that were established through discipleship training, churches that are sending shock waves all over the world. (It is difficult to express in words the depths of our gratitude and happiness.)

Now we do not need to search around to witness the powerful effects of discipleship training. The question of whether we are able to find such a place or not, is now dependent upon how hard we look, for the reality of discipleship training can be witnessed in so many churches all around us. In the first few years, when the CAL (Called to Awaken the Laity) Seminar began, one of the most important objectives for participating ministry workers was to go and witness for themselves the active ministry taking place at SaRang Community Church. Circumstances, however, have changed. Now most participants simply visit SaRang on their own because they have been deeply impacted and challenged by surrounding churches, which had themselves come to a turning point through the ministry of discipleship training. This development was not simply due to the training role taken on by SaRang Community Church, but it indicates that many fellow churches have come together to take on the joint responsibility of ministering to the laity through discipleship training.

I would now like to introduce several churches that I am convinced will be of great help to ministry workers. The New Central Church located in Pusan, is an excellent example of how a well established church with a long tradition can be changed through discipleship training. When a new pastor was appointed to that church about 10 or so years ago, there already existed an influential senior pastor. Most of the congregation was comprised of senior elders who were bound by fixed ideas. There was severe antagonism between the congregation and the full-time church staff, leaving many scarred. In short, this was the perfect example of an established church, having all the essential qualities that generally typified a well established church. No matter how one tried to look at it, this was a church in which discipleship training seemed an impossible goal. It would certainly be doomed to fail. However, today in that very same church, great miracles are taking place and many other established churches are now being encouraged through it.

In America, there is a church shouting out a powerful message of the potentials of discipleship training ministry to the more than 3,000 Korean-American churches, where many Korean-Americans find spiritual refuge. This is the SaRang Community Church of Southern California. For the past 10 years, hundreds of ministry workers from among the Korean-American churches were challenged by the vision of discipleship training. Yet most of them abandoned this ministry halfway through, without ever growing to see the ministry bear fruit. Many also claimed that the Korean-American church was simply not suitable ground for discipleship training. They claimed that it would be more harmful to confront Korean-Americans with the concept of 'training', since it was not training that they needed, but rather constant care and comforting. However, the SaRang Community Church of Southern California has been disproving established opinions, demonstrating that Korean-American churches are indeed fertile soil for fruitful discipleship training. There are already many leaders who have again taken on the challenge of a discipleship training ministry, having been inspired by that church. It is a great blessing for all Korean-American churches that God planted such a church in America overflowing with inspiration.

Still another church that deserves our attention is Yeomkwang Church, located in Taean, Korea. Without any actual evidence, it is difficult to judge whether a discipleship training ministry can be successful in the farming villages of remote districts. However, for the past 10 or so years, Yeomkwang Church has played a big part in helping wipe out these fears of uncertainty. Being convinced that there is no royal road to lay ministry apart from discipleship training, even for ministries conducted in farm villages, this church advocated discipleship training with greater strength and conviction than any other church. It has already become a powerful ministry, attracting the attention of many ministry workers. I am confident that we will soon witness in rural churches the miracle of the laity devoting themselves as disciples of Christ no less than what we have witnessed in the churches of the larger cities.

There are many other churches that are just as wonderful and significant as those three that have been mentioned above. Since I am unable to introduce them all to you in detail due to limited space, I regretfully only list their names. I trust that a day will come when their inspiring stories will also be shared with the world.

Korea:

Seoul Donam-dong Church (Pastor Tae Soo Han)

Seoul Beautiful Church (Pastor Jong Po Kim)

Seoul Chamsil Central Church (Pastor Ju Chae Jung)

Seoul Chung-Jung Church (Pastor Sung Suk Oak)

Seoul Hong-Seong Church (Pastor Keun Soo Lee)

Seoul Songpa Cheil Church (Pastor Byung Shik Park)

Seoul Yeongdong Church (Pastor Eun Jo Park)

Seoul Disciple Church (Pastor Sam Ji Jung)

Seoul Jiguchon Church (Pastor Bong Hee Cho)

Pusan New Central Church (Pastor Hong Jun Choi)

Pusan Kaekum Church (Pastor Song Ho Park)

Taegu Dong-Heung Church (Pastor Hyung Shik Kim)

Kwangju Bansok Church (Pastor Jong Won Choi)

Taejun Saeronam Church (Pastor Jung Ho Oh)

Taejun Jungrim Seongkyul Church (Pastor Hyung Kyo Jung)

Ansan Dongsan Church (Pastor In Joong Kim)

Yangsan Samyang Church (Pastor Yeon Chul Jung)

Yeosoo Sandol Church (Pastor Min Chul Shin)

Ulsan Citizens Church (Pastor Jong Kwan Lee)

Ulsan Big Light Church (Pastor Tae Hwan Cho)

Iri Central Church (Pastor Ju Hwan Oh)

Ilsan Peace Church (Pastor Sang Tae Choi)

Ilsan Bethel Church (Pastor Kwang Sok Park)

Jinju Seongbuk Church (Pastor Choon Soo Lee)

Changwon Namsan Church (Pastor Song Beom Lee)

Changwon One Light Church (Pastor Hee Ku Yun)

Chonan Presbyterian Church (Pastor Jung Ho Lee)

Taean Yeomkwang Church (Pastor Jong Chun Kim)

Pyungchon New Central Church (Pastor Choong Shik Park)

Pyungtaek Daekwang Church (Pastor Chang Don Bae)

Mokpo Salt and Light Church (Pastor Hyun Yong Cho)

America:

Sarang Church of Southern California (Pastor Jung Hyun Oh)

New Jersey Chodae Church (Pastor Yong Jin Cho)

New York Onnuri Church (Pastor Mun Hui Cho)

LA Pyungkang Church (Pastor Jung Hoon Lee)

Philadelphia Antioch Church (Pastor Sung Ki Ho)

Maryland Sanjunghyun Church (Pastor Byung Hwan Lee)

New York South Church (Pastor Sang Il Park)

Japan:

Kujiha Christ Chuch (Pastor Endo Akio)

Sendai Lovely Seongseo Church (Pastor Fujimoto Kouetsu)

Shuttofukuinyurigaoka Christ Church (Pastor Shiba Mitsumasa)

Nerima Grace Chapel (Pastor Ogasawara Takashi)

Nagoya Church (Pastor Kedo Genji)

Kasugai Gospel Freedom Church (Pastor Yoshia Masaharu)

Akashi Church (Pastor Yamawaki Hisaji)

Chapter 28: Roots of the Korean Church

As the Korean church was first being established, it was greatly influenced by the Nebius method of ministry. In 1890, Korean missionaries invited to Korea Reverend John Nebius and his wife who were doing mission work in Chifu, China. For two weeks, the Korean missionaries spent time together with the Nebius couple, learning the fundamentals of missions that would guide the future of Korean missions. Among the Nebius principles, one in particular draws our attention. This is the first principle, which essentially encourages all believers to become individual workers for Christ where they are, and also teaches the laity to work diligently in their given occupation, living lives that reflect Christ to all those around them.[1]

Let me outline a few important implications coming from this principle. These were what molded the spirit with which the entire congregation of the early Korean church was mobilized, the same spirit that made possible discipleship among the laity.

The first implication is that underlying the principle of the lay ministry was an education-centered ministry. At the core of the

Nebius method was not only the simple raising of individual lay believers and training them, but also raising the productivity of the entire church. Based on the interdependence of the church, the principle urged that all laity become individual workers for Christ. Further, based on the understanding that the whole church has been called to be witnesses of the gospel to the world, it emphasized that each and every individual live so as to reflect Christ in their lives. In light of this, it becomes clear why the church at that time placed priority on teaching rather than on preaching. This is not to say, however, that preaching did not play an important role. Rather, it is to say that the ministry emphasized the importance of training the laity in the word no less than preaching to the laity. Thus at the time, gatherings akin to Bible study groups or discipleship training classes were prevalent, greatly influencing individual spiritual growth and personal evangelism.

The first Bible study class was formed in Seoul in 1890, when Dr. Horace Underwood began to gather together with seven students in his private study. In 1901, a general mission policy was adopted, with the aim of establishing Bible study groups everywhere that missionaries went. Four years later, 60% of the entire nations church population were attending one or two Bible study classes. Statistics also show that in 1909, there were approximately 800 Bible study groups within the Northern Presbyterian Mission District alone, with over 50,000 people receiving teaching there.[2]

Inherent in these testimonies to the rapid growth of the early church is the implication that teaching has a wider sphere of influence than preaching, and its character allows it to concentrate more on details. While preaching may be the more appropriate method of proclaiming the gospel to the world, teaching has its strength in being able to minister to both the church and the world, meeting their needs through the Word. Again, preaching requires only a simple response from listeners, while teaching requires intellectual interaction with those who are learning, widening their thinking in the process.[3] Thus, those who desire to grow in wisdom and maturity so as to be able to discern good from evil, must be trained thoroughly on solid food (Hebrews 5:14).

During the time of the first church, men and women, and even children, were all students, while they taught at the same time. Each was nurtured by those more mature in faith than they, and in turn, each taught those with weaker faith than theirs.[4] As Nebius pointed out, through this kind of interdependence, the early church came to be a church in which the laity could each apply their gifts and develop them, and they were thus able to mature in knowledge, strength and efficiency.[5]

A second implication is that underpinning the Nebius principle was a family-centered ministry. The church in its early years could not avoid using the family as a base for missions and ministry work. Since all the early churches appearing in the Bible were family churches, there was no reason why it should have been any different for the early churches of Korea. It would be misleading, however, to conclude that the early Korean churches were family-centered simply due to circumstances. This is because, despite the fairly miserable conditions existing in the churches a short while after being established, they positively sought to equip themselves with basic necessities. By concentrating on family meetings, church leaders at the time were able to stay aware of the many spiritual changes and influences that were taking place in the world of the laity. 'Living room' meetings for men grew more and more popular, and 'inner room' meetings for women were being pursued with interest. At these meetings, men and women were able to meet together and receive spiritual training through Bible studies. The meetings also provided a wonderful opportunity to invite unbelieving friends and neighbors to share the gospel with them.[6]

Thirdly, inherent in the Nebius principle was a personal evangelism-centered ministry. In the early days, the laity of the church were all evangelists. They did not evangelize with any specific mission strategy, or under the compulsion of leaders. Rather, their enthusiasm for evangelism was merely the outward expression of all the capabilities they had developed through the training-centered and family-centered ministries. Herbert Kane described this phenomenon as follows.

Beginning in 1895 and for the 10 years following, there was consistent and continual growth in over half the mission districts. In the year 1900 alone, the number of churchgoers increased by 30%. New believers continued to emerge, even after the missionaries had already reached their limit in the ability to teach them, and the doors to evangelism were opened as far as even the remote areas where missionaries could not otherwise have set foot. For the most part, these phenomena did not arise through any form of organized evangelistic movement, but rather, it was the result of the personal evangelism of believers, who shared the gospel with everyone in a simple and sincere way in the course of their daily lives.[7]

There were, of course, more than one or two methods of

evangelism that the early church used. It is clear, however, that the most effective method of evangelism was through personal contact.[8]

Between 1909 - 1910, a movement developed to save one million souls. Each individual devoted a day during the week for personal evangelism, and statistics show that the total number of days that the laity devoted to personal evangelism was over 100,000 days nationwide.[9]

What we learn from all this is that in order to discover more about the ministry of the early churches, we need to clearly understand three inherent characteristics of those churches as mentioned above.

Behind the fact that Korean churches are now among the most successful results of world missions, lies their spirit of ministry centered around the training of the laity. The basic intent of the first church in Korea was not to establish a missionary-centered nor staff-centered church, but rather, to establish a laity-centered church. They took on a biblical approach, emphasizing the training of the laity, that they might serve one another within the church, and also emphasizing the dispatch of witnesses to the world, that they might witness Christ through their words and their behavior. With such intentions, small group meetings such as the living room and the inner room meetings, were used as a cradle for the raising of disciples.

Our present environment is so entirely different from that of the early churches, that we cannot even compare ourselves with them. From a methodological perspective alone, we probably could not even imitate the methods used by those early churches. We are more than able, however, to assume at least the spirit of these early churches, which was so precious and fundamental to their ministries. Indeed, now is the time for us to rediscover that same spirit, the great inheritance that those who went before us have left behind, and rekindle that spirit within our own ministries.

Chapter 29: Strengthening the Roots of SaRang Church's Discipleship Training

Yesterday and Today

When SaRang Church first opened its doors in July 1978, there was only one thing that it possessed: the pastor's vision of establishing a solid discipleship training program. Although there were only ten church members at that time who didn't know precisely how to go about realizing their pastor's vision, they were zealous to give their support as one body of Christ. While surrounding older and well established churches went about their teaching methods, SaRang Church followed a different approach. It wasn't that the teaching programs of the other churches were no good, rather, SaRang Church felt that their pastor had something better in store. Discipleship training was such a strong and convicting vision for me and the early members that it continued to be the main focus for SaRang Church.

During the first few years of establishment, SaRang Church had to overcome a great many trials and tribulations. In the small space of a basement, the first few years were bittersweet. There were joyful and persevering servants of God who gladly gave their time and energy to do social work, but there were others who could not adjust well to the church and left with hurt and pain. There were also times of extreme financial hardship when the church members could only gaze up at their pastors face during consultation. Yet amid all these circumstances, there were actually more jubilant and encouraging moments than difficult and painful ones. Time flew by quickly, and the sense of anticipation for the discipleship training bud to break into full bloom at any moment made sitting still for one hour seem endless. That is why even when during a blistering hot summer there was a staged demonstration protesting the construction of SaRang Church, when the construction stopped because of bankruptcy, and when there were Sunday worshippers packed like sardines in the church, struggling to breathe properly in the extreme summer heat, I just could not let go of the vision for discipleship training. Where would be the joy in ministering without discipleship training? This question reoccurred in my mind daily, without fail.

There came a year when I had to physically abandon everything. Yet, through the Lord's perfect strength, His will of building discipleship training at SaRang Church came alive and continued to grow tremendously as one body of Christ. The one thing that changed after I recuperated from my fatigue, was that I no longer trained the small groups. It was unfeasible for me to teach the vast number of small groups, so together we assigned a handful of believers who ministered to the small groups.

In response to this, some members expressed their disapproval over what appeared to be favoritism shown by the pastor. As a result, over forty associate pastors were assigned to the important responsibility of administering and teaching the various small groups. As the senior pastor, I was responsible for these associate pastors who were to spread the teachings of the Gospel and make disciples of Jesus Christ.

Over 20 years have passed since SaRang Church began its discipleship training. I believe our roots may be compared with the roots of a 20 year-old cedar tree. Discipleship training has grown to be healthy and strong while its roots are deeply embedded in Christ. Discipleship training is the core of the ministry and is producing great results. When looking back, one cannot state that small efforts produced great results. In ministry, every fruit has a reason for its existence, as does every step of improvement and growth. One thing is for certain: To this end I labor, struggling with all His energy, which so powerfully works in me (Col 1:29), and we view the things accomplished and the efforts made in the long run. Over the past 20 years, I have ruthlessly abided by the following principle: to put all my efforts into establishing the deeper roots of discipleship training which would serve the community in great ways. There are many other secondary principles, but chief among them is the vision of growing and improving discipleship training so that it provides a practical use for believers.

Going in the Right Track

Discipleship training is not one of the many different ministering methods that we can choose. Discipleship training is the essence of a sound church, and it serves as an unique model for developing an intimate relationship with Jesus Christ. A believer who turns on the engine and begins discipleship training must finish the race and complete the training. The discipleship trainee shouldn't give up when he feels inferior to others, when he hears criticism, when he doesn't see any signs of spiritual fruit, when he's sick and tired and wants to quit, when there appears an easier way, or when there's a huge mountain blocking his way. There must not be any hint of regret. Discipleship training is the ministering method that was taught by Jesus Christ our Lord, the head of the church. It may not be disregarded or abandoned. Saying that we are lacking is no excuse for not completing God's work.

I believe that whenever SaRang Church's members looked at me, I prayed that they would see qualities of steadfastness, determination, and consistency. I would have left the ministry if not for discipleship training and the spiritual gifts it provided. With that strong and positive vision, I was determined to adhere strongly to the God-given task that we had begun.

One day, less than a year after SaRang Church had started, a male deacon whom I had known since childhood asked me a question. "Pastor, are you going to continue your pastoral duties this way? Surrounding churches are holding revival meetings and already have hundreds of people worshipping at their churches, while day and night we lead a handful of people in discipleship training. At this rate, when are we going to catch up with the other churches?" When I heard that question, all I could say was, "I'm going to continue ministering in this way." Now I can't honestly recall having had this dialog with the deacon. He, however, never forgot. It had such a powerful impact on him that three years ago, he reminded me of it as he recounted the story to others. This episode, he said, showed the resolute nature of my vision for discipleship training, and how we never strayed

281

from the vision by following the trends of other churches. By the grace of God, I am happy to say that nothing has changed in these principles as I pastor SaRang Church.

In ministering, there are numerous temptations. Pastoral leaders face decisions that are troubling and worrisome. Will things work out if they're done this way or that way? The cruelest temptation is one that cuts out the life of discipleship training as it grows in effectiveness. There is the temptation to turn discipleship training into an easier, huge, lecture-type class rather than keeping it in an intimate and accountable small group setting. There is also the hasty and unfulfilling temptation to quit discipleship training and create an inspirational service designed to stir and revive the laymen.

Another temptation is attending a variety of seminars to hear success stories and experiences. Yet they only serve like a medicine to help us temporarily, and should not be considered a panacea whereby we stop working for the Lord because we think a permanent remedy exists. No mother would feed her child medicine instead of nourishing food for breakfast, lunch and dinner. In the same fashion, seminars should not become the main focus of leaders. Running from church to church to find the correct and successful way of ministering is useless. Unfortunately, some pastor their churches with reference to the many seminar binders displayed on their bookshelves. If we are totally devoted to discipleship training, then there is really nothing else that can take away our focus from developing and training disciples of Jesus Christ. In this short life of ministry, how can we find the time to fully concentrate on 2 or 3 other ministering methods?

Up to the present day, SaRang Church has never strayed from

its vision. We have been steadfast in the single vision of growing and strengthening discipleship training. The only way to deepen the roots of discipleship training is through concerted efforts and many prayers. The church is thus able to trust me as their steadfast pastor through continued dedication to the single vision and perseverance in difficult times. Changing methodologies have provided temporary stimulation and excitement among church members, but no trust for the vacillating leader. If a pastoral leader cannot eradicate uneasiness when the question arises, 'How long will this go on?', then it is impossible for the leader to take on the responsibility of discipleship training.

Unbroken Strength

One of the many difficulties that I encountered was the number of outside requests to give lectures about discipleship training. The most difficult was refusing to give seminars and lectures to other churches and Christian organizations who held a deep interest in discipleship training. The main reason for turning down such requests was the belief that in order for discipleship training to continue successfully, I needed to remain at the church and focus solely on it. It would be a violation of principle if I were to begin traveling to other places in order to give lectures and hold seminars. Even if there is a capable group of pastoral leaders who carry out their responsibilities in managing discipleship training, I believe the head pastor must be present to oversee and give his undivided attention to discipleship training so that no great mishaps occur in the future.

If a church does discipleship training well, the church's pastor may eventually become famous and travel often to speak to other churches. As a result, the successful discipleship training program may tumble and become merely a Bible study class. Pastors should carefully consider the requests to speak at other churches and specifically limit the number of lectures or seminars that may be made. There is one principle for pastors to keep in mind: refuse any requests that may cause your discipleship training to deteriorate.

I most often politely refuse nine out of ten requests to speak at other churches. I'm told this earned me the nickname of being the man who digs his hole and sits in it . Undoubtedly, this is not an attitude that I insist is Gospel truth. Such an approach may be a stumbling block to other churches who believe that sharing experiences and knowledge about discipleship training can be used for the furthering of God's kingdom. Aside from speaking at other churches in special cases, your primary method of furthering God's kingdom is giving undivided attention to your own church and striving to make sure things do not go wrong.

There is another rule to follow in order to make discipleship training more substantial. Some may view it as being rather extreme. Nonetheless, there is a lot of significance and truth to it. When SaRang Church first began, I made an agreement with the church elders. We agreed not to hold any positions in Christian organizations or associations for pastors and elders. The reason was that the focus would shift from SaRang Church to other responsibilities associated with positions in Christian organizations. Surprisingly up to this present day, our promise has not been broken. The message conveyed here is that church leaders must concentrate on the church if discipleship training is to remain vibrant and healthy. How can anything good be produced if thoughts and minds are scattered?

Struggling to Continue Growing

Let's think for a moment. Is there anything in this world that would put more pressure on a pastor than desiring to become a disciple of Jesus Christ? The more profound the reason for becoming a disciple of Christ, the more focused and upright a person becomes. Subsequently, the pastor who starts discipleship training must wear chains on his feet and be determined to follow through in his ministry. How can someone teach another to become a disciple of Jesus Christ if he himself doesn't make any effort or have a desire to live and be like Christ? During discipleship training ministry, if there is no change or improvement seen in the leader, then the training may as well not exist. Therefore, it must be communicated from the outset that discipleship training may create many difficult and ugly moments which produce stress and place a burden on the leader.

In order to express himself, a pastor cannot open up his feathers like an extravagant peacock. This should not be allowed in his sermons nor in the small groups. A pastor is a sole and lonely combatant. Only under the Lord does a pastor shed his tears and pour out his sweat. However, strangely enough, the church knows exactly how much effort the pastor puts in as well as all the growth within the church. The pastor is a positive and visible image of authority to the church members.

SaRang Church exists in an environment in which it cannot afford to remain status quo. It must continue to grow and run ahead. I ask, "How can a pastor sit back and relax while the churchs laymen are running ahead striving to become like Christ?"

Under these circumstances I faced many challenges and

continually tried to think of self-improvement measures. I believe
that a desire for the church to grow should be natural and
inherent in a pastor. There were moments when things were
burdensome and it was tempting to run away from them all. At
times there were impulses to let go of everything because the
church was exhausted. However, I thank God that at SaRang
Church we continued to persevere and never showed even a
slight suggestion of giving up through difficult and painful
circumstances. It would be frightening if someone would ask, "So,
based on your self-growth, how sufficient and satisfied are you?"
There would be nothing for me to say. However, by focusing on
advancement, the church is confident that the pastor who
watches over the church day and night will be able to reply
positively to that question. Subsequently, when discipleship
training has somewhat found its place, it creates a good
environment for both the pastor and the laymen to improve. I
have no doubt, showered by the grace of God, that through
sacrificial giving and receiving of one's self we receive the
blessings of God.

No Training, No Work

From the very beginning, SaRang Church has seemed a solid
rock because the leaders of the church were all well-trained. We
established a rule that anyone who wanted to be involved
deeply in the various teaching ministries needed to first receive
the proper training. These ministries are: the teaching of God's
Word to others. For the first 2-3 years after SaRang Church was
established, there were some discipleship trainees who were
concurrently teaching. After those early years, however, there

have been no such cases. If a person was not trained and prepared, then their work did not begin. Even though a person appeared to be very spiritually in tune with God, no responsibility was given to that person unless training was first received. Because of this, several people who came from other churches expressed some discomfort. In unfortunate cases, some people left the church altogether. Nonetheless, SaRang Church and I as its pastor remain steadfast to these principles.

With the firm rule of not allowing anyone without verifiable training to minister to others, SaRang Church has been able to plan and provide timely and suitable responsibilities for those who complete their training. Even though a person may have experience and appear to have a strong faith in God, if that individual does not humble himself and receive the proper additional training, then he cannot receive recognition from SaRang Church.

As more people stepped forward to receive training, the standards of discipleship training improved and the level of difficulty increased. As a result of these strict regulations which require such a thorough discipleship training program, I am not aware of any case where a worker was misused in the church. Looking over our past experiences in training, SaRang Church never thought of easing the rules or sacrificing the quality of our program from the very beginning.

Disturbances came from every direction. But it was difficult to find a small hole through which they could penetrate. Every trainee knows beforehand and prepares to overcome the difficulties and possible pitfalls that he or she may face during the course of discipleship training. How important is this in securing peace and stability within the church? Up to this day, there has been no incidence of improper lay training, nor any significant problems to shake the foundation of the church. From the outside, SaRang Church may be viewed as a church which has attracted many high quality laymen. One thing is certain, however, the church has received abundant grace through its focused efforts to substantiate the principles of discipleship training.

Desiring Balance and Rhythm

The church must take careful consideration to avoid luring a discipleship trainee or a member into the teaching ministry and making excessive demands. While there is a time to work hard and put in all one's effort to work for God, there is also a time to sleep and rest so as to preserve a close spiritual relationship with God. No one can go through each day with tightly clenched fists. There is a time to clench the fist, and a time to relax the hand.

When discipleship training first began, it was novel and exciting. For twelve straight months, all the church leadership did was work, work, work. Additionally, when leaders were given the responsibility to take care of a small group, they were busy running here and there all year long to individually train their small group members.

A person who keeps running like an athlete, however, cannot last long spiritually. In order to continue the race, there must be a harmonious balance of work and rest. The balance and rhythm varies from person to person.

It is important to prevent imbalance in discipleship training. Continuously meeting in a small room behind closed doors to study the Bible is not mandatory. Once in a while it is advisable to meet outdoors in places like a retreat center or at a park to share and spend time in prayer. After the training ends, meeting with other discipleship trainees to continue growing in Christ is highly recommended. In this way an individual can continuously be challenged to deep contemplation of the Word. If one looks at the Bible with a simple mind and an unclear objective, it is like reading the Bible with your eyes closed. There should be opportunities for the disciple to organize a system in which to learn or extract more from the Word. The lack of a personal system of study can become a weak point either in discipleship training or in a teaching ministry.

By God's grace, SaRang Church has been able to maintain a good balance and rhythm to this day. Subsequently, discipleship training has flourished and many other programs have been born. To replenish and satiate the needs of the laymen, we have established a Bible college. There are regular seminars on family life, and well known guest lecturers who give seminars on special topics. In addition, in the summer and fall seasons, leaders and trainees are given four months off for rest and leisure. Those who at first protested four months of rest are now the ones who eagerly await this vacation period.

In addition, there are many opportunities for leaders and members to participate in social services. At one time, while trying to establish a rhythm and balance, we loosened up the strict training rules and schedule. This caused an adverse spiritual reaction. Although it was a difficult challenge, the church persevered and overcame the trial. Currently, discipleship training is secure and is a channel through with disciples can eventually train and teach other laymen.

Any church which is serious about discipleship training should establish these essential principles and put them into practice. Stated again, the blessings that flow from focused discipleship training are great, but they do not come simply by chance to those who sit around and wait. In order to progress, a church must first sow its seeds. Make all the necessary efforts without taking advantage of anyone or merely relying on others.

Chapter 30: From Discipleship Training to Sprout Leader Training

The beginning stage of our discipleship training was more of an experimental cultivation in a new ground called the church. Unlike a homogeneous group of all college students, it was difficult at first to assess its outcome since we began with a small group of men and women, old and young, rich and poor, educated and uneducated. Not only that, I had not yet organized my philosophy of ministry in a systematic manner. Even my teaching materials were borrowed from outside mission organizations.

The most important fact I had to recognize was that discipleship training was being utilized in a regular church ministry situation. It was essential that I stay open-minded. During the experimental period, I had to remain teachable and develop a very flexible attitude. Gradually I learned to hold fast to the basic framework of discipleship training while being able to promptly release anything that needed modification. Only the best could then remain. The result was the framework of the training program that is now bringing an abundant harvest for SaRang church.

The Beginnings of Mens' and Womens' Groups

The first womens' group met a crisis and was gone in less than six months. Only my wife remained out of the six original members. But a new group was soon formed when several married women with appropriate qualifications registered for our discipleship training. From that moment on, womens' groups proliferated rapidly.

The Holy Spirit worked so mightily that the Word of God brought repentance and the reshaping of womens' lives whether they had believed from their mothers' womb or just became Christians. The diligence and dedication of the first womens' groups became a driving force in the revival of the church, to the point of creating groups called Upper Rooms just to teach the increasing number of new members. There were no leaders who had been fully trained; only sprout leaders in training. Taking into account the special circumstance of the embryonic stage, after only eight months of training eight women deacons were chosen to double up as sprout leaders.

It is regretful that I am not able to tell all the amazing things that happened in those Upper Rooms. As I write, many of those sprout leaders are still running the race. Most are now in their fifties or sixties, but their fervor and dedication have not changed a bit. I am so thankful that at any time I can always confirm the potentiality and greatness of the laity in them. Today there are thousands of other women leaders who have followed those original core leaders. Their faith and calling to work together with the pastor is expanding the purpose of God on this earth by His church.

A mens' group began a year later than the womens' group because at first there wasn't enough men to start a group. Eight out of the first twelve were coerced by their faithful wives to attend. Most of them needed to learn the basics of the Christian faith rather than be trained in discipleship, so I had to exercise a lot of patience with these men. For the first couple of months, in order to make certain they would attend, I would personally go and pick them up by car. Many times our study ended in frustration because their hearts were not open. They had no experience of God's saving grace even though most were descendents of Christian men who had long records of faithfulness. These men were proud and confident with no apparent shortcomings. They were dignified even in their reasons for not believing and obeying. They saw no problems in considering themselves more righteous than God.

After about six months, from the most obstinate and down, God started to touch each one. From then on, the group atmosphere changed, as if the darkness disappeared in the light. Their expressions were full of joy and peace, and their conversations were laced with thanksgiving and love. With this change in their persons, their family and social lives changed. Soon, many delightfully shared with their family's testimonies of what happened during the previous week. Within four and a half years of the inception of the church, many from this original group were appointed as elders.

Following in the footsteps of those first women, through discipleship training hundreds of men at SaRang have entered the race for the kingdom of God as faithful lay leaders. Only

Jesus knows about what is happening in the Upper Room meetings they are leading and what is being done in their workplaces. However, it is not hard to meet people in the church who were saved through them or who are growing in the Lord through their efforts. Even today, Jesus, the head of the Church, is using their mouths to teach and proclaim, and their hands to heal.

There were many obstacles to overcome in order to train the men. They were far more unyielding and difficult than women were. The initial womens' group failed in the first round, but the second mens' group experienced similar setbacks soon after it started. The most difficult problem was that compared to the women, there were not that many men to choose from. In SaRang Church, for many years, male membership was less then twenty percent. Most were coming to a church for the first time, so it was only natural that women were leading the way.

My desire to forcefully continue the mens' discipleship program at the same pace as the womens' brought on disaster. The men, apparently, were too busy. It was tough to know when the right time to conduct the training was. We first tried evenings, then met early in the morning. When that didn't work we tried Sunday afternoon. The men with very young faith soon gave up. Over the years since then, it is my observation that men are not as spiritually sensitive as women, some to the point of being incorrigible. Training men takes a greater spiritual warfare. If the leader loses spiritual power, he will not be able to continue for long. On the other hand, once men taste the grace of God and are transformed. I have also observed that fewer things hinder their growth with less frivolity than women.

Discipleship training today is the nerve center of SaRang church. It has become a gateway to discovering lay leaders. Each year hundreds are selected, and the number of applicants sometimes is double the number of personnel needed. Requirements for selection as leaders are stringent. Once they are in the program, the intensity of the training is so high, it sometimes feels like a boot camp. But even so, their faces are full of joy and pride. As the senior pastor, I receive an overwhelming number of personal letters from them every year. They want to share the grace they experienced through discipleship training. They express their heartfelt thanks to God and the leaders for the opportunity. As I read these letters, I am filled with praise to God for how worthwhile the effort has been.

The Necessity of Ministry Training

When the church was taking shape and the discipleship training was on track, I started to develop an appropriate training manual for the church. After it went through dozens of revisions and additions over a period of many years, this material has evolved into Activating the Laymen: Discipleship Training and Ministry. This new manual brought epoch change to the training program of SaRang Church. Formerly, the emphasis was on strengthening the foundation of the gospel and faith, along with pursuing mature character in Christ and holy living. When the materials were revised, a Ministry Training (at first it was called Advanced Discipleship Training) manual was added as a supplement to provide a practical follow-up to discipleship training.

In order for the lay members to have a co-ministry with the clergy, it takes more than just good faith and character. A correct understanding of who one is, and the new paradigm that comes from sharing a ministry philosophy with the clergy are needed. Another essential is the ability for self-examination to confirm which spiritual ministry is appropriate with the gifting we have received. All of this is too much to be included in a one-year discipleship training process. That is the reason why we added another year-long course, Ministry Training, as a supplement. This course seems to confirm the difference between an established church's discipleship training and that of a mission organization. Since the full development of our ministry training materials, unless there was a special reason not to do so, anyone who finished discipleship training at SaRang Church has also proceeded to the second year of training.

As the church grew and the number of applicants continued to increase, I transferred the first phase of the training to a team of assistant pastors and concentrated only on the follow-up ministry training. Because three discipleship groups were transformed into one ministry group, however, it was slightly unsatisfactory as an organic teaching environment. The group members had become accustomed to a small group setting. Being part of the new larger group took some adjustment on their part. I felt the number of members was not as critical because, unlike the discipleship training, there were more short lectures from the leader, and it was more persuasive in tone than conversational. But, I think a group of over 25 people is too difficult to handle. No matter how much thoughtful consideration is given, individuals can lose the focus of the training. (For a reference of dialogues between leader and trainee during ministry training, please refer to Appendix I).

Every passing year brought more confirmation of the enormous contribution of the ministry training process to producing lay leaders. A lay member who is convinced of his calling is a competent minister both in the church and out in society. A healthy doctrine of the church sees a lay person in co-partnership with the pastor in ministry philosophy. A layman who has discovered in the Word of God a definite theory and methods of serving others, will successfully lead an Upper Room group. Those who feel the need to learn God's Word more systematically and in depth will diligently strive to improve. Each of these things can be observed in numerous brothers and sisters who have gone through our ministry training course.

Evangelism Explosion Training

Both discipleship training and ministry training do, however, have weaknesses in teaching about evangelism. It is true that the courses teach that laymen are disciples called to spread the gospel, and that the existence of the earthly church is to save the world. But in reality, because the trainees are not given an opportunity and place to evangelize, there is a danger that evangelism might be viewed as little more than an impractical proposition. Jesus took the disciples with Him, showed them how He proclaimed the gospel, then instructed them to do likewise. But, given my ministry context today, I know that I do not have a reserve of energy to imitate Jesus' pattern. The fact of the matter is, if the pastor does not go out into the streets during evangelism training, then it carries no real meaning. To alleviate such weakness in the SaRang training materials, an evangelism explosion program was introduced. Anyone who finishes the ministry training has to complete this four month program.

For over ten years, SaRang Church has received abundant

blessings through this evangelism explosion program. The celebrations of new believers never ceases because so many lay leaders who have gone through this training are working with passion. There are even some among them who have crossed national boundaries to set off the explosion of the gospel in different countries. This program exhibits a powerful force that opens the people's mouths, a deep spring that makes the joy of salvation constantly overflow in people. I am confident that an extraordinary number will still be coming to the bosom of God through this training.

Sprout Leader Education

Spiritual demands increase in lay people as they conclude all the training requirements and join the practical ministry. In some ways, the pastor now has a greater burden than ever. In order for them to successfully maintain their ministry, I believe the pastor has to constantly provide them with needed materials. He must always seek to fill their spiritual needs.

Spiritual ministry is a type of warfare. The power of darkness, which was dormant when a person did not minister, now persistently approaches the believer to challenge and tempt. Those who are more active, therefore, in ministry will experience greater spiritual stagnation. It is easy to mislead other people when the first excitement is gone and mannerism replaces genuine diligence. Lay ministers need to grow until they are almost obsessed with the idea that they cannot remain the same if they want to have spiritual impact or authority as lay leaders. They also need to have some spiritual discernment and counseling techniques in order to carry out their ministry. The program we have provided to fulfill such needs is the 'sprout leader' education. This is a program that has no graduation. As long as a person is in lay ministry, he or she is part of the sprout program.

Men and women meet separately in the SaRang sprout leader education. For the last twenty years, women sprout leaders have been meeting every Tuesday from ten to twelve in the morning. I personally consider this as a golden time and carefully prepare for it. It is not easy to guide thousands of sprout leaders gathered in one place, but there is a special sense of spirit, unity, and inspiration at these meetings that isn't found in any other meetings at SaRang Church.

Depending on the circumstances, we spend more than an hour praying together. Often times worship and the grace of God make us forget what time it is. After worship, using the Upper Room materials I've written, the main point of the scripture passage to be studied is summarized. I always regret that, due to the time factor, I am not able to give more meticulous ideas for the inductive study method. But it is not desirable to spoon-feed them. There are times when their faces are downcast after hearing admonishment. I count it a blessing that as a leader I can give corrections without any anxiety. This cannot be done unless they are his spiritual children. I always yearn for this time with the sprout leaders. It has become a time of replenishing for me, a time of seeing the vision once again.

Our mens' sprout leader class is yet to be stabilized. Sprout leaders are the senior pastor's responsibility and must be taught by him. Yet because of their lifestyle, it is distressing to me that they cannot set a proper time to meet. The most appropriate time for them might be on Sunday afternoons. But it is not a

good time for me after leading 5-6 services already that day.
Given these concerns, our mens' group does not meet every
week. Instead, male sprout leaders prepare by listening to tapes
of my teaching our womens' group. The first Sunday afternoon of
every month is reserved for the men leaders to meet and pray
with our assistant pastors, and then share the appropriate
information by districts. I will often come in during these times to
give a short lecture or answer questions. It is not a satisfactory
solution, but I find comfort in the increasing number of mens'
groups and that many men are experiencing amazing
transformation through these groups.

When laymen are well trained and have become able ministers,
most do not want to release their newly gained ministries.
Sometimes they are fearful that the leader might ask them to
step down. If their family situation does not allow them to
continue their ministry, they want to get back into it when the
situations improve. What joy is there in Christian life, they say, If
you are not doing the ministry? Maybe this is why members who
emmigrate or are appointed to a foreign office witness to the
people around them and often start an Upper Room group.
Sometimes this becomes a bone of contention with a local
Korean church. Most of the time, however, it empowers the local
pastor.

Additional Programs

SaRang Church operates many additional programs to aid
sprout leaders and other lay leaders in ministry. There is a
tendency to want to learn more as you work. It is true that
studying only the Upper Room materials is not enough to make a

sprout leader effective. In order to use those materials correctly, it takes a great effort. A summary of the Old and the New Testaments, systematic theology, counseling techniques, and more are all needed. We offer many classes for this from the laymens' college. Lay leaders and other lay members alike may register and learn at any time according to their convenience. We also offer the Crossway method of learning the Bible over a period of few years in an interesting and systematic manner. A special speaker is invited during the Winter Break to give a series of lectures on counseling for a week. Leaders with expertise in counseling operate seminars on family and marriage problems. Consistent training in prayer is done through an intercessory prayer group that meets every Thursday evening.

We are doing everything we can to activate the laity, but we do recognize that there are matters which we haven't yet covered. We know that the Church will always be in a state of incompleteness till Christ returns, so even though we lack much, we remain thankful and satisfied.

I would also add this note of caution. Because it is the program of a large church, imitating it might prove to be difficult for other sister churches. Yet regardless of the size of the church it should not be too difficult to figure out the basic program that can be applied to each local situation.

Chapter 31: Bring in the Harvest with Joy

It has been more than twenty years since the roots were put down in SaRang Church's discipleship program. Today we have the huge advantage of being able to see both the positives and the negatives of awakening the laity. Nothing can be hidden and everything is in the open. Let me share with you some of the abundant fruits that are being joyfully harvested.

In all honesty, I don't think I could have even imagined in the beginning the extent of the potential of the laity. No matter how I tried, I could not have predicted that discipleship training would have brought in such fruits in ministry. This speaks eloquently of God's overflowing grace on all things that we ask and wish for. This grace is not encountered by SaRang Church alone. Many previously introduced ministries that are managing effective discipleship training can show similar evidence of God's grace. I even dare to say, "Please do discipleship training. You will joyfully see the same fruit".

Chapter 17 describes in detail the changes that occur in the nature of the church when discipleship training puts down healthy roots. However, an improved nature does not adequately describe the situation in SaRang Church. SaRang was founded with discipleship training as its very core. As a result, many changes in the nature of already established churches that are being discovered during discipleship training were already embedded from inception in our church. I will, therefore, only introduce a few aspects that seem most important.

A Powerful Mindset Can Lead the Community of Believers

As a church exists for many years, it is natural that it develops its own mindset. Different mindsets guide different churches differently. The primary factors which contribute to each mindset are the philosophy of ministry of the pastor, how many are influenced by it, and how deep does that influence go. Identify these and you begin to understand the vast differences from church to church.

Discipleship training plants a strong sense of calling in the laity as the ones who are being sent into the world. It gives them a clear sense of self-identification as being the core of the church's existence. It erases any doubt they might have about their stewardship, which requires that they, along with the clergy, stand before God's judgment seat at the end of the age. They realize that any position given to them by the church is not an honor, but a ministry to serve. They don't forget that for a healthy Christian life there is mutual accountability between all brothers and sisters in Christ. They are aware that church life and social life are both indivisible living and holy sacrifices, so they behave accordingly. Consequently, when these beliefs are cohesively brought together, consciously or unconsciously, they become a powerful mindset, which will lead that particular body or community.

Recently, a survey project was carried out at SaRang Church using 645 lay leaders and 330 laymen as subjects. (Refer to Appendix 5) 94 percent of the lay leaders described themselves as called on an equal footing as the clergy. More than 67 percent were sure that their calling was received through the discipleship training and ministry training programs. Eight out of ten pointed out the atmosphere of the SaRang Church as the impetus for becoming a lay leader. In other words, they joined leadership because of the sense in the church environment that they would not be recognized unless they were dedicated. A probable conclusion is that in addition to their sense of calling, they were influenced by a general mindset which condemns idleness.

There is another statistic which proves how prevalent and continual this thought is in our church. 70 percent of the participants answered that they are mentoring a few people around them to be lay leaders in their footsteps. This demonstrates a mindset which is not static but is being transmitted on to the next generation.

The quickest way to find out what influence this mindset has on ordinary believers in SaRang Church is to ask those who have just registered with the church and are being nurtured in the new family classes. This group consists of both new Christians and established Christians who are transferring from other churches. Of these, about 72 percent showed a desire to receive discipleship training. 7 percent felt oppressed by the atmosphere of the church that emphasizes the training, and 25 percent had feelings of half-and-half. Along with it, there were more that 70 percent who digested this mindset as a natural and reasonable phenomena. I believe this is excellent survey material that shows a glimpse of how influential the unspoken and unseen mindset, stemming from the pastor's philosophy of ministry, is on the collective consciousness of the laymen.

Why is it that being a sprout leader, a leader, or a Sunday school teacher provides more spiritual authority than a position as an elder or deacon? Why do meetings in which the Word is shared and where each person is encouraged prosper more than meetings in which church administration is discussed? Why do many people spend more time together to evangelize, serve, and learn than at church functions which are often found in other churches? Why is the worship so unique? Why are their words so full of confidence? Why does the church not experience exhaustive and destructive problems within? Why is it that nine out of ten have strong pride in being members of SaRang Church?

There is only one possible answer to these questions. It is because an invisible mindset, which is shaped by discipleship training, controls the entire body of the community. This mindset of SaRang Church, a church that insists on discipleship training, is the most important thing I want to share because I firmly believe that it is a precious inheritance that can sustain the life and health of the church.

Healthy and Continuing Church Growth

Church growth does not happen only through one element, but when many important factors are in harmony. SaRang Church cannot escape this truth. Therefore, I do not say that discipleship training is the only unique reason for the church's growth. For instance, some people who attend the church for the first time do not return the next week because of the discipleship training programs. No matter how well the members are trained, if they do not have any means to keep the ones they have witnessed to, it will surely hamper the growth. But we should not overlook the fact that there is one element which is leading our growth.

In our case, the invisible but leading factor in our growth is clearly discipleship training. The training itself awakens the members to a sense of calling. So, as long as it is being done properly, the church will not be able to stay mute. The more trainees there are, the more influence on other believers, the more it will explode outside of the church.

For the first seven years of SaRang Church until the opening service in the church building, the yearly increase in the weekly Sunday attendance was 40.2 percent. Since then, for the last 14 years, the growth persisted at 24.7 percent in Sunday adult attendance. In 1997, as an example, new membership in the adult congregation from college age and up was 3,197. Among them 38.7 percent, 1,236, were first time believers who joined the church. The average growth percentage might have dropped, but a church that can evangelize four out of ten people cannot be underestimated. Everyone would agree that this feat could hardly be expected if the church was not operated by trained lay people as the main engine. SaRang Church lacks major space for worship, education and ministries. Still, I believe it is able to sustain the growth because the seeds that were sown in tears have grown and are bearing fruits a hundred times over. Healthy growth must be maintained little by little and continuously. I don't know of any other element that could guarantee such growth as that achieved through discipleship training.

Expansion and Diversification of the Ministry Field

Trained people must work. Without meaningful work they are like marathon runners who practice for many years and yet fail to run a race. So the leader must not only train but must also actively seek a ministry field for those trained. If the leader is unable to find a ministry field or create a niche, then the training should pause for a while. It is better to eat less than to become spiritually obese by just sitting around and studying the Bible. The reason SaRang Church did not become tired of running on the single path of discipleship training is that the leaders had persistence to constantly open up new fields of ministry for the trainees to start out in.

Our most basic field of ministry is the Upper Room small groups. It consists of a group Bible study meeting led by a sprout leader for the purposes of evangelism, nurturing, and fellowship. Anyone can attend and the participants are referred to as sprout members. The life of the Upper Room is in constant growth and reproduction. An Upper Room group with around ten people is like a small church. A sprout leader is a little pastor and the sprout members are the young sheep that the leader is responsible for. Without fail we can see Jesus Himself teaching, proclaiming, and healing throughout these Upper Room groups.

A survey done among the sprout members shows the extent of the spiritual influence sprout leaders exert on them through the Upper Room groups. Nine out of ten answered without hesitation that they considered their sprout leaders to be their spiritual parent. This may also be the reason why they replied to survey questions that they are deeply grateful to the leaders for their dedication and service. With such an open heart toward the sprout leaders, it is no wonder that 85 percent acknowledge that they look forward to and enjoy their Upper Room meetings. Most of them feel loved and sense an obligation to the Upper Room for the systematic studying of the Bible and for the many prayers they receive. On top of that, 92 percent of sprout members admitted that they began to love SaRang Church through these meetings. What more could be said than these findings to confirm the enormous work the trained lay leaders are doing?

The Upper Rooms insure the health of the church. Bible study is not the main reason for these meetings. Rather, it is another place where Jesus' disciples can be made. It is also a place of love where the body of Christ is formed by parts of the body that serve one another. There, new lives are born. There, young lives are nurtured. Multiplication of the Upper Rooms has a direct connection to the growth of the church.

We have more applications for the sprout leader's class than we can provide every year though there are some who do not continue due to personal circumstances, but more likely due to the proliferation of the Upper Room groups. This is a sign of the health and prosperity of the program. Presently, 65 percent of the total membership of the church from college age and up are enrolled in the Upper Room groups.

At times, it is beneficial to give only one or two sprout members to a leader in order that the group start out like a church planting ministry. In SaRang Church, some male sprout leaders are given this type of ministry. This happened especially in the beginning of the Upper Room ministry. One such leader is now an elder, but at that time, after having just finished discipleship training, he started a first Upper Room group with seven sprout members. Soon, however, the members dropped out until only one drunkard came out to make trouble. This hardship continued for two months. This leader could have taken over another group, but he refused, still praying and witnessing earnestly. He repeatedly said that it was a precious opportunity for God to work on his pride and endurance. Surprisingly, he overcame the spiritual warfare and saw his Upper Room flock multiply into four other groups within a year. SaRang Church is full of stories like that. God sometimes works on the leader rather than the group. At times, an Upper Room might have to be sacrificed in order to raise a sprout leader, because a competent leader is not made overnight.

Just as important as Upper Rooms is finding a place of charity work where serving with love can be put into practice. For the first ten years of our church, we could not develop any kind of charity work where loving hands were in demand because there were not enough leaders to send. Almost everything was invested in the Upper Room ministries where people were served with the Word. But now, there is extensive charity work in operation through our church. There is a constant increase in the number of members who prefer to be part of the charity ministry according to their gifts, and in the number of lay ministers who manage both the sprout leader positions and charity work simultaneously.

If a member becomes predisposed to just studying the Word in the Upper Room meetings and partaking in fellowship among other members for a prolonged period of time, then his or her Christian life could become diseased. Both sprout leaders and sprout members, therefore, should be encouraged to go out periodically and serve others who are in difficult circumstances. For those reasons, many of our trainers and their trainees carry on ministries with the physically impaired, in the slums, with teenage girls, in youth hostels, with the elderly and homeless, with homosexuals, and with rural and hospice ministries. None of these ministries are accomplished without the love of Christ. Without question I believe these are things that must be accomplished by the church that has been sent into the world. If the church is apathetic or powerless to be the light and the salt in society, then that church is not the church that Jesus would want. SaRang Church will unceasingly open up places of charity work. Last year, the City of Seo Cho entrusted a local community welfare office for our church to operate. We are also working with the city government after launching a volunteer organization that can penetrate deep into our community.

Rise in the Lay Leadership

When discipleship training continues steadily, it is only natural that there is an increase in trained lay leaders. Even with several natural factors of decline taken into consideration, there will still be a moderate increase in trained leaders. Some margin of unexpected circumstances could crop up during the nearly 2 and V 2 years of training it takes to produce one lay leader at SaRang Church. The number of applicants for training could diminish. There could be no more people to train, or people might evade the training because of the long time frame required. All these things could be stumbling blocks to the continual development of lay leaders. Thankfully, SaRang Church has not yet wrestled with such problems.

Approximately 10 percent of the adult membership at SaRang Church is currently serving as lay leaders. In other words, it is a place where nearly 3,000 little Jesus are working together with the pastor. This percentage is not trivial compared to the total size of the church. Any church, regardless of the size, that has one of ten who are dedicated and trained is a healthy body. What is lamentable is that in many churches, those who are making up the workforce of ten percent haven't even received proper training. The important fact here is not the numbers, but that these are spiritual children and co-workers of a pastor who has thoroughly trained them.

The distinguishing feature of trained lay leaders is that they are completely equipped by the pastor's philosophy of ministry. The pastor, therefore, can rely on them for anything without any worry. More importantly, because they are prepared leaders, they will see much fruit. Most of them feel the ministry is worthwhile. According to the survey previously mentioned, 98 percent of the leaders in SaRang Church perceive themselves as God's instrument in building the church. Because they have been trained, 80 percent of them are able to balance their church ministry and family life. Interestingly, less than 2 percent of that number replied that their office life was also in harmony with their church ministry. It is amazing that 59 percent believed that the most appropriate ministry for them was being a sprout leader to serve others with the Word. Close to 88 percent said that their ministry is bearing fruit, testifying that God is working through them. Almost 93 percent said that their ministry makes them feel worthwhile and joyful. These statistics provide evidence of how beneficial these trained laypersons can be to a church, and how strong and healthy their spiritual life can be.

Building Understanding Hearts for Spiritual Ministry

Generally, one of the distressing things that a pastor experiences is misunderstanding and complaining that arises from misconceptions about spiritual ministry, from the elders on down to the lay leaders. There is a vast difference between dealing with precious souls and dealing with the administrative work of passing the paper, or between serving the body by nurturing weak souls with the Word and settling a matter at a church board meeting or deacon's meeting. Administering or operating the church ought to be interpreted as a spiritual ministry to keep the believers sound. But the reality tells otherwise. Most churches do not have a firm foundation for building understanding hearts for spiritual ministry.

From its inception, SaRang Church has laid a firm foundation of understanding care for souls because the members have been participating in the spiritual ministry along with the pastor once they were trained. This is not only a great blessing for the pastor, but also a precious treasure for the church as a whole.

The attitude of an elder who is a sprout leader struggling day and night to care for and nurture ten or more souls is clearly different than an elder who sits in a board meeting killing time by looking through the minutes. I often hear these words at our church. "Pastor, how exhausted you must be caring for so many souls. With only a few sprout members, I'm having a hard time. Take heart. We are praying for you." It might sound insignificant, but those are words from people who understand what spiritual ministry is all about. It is a certainty that when the number of members who understand and feel the same as a pastor gets larger, that church will demonstrate increased power. In this sense, as the senior pastor of SaRang Church, I am not lonely. My heart is secure. My support is strong.

Dependence and Love toward the Pastor

Unless there is a particular reason, laymen in any church love and depend on their pastor. This subject matter might, therefore, appear slightly redundant. But what counts is the kind of love and dependence it is. Imagine a hard working pastor who does not hold back sweat and tears to help each person become fully devoted to Christ. This is the image of a pastor who does discipleship training. Of course, other pastors who are not doing this type of training are also just as dedicated in caring for their sheep. However, compared to the sweat of a pastor as worship leader, preacher, visitation pastor, or senior administrator, I believe the sweat and tears of a pastor who intimately shares the sorrows and joys of discipling touch hearts more deeply. In some ways, though it is the sweat of the same pastor, what determines whether or not it touches the depth of their hearts is how it was shed. The truth is that a pastor who does discipleship training, more than those who do not, moves the hearts of the believers in a profound way and will receive more of their affection. It is the same principle as a son feeling more love and gratitude toward a mother who worked hard to send him to school than a mother who already had a lot of money to give.

It might seem impertinent, but I would really like to share something. Any pastor who does discipleship training is plainly exposed before his people. If you want to be hypocritical, you can't, and if you want to just roll along, you can't. Truth is transmitted as truth, and a lie is transmitted as a lie. So to develop his sheep into disciples of Jesus, he must exert all his strength, fully concentrate, and willingly sacrifice. This attitude of honesty will move people. A true pastor is not respected because he demands it, but because it comes to him naturally.

He does not need to beg for love and does not have to stiffen his neck to show authority. Even if he does nothing, he will be loved. I would venture to say that this is an overflowing bonus justly earned by a pastor who does discipleship training.

People often times anxiously say that if the lay members become too smart, the clergy gets hurt. But SaRang Church is a place where the opposite is true. This is not a phenomenon without a reason. Not only the senior pastor, but also many associate pastors are receiving trust and love from the members. I can daringly say, "Do you want to receive trust and love? Lower yourself and make disciples."

Chapter 32: Remaining Problems

Can a church become extraordinary if discipleship training is carried out well? Will there be other problems under the surface? The answer is simple. A church will not become perfect or exist without any problems just by carrying out discipleship training. Discipleship training might solve many problems, but establishing discipleship training could also bring in other new problems. I believe SaRang Church is a good example and forum from which to view such problems.

Endless Challenge and Responsibility

When the laity are spiritually awakened, their expectations of the pastor increase. People who are growing in their faith and are willingly dedicated need proper nourishment which will support their spiritual strength. This is a cross that the pastor alone must shoulder entirely. Yet this might not be as difficult as having those who pursue maturity look to their pastor to be a model of Christian living. To be frank, it is difficult to draw a line regarding what level one must reach to say that he is more like Jesus, or at what stage one can be called mature. But committed people want to see something a little more visible. This is an exorbitantly heavy pressure on the pastor. They do not demand specifics with their lips. But they do draw invisible lines which say that a pastor who teaches must at least be at one certain stage, or practice at least that much. Just because a person is a pastor does not mean, however, that his methods and practices are perfect, or that he has already reached a certain level. So the difficulty for a pastor is, the more he does discipleship training, the more obligated he feels. Where the Spirit of God is, there is peace, but it is not going to be easy to shake off the Christ placed yoke of carrying out discipleship training. Perhaps true freedom from that burden will not come until it is time to be lowered into the tomb.

Higher Demand for the Role of the Clergy

Theoretically speaking, it is safe to assume that the more lay leader's discipleship training produces, the less need there will be for professional clergy. It is the same as asking what else is there for the clergy to do when there are so many active lay people in the church. When SaRang Church began, it started innocently with a similar notion. There was even a vague expectation that there might be a reduction in church expenses because of discipleship training. But now, we concede that such thoughts are logically far from the truth. With an increase in the number of lay leaders, we are facing a reality that requires the use of more professionally paid staff, rather than less.

Why are there such adverse conditions at present? Well, as I stated earlier, lay leaders can be exorbitant spiritual gluttons who are not easily manageable. They also must work through many kinds of spiritual valleys, often the same that a pastor faces during his ministry. This means they often require more help and care from the pastor than other regular believers. Of course, they do carry and support one another, but that still cannot take the place of a pastor. This is the first element that stimulates a greater demand on clergy.

Additionally, when a church undergoes growth through lay ministries, there is often an increase in the number of ministry groups that the lay leaders are unable to fill. A pastor or staff member must often fill these voids to some degree, until lay leaders can be properly trained. Accordingly, there is a need for more pastors to be available for discipleship training. If an adequate number of clergy is not assigned to carry out a team ministry, then before long, the senior pastor will reach a status quo in his impact.

At SaRang Church there are about seventy pastors. We want to reduce that number, if possible, but the prospect is that it will increase. This is opposite to our expectations. Yet, it might remain a problem that cannot be solved in the near future.

Idealistic Theory Toxicosis

The focus of discipleship training is Jesus, Himself. This makes it vulnerable to idealistic theory and standards. As a result, the way new disciples view the church will naturally move towards idealism. Is idealism wrong? Of course not, but the adverse side effect of an idealistic view of the church may be serious. The earthly church is definitely not perfect. No matter how hard a leader challenges people to become disciples of Jesus, the leader is only an imperfect pronoun. Nevertheless, many lay people unconsciously view the pastor and criticize the church through an idealistic lens. This is potentially explosive.

A person who is immersed in an idealistic theory can react hysterically whenever standards are not met. The idealistic theory, instead of showing tolerance for something insufficient, weak, or even slightly wicked in appearance, always demands perfection. Consequently, the idealist is completely caught by surprise if a pastor shows some slight imperfection. The reaction to some insignificant incident at the church may be the same fear as if there had been an earthquake. Idealistic theory weakens people. It takes away energy needed to adapt to reality. As we are aware, when a person stays in a germ free environment for a long time, his immune system is low and he will quickly contract a cold virus or other germ when he enters a realistic environment. In some ways, idealistic theory is comparable to a germ free environment. The theory, however, ought to remain the target toward which we aim, and not a drug that poisons us.

There have been times during my role as pastor of SaRang Church that I have been upset with some members who appear to be addicted to such idealistic theory. It is of no concern during times when the church is under easy sail, as we are, by God's grace, experiencing now, but I am anxious that these idealists might take false steps when there is a new spiritual germ or virus that must be fought. Many believers in well established churches, who have experienced various trials during their long Christian life, have already developed an immunity for these spiritual germs, so they are not easily shaken even when faced with disappointments in the church. The members of SaRang Church have yet to be immunized. As their pastor, I am worried sometimes whether they can become strong soldiers of Christ and be victorious.

A High Threshold

A church that uses the word 'train' will automatically conjure up images of strong and intense men and women. This misleading term was one of the problems SaRang Church wrestled with from its inception. We tried various ways to soften the image somewhat, but just as an expressionless person's face instantly returns to it after a slight smile, we still seem to reflect the same intensity. This does not necessarily have only negative effects. For example, if a person applies for membership at SaRang Church knowing full well how intense it is, then no doubt he or she is a quality believer who wants to be trained and put to work. The image of intensity also has the effect of making an unqualified person avoid being drawn into membership. Once a person is a member of the church, even with an extreme and demanding leader, it will help that person to obey. Above all, a new member will be nurtured to become a strong believer. These are positive things that an image of intensity will bring to a church.

The negative effects, however, should not be carelessly skimmed over. For example, the image of intensity has a tendency to create a difficult climate for so called successful people in the world to adapt to. It is not that they don't want to participate, but demanding conditions may not allow them to commit to discipleship training. Yet the church cannot take their situation into special consideration and treat them on an unequal footing with the trained leaders. So, naturally they have little opportunity to serve. This does not mean that people of that class do not become members of the church. It is just that, generally, there are not as many business and professional people at SaRang compared to other large churches. Although about half of the high ranking people in Korean society identify themselves as Christians, in reality, most do not affect the society at all. Quite the opposite, many cover up the glory of God through all kinds of scandals in which they are wrapped up in. It is heartbreaking to think that they cannot easily enter the church because the commitment threshold seems so high, even if that reason is discipleship training. If, however, it is the practical responsibility of the church to train these people, using whatever means, so that they can do their best as those called in their area of social standing, then I wonder if SaRang Church has yet to overcome an important but unavoidable weakness.

There are of course many more than the few things mentioned above that must be overcome. To reiterate once more, the earthly church, however hard it tries, cannot achieve perfection. Yet, just as the presence of bad germs in the air promotes strong immunity in our bodies, I believe the presence of weaknesses that are difficult to overcome in the church will help develop the quality and strengthen its nature. No matter how huge the remaining problems might appear, they cannot be compared to the fruits of discipleship training. And so, today, SaRang Church is committing all of its resources to the awakening of the laymen.

Chapter 33: Twenty-first Century, a Wide Open Door

Discipleship Training is a Key to Tomorrow's Church

What should the Church be like in the Twenty-first Century? It is the question I hear all the time. Many plausible prognoses are pouring in. Undoubtedly the Church in the information age will not wear the same clothes as the Church in the industrial age. On the outside, it might appear to be the same clothing, but in reality, the designs and colors are quite different. Some people humorously compare a DC-3 plane with propellers to a Boeing 747. The two planes appear to be alike at a quick glance, since they both have wings, windows, seats and wheels. But the two are vastly different in many points, such as speed, capacity, cost, complexity, and noise level.

By the same token, the Twenty-first Century Church will be a new model of the Church of the previous century. From its expense to its complexity, it will be different in many ways. Be that as it may, both models are the body of Christ and possess an identical purpose of existence all glory to God.[D]

From this stance, someone may ask whether there is a ground on which discipleship training can stand in the Twenty-first Century. A person could ask such a question if he or she views it as one of the methods of ministry that was utilized only in the industrial society. The question means nothing, however, to a person who perceives making disciples as a Biblical method of ministry free from the change of times. Thankfully, many scholars on the future Church are unanimously of the opinion that the ministry of making disciples is a decisive key that will affect the life of the Church in this century. Pastor Sung Hee Lee, a prominent leader figure in the Korean churches, has warned that in the Twenty-first Century, the church must transform from a visitation ministry into an education ministry; from a great congregation ministry into small group ministry; from Sunday church into everyday church; from a gathering church into a sending church; from clergy centered to laity centered; from the authority of the pastor into leadership of the pastor; and from discipleship training into apostolic training."

I think the reason he distinguishes discipleship training and apostolic training comes from an incomplete understanding of the definition of a disciple. We must not lose sight of the fact that within the command of Jesus to make disciples, there is embedded an apostolic calling to be sent into the world. Nonetheless, for the future ministry's sake, we must carefully evaluate the presuppositions concerning the need for transformation. The interesting point here is that the content of the change proposed is mostly indirect suggestions about the necessity and importance of discipleship training. In other words, the Church in the information age needs a resolute philosophy of ministry to raise up laymen as disciples of Christ more than ever before.

There is more amazing data that supports the opinion that discipleship training will indeed be the basis of the Twenty-first Century Church ministry. Recently, 5,000 pastors in America were subjects of a survey. The content of the questionnaire was on what they thought was the most needed element to strengthen, equip, and revive the Church of the Twenty-first Century. The results of the findings were stunning. Almost 100 percent of the pastors replied that it is first or second in their priorities to unearth the laity and train them to become partners in ministry. [12] How could this urgency be applied only to the American churches?

Just as the defiance of children at home gets tougher as time goes by, so there is a possibility that the defiance of the members of the church could increase. Parents lose power to control their children little by little. In the same way, a pastor forfeits his influence over the laity a little bit at a time. Under these conditions, the first thing a pastor must do is to recover the laity's Biblical position and role. If they are properly taught before they deviate, then they will fulfill their role with sympathetic force, rather then defiant force. But if the opportunity were to be missed, then it would be most difficult to handle. Rather than to teach them as a congregation, it is better to reach them as a small group. I believe there is no better way to help them stand up in faith than through a personal meeting. This will become even more so as time passes.

During one of his missionary journeys, Paul had a short opportunity to stop over at Troas before he moved his ministry from Asia to Europe. The door was open for the gospel right in front of him, yet he left the place. When he could not meet with Titus, a co-worker, his heart was troubled. Much as it was difficult for Paul to carry on the mission without Titus, so we pastors from now on are unable to do powerful ministries without the lay leaders. Before trying to save many souls at once, our eyes should turn to developing one person as a disciple. Before installing state of the art multimedia systems in the church, we should have the vision of finding lay people who can become co-workers in the ministry. Lay members who are properly trained in the hands of the Holy Spirit through the Word of God, will not mutate no matter how much the world changes. They will not leave the pastor's side even if many others fall away. Unless we are emptying all our strength into molding lay co-workers like Priscilla and Aquila, who would not have hesitated to give their lives for Paul, it is anybody's guess what the future holds for the church.

It Is not Too Late to Begin

SaRang Church has been conducting an 'Awakening the Laymen Discipleship Training Pastors Seminar' in order to assist and encourage pastors who would like to have discipleship training in their churches. Over five thousand pastors in Korean and immigrant churches around the world were able to bring back a new vision from these seminars. In addition, hundreds of churches in Japan were able to turn the direction of their ministry into a discipleship training mode.

Although it is a short weeklong seminar, it is a highly intense program structured with three points: theory, practice, and field studies. The methodology of the discipleship training isn't presented in an encyclopedic fashion. The priority of the training is to change the paradigms planted firmly in a pastor's mind. The fact is that a renewal in a pastor's ministry begins with a transformation of those paradigms, not in the specific methodology of the program. Above all, a distinctive character of this seminar has been for pastors to have several opportunities to visit the small groups of SaRang Church.

The pastors who have attended these seminars and have gone back to their churches with the vision of establishing discipleship training have encountered great success. This suggests that the possibility of being successful in discipleship training in Korean churches is very high.

But I believe a church in any nation can start and keep a discipleship training ministry continuing as long as the pastor is willing to change the old paradigms that he may be comfortable with now. It is wise on the part of the pastor to start discipleship training at a time when members of the congregation are still open to radical change. When Paul arrived in Troas, the door to evangelism was open wide, and so the door to awaken the laity is open wide before us right now. The problems with establishing change lie with the pastor. If he would like to have a ministry that is healthy, productive and a leader of society in the Twenty-first Century, then he should not dream of doing it all by himself. The leadership of a pastor who wants to know what he can do for the lay members will no longer have any power. Now is the time to develop a leadership that focuses on what I can do with the laymen. Opportunity does not always arise. Now is the time to redefine the ministry philosophy to properly train lay people to become Jesus disciples. This is our opportunity to rest on the foundation of discipleship Jesus taught so that the laity can stand up intact. Lord, may your disciples be raised up like swarms of bees in this country. Amen.

NOTES

Part 1

1. Neil Brown, *Laity Mobilization* (Grand Rapids: Eerdmans, 1971), 78.

2. "Monthly Econo-Political Culture", *Kyung Hyang Daily Newspaper* (Korean), February, 1984, 198

3. Bill Hull, *Disciple Making Pastor* (New Jersey: Revell, 1988), 24-25.

4. Alister E. McGrath, *Spirituality in an Age of Change* (Grand Rapids: Zondervan, 1994), 49.

5. Howard E. Butt Jr., "The Layman as a Witness," *Christianity Today* (Vol.XII, No.23), 11.

6. Kil-Sung Choi, "Some Characteristics of Minjoong Faith", in *Monthly Chosun* (Korean) (Chosun Daily News Co., December 1982), 73.

7. Hans R. Weber, *Evangelization* (New York: Paulist Press, 1975), 64.

8. Hendrik Kraemer, *A Theology of the Laity* (Philadelphia: Westminster Press, 1958), 65ff.

9. John Stott, *One People* (Downers Grove: InterVarsity Press, 1971), 11

10. Quoted in Michael Green, *Evangelism in the Early Church* (Grand Rapids: Eerdmans, 1975), 172.

11. Bill Hull, *Disciple Making Pastor*, 126.

12. John Stott, *One People*, 28.

13. Ibid., 28.

14. Hans Kung, *The Church* (New York: Image Books, 1967), 169.

15. Ibid., 58.

16. Quoted in John Stott, *One People* (Downers Grove: InterVarsity Press, 1971), 30.

17. Quoted in D. Douglas, *Let the Earth Hear His Voice* (Minneapolis: World Wide Publishing, 1975), 398.

18. Hendrik Kraemer, *A Theology of the Laity*. 72.

19. John Stott, *One People*, 42.

20. John Calvin, *Institutes of the Christian Religion* (Philadelphia: The Westminster Press), 110.

21. John Stott, *One People*, 42.

22. Quoted in Anders Nygren, *This is the Church* (Philadelphia: Muhlenberg Press, 1952), 272.

23. Quoted in John R. Crawford, "Calvin and the priesthood of all believers," *Scottish Journal of Theology* (Vol.21, No.2), 152.

24. John Calvin, *Institutes of the Christian Religion*, 127-128.

25. John Stott, *One People*, 47.

26. Oscar Feucht, *Everyone A Minister* (St. Louise: Concordance, 1977), 63.

Part 2

1. Lynne & Bill Hybels, *Rediscovering Church* (Grand Rapids: Zondervan, 1995), 58.

2. Rick Warren, *The Purpose Driven Church* (Grand Rapids: Timothy Publishing House, 1995), 77.

3. Hans Kung, *The Church* (New York: Image Books, 1967), 120.

4. Peter Kuzmic, "The Church and Kingdom of God", *A Thesis from Wheaton International Evangelical Conference'83*, 22-49.

5. Hans Kung, *The Church*, 120.

6. Stephen C. Neil, *Creative Tension* (London: Edinburg Press, 1959), 112.

7. Harry Boer, *Pentecost & Mission* (Grand Rapids: Eerdmans, 1975), 18.

8. John H. Piet, *The Road Ahead* (Grand Rapids: Eerdmans, 1970), 11.

9. Ibid., 12.

10. Ibid., 28.

11. John Calvin, *Commentary on the Epistles of Paul the Apostle To The Corinthians* (Grand Rapids: Baker Book House, 1979), 414-415.

12. Quoted in Harry Boer, *Pentecost & Mission*, 19.

13. Hans Kung, *The Church*, 120.

14. Francis Schaeffer, *The Church of the Late 20th Century* (Korean Translation) (Seoul: Word Press, 1972), 95.

15. See F. L. Cross, *Oxford Dictionary of the Christian Church* (London: Oxford University Press, 1958), 74-75 ; also, R. B. Kuiper, The Glorious Body of Christ (London: Banner of Truth, 1967), 68.

16. There is no question that I have been greatly influenced by Han Kung, especially in the area of the apostolic nature of the church. His main points - "all Christians are called" and "all Christians are called into the service of God" - are the two most important contributions that he has made to me personally. However, I also see some dangers in his theology. First, while emphasizing God's people as God's priests in the New Testament era, when it comes to the topic of the

position of the pope, he is not very strongly opposed to it as he is about Catholicism in the rest of his discussion. He said in his book, The Church, "the enormous burden of responsibility, of care, of suffering and anxiety which weighs upon the Petrine ministry - provided that Peter's successor is truly a rock, key-bearer and pastor in the service of the whole church." (Kung 1967, 605) "For the Catholics this 'specialty' is the pope. But in a sense they are not alone' the orthodox Christians too have their 'pope'; their 'tradition'; and the Protestants too have their 'Bible'... (Kung 1967, 609). Despite making some critical comments regarding the authority of pope, statements like these indicate that Kung still has come limitations in regard to his position on the pope. Secondly, in his discussion of the church as the creation of the Spirit, he commented that "the Spirit of God, if domiciled in the church, is not domesticated in it. He is and remains the free Spirit of the free Lord not only for the Catholic city, not only of Christians, but of the whole world." (Kung 1967, 223) There is no question that he seems to indicate the possibility of salvation outside of the Christian faith, by non- Christian religions of the world.

17. Jong Sung Lee, The Doctrine of Church I (Korean), 164.

18. Hans Kung, The Church, 443-444.

19. Ibid., 458.

20. Ibid., 458.

21. Ibid., 459-460.

22. Gottlob Schrenk, Theological Dictionary of N.T. Vol III, 54.

23. Carl Kromminga, Bring God's News to Neighbors (Nutley: Presbyterian & Reformed, 1976), 110.

24. Stephen C. Neil, Creative Tension, 9.

25. F. F. Bruce, *The Book of the Acts* (Grand Rapids: Eerdmans, 1975), 39.

26. Harry Boer, Pentecost & Mission, 103.

27. Robert E. Webber, *Common Roots* (Grand Rapids: Zondervan, 1978), 84-90.

28. S.C. Farris, *Dictionary of Jesus and Gospels*, 892.

29. John Stott, *One People* (Downers Grove: InterVarsity Press, 1971), 44.

30. Hans Kung, *The Church*, 481.

31. Ibid., 487.

32. John Calvin, *Institutes of the Christian Religion*, 110.

33. J. H. Bavinck, *An Instruction to Science of Mission* (Philadelphia: The Presbyterian & Reformed Publishing, 1960), 68.

34. Hendrik Kraemer, *A Theology of the Laity*, 147.

Part 3

1. James A. Todd, "Participation," *Encounter*, (Winter 1973)

2. Schrotenboer, "The Unity of the Church in Mission," *A Lecture for Reformed Missions Consultation* (Grand Rapids:Calvin Theology Seminary, 1976), 8.

3. Carl Wilson, *With Christ in the School of Disciple Building: A Study of Christ's Method of Building Disciples* (Grand Rapids: Zondervan, 1976), 8.

4. William Barclay, *The Mind of Jesus*, 89.

5. Ibid., 92.

6. Mark Sheridan, "Disciples & Discipleship," *Biblical Theology Bulletin* (October 1973), 255.

7. Michael J. Wilkins, *Following the Master* (Grand Rapids:

Zondervan, 1992), 281-289.

8. Barth, *A Linguistic Key to the Greek NT* (Regency, 1980), 531.

9. W.W. Klein, *Dictionary of Paul and His Letters* (IVP, 1953), 459.

10. Michael J. Wilkins, *Following the Master*, 24-47.

11. Ibid., 235.

12. Rudolf Bultmann, *The History of the Synoptic Tradition* (Basil Black Well: Oxford, 1963), 160.

13. John Calvin, *Commentary on a Harmony of the Evangelical Vol I* (Grand Rapids: Baker, 1979), 471.

14. William Barclay, *The Gospel of Matthew Vol I* (Westminster Press, 1958), 407.

15. Ibid., 408.

16. John Calvin, *Commentary on a Harmony of the Evangelical Vol I*, 472.

17. Michael J. Wilkins, *Following the Master*, 25.

18. K. H. Rengstorf, *Theological Dictionary of the N.T. Vol. IV*, 427-431.

19. Ibid., 446.

20. Norval Geldenhuys, *Commentary on the Gospel of Luke* (Grand Rapids: Eerdmans, 1968), 399.

21. H. Strathmann, "martus," *T.D.N.T. Vol. IV*, 492.

22. K. H. Rengstorf, *T.D.N.T. Vol. IV*, 492.

23. See Harry Boer, *Pentecost & Mission* (Grand Rapids: Eerdmans, 1975), 118-130.

24. Robert Recker, *Witness in Word and Deed* (Grand Rapids: Baker, 1975), 375.

25. K. H. Rengstorf, *T.D.N.T. Vol. IV*, 455.

26. Philip Schaff, *History of the Christian Church Vol.II* (Grand Rapids: Eerdmans, 1967), 20-21.

27. T. F. Torrance, *Service in Jesus Christ* (Grand Rapids:

Eerdmans,1975), 1-2.

28. D. Bonhoeffer, *The Cost of Discipleship* (New York: Macmillan, 1975), 79.

29. H. W. Beyer, "diakonia." *T.D.N.T. Vol. II*, 85-86.

30. John Stott, *The Epistles of John* (Grand Rapids: Eerdmans, 1975), 143.

31. Lawrence Richards, *New Face for the Church* (Grand Rapids: Zondervan, 1970), 38.

32. Finke, *The Churching of America*, 1776-1990 (Rutgers, 1992), Chapter 7.

Part 4

1. Sung Hee Lee, *The Great Prediction of the Future* (Korean) 302.

2. John Stott, *Issues Facing Christian Today* (Basingstoke: Marshalls), 26.

3. Henri Nouwen, *Bread for Journey*, (Harper Collins) February 27.

4. Francis M. Dubose, *Classics of Christian Missions* (Nashville, Broadman, 1979), 44.

5. John Stott, *One People*(Downers Grove: InterVarsity Press, 1971), 45-46.

6. John Calvin, *Institutes of the Christian Religion IV*. P.52

7. John Piet, *The Road Ahead* (Grand Rapids: Eerdmans, 1970), 57.

8. Oscar Feucht, *Everyone A Minister* (St. Louise: Concordance, 1977), 97.

9. Aubrey Malphurs, *Developing a Vision for Ministry* (Grand Rapids: Baker, 1992), 10.

10. Robert Coleman, *The Master Plan of Discipleship* (Old Tappan: Fleming Revell Co., 1987), 21-37.

11. Ibid., 82.

12. Ibid., 83.

13. Michael J. Wilkins, *Following the Master* (Grand Rapids: Zondervan, 1992), 22.

14. Paulus Scharpff, *History of Evangelism* (Grand Rapids: Eerdmans, 1966), 126.

15. B. K. Kuiper, *The Church in History* (Grand Rapids: Eerdmans, 1955), 342-343.

16. Lawrence Richards, *Creative Bible Teaching* (Chicago: Moody Press) 31.

17. Lynne & Bill Hybels, *Rediscovering the Church*, 130.

18. Lawrence Richards, *A Theology of Church Leadership* (Grand Rapids: Zondervan), 319.

19. J. Verkuyl, *The Message of Liberation in Our Age* (Grand Rapids: Eerdmans, 1970), 106.

20. Ernest G. Bormann, *Effective Committees and Groups in the Church* (Minneapolis: Augsburg, 1973), 12.

21. Clyde Reid, *Groups Alive-Church Alive* (New York: Harper and Row, 1969), 16.

22. Lawrence O. Richards, *A New Face for the Church* (Grand Rapids: Zondervan, 1970), 157.

23. Irvin D. Yalom, *The Theory and Practice of Group Psychotherapy* (New York: Basic Books, 1975), 70-104.

24. Navigator, *Bible Study Methods*, 56.

25. Ibid., 22.

26. LeightonFord, "Jesus as a Model for Leader," *World Evangelization* (March/April 1995), 6-10.

27. Clyde Reid, *Groups Alive-Church Alive*, 82.

28. John Stott, *One People*, P.527.

Part 5

1. Nak-Jun Baik, *The history of Protestant Missions in Korea* (Korean), 151.

2. J. Herbert Kane. *A Global View of Christian Missions*, 265.

3. John Piet, *The Road Ahead* (Grand Rapids: Eerdmans, 1970), 57.

4. Suk-San Chung, *The Evangelization of Korea and the Neveius Principles* (Korean), 68.

5. Ibid., 68.

6. Nak-Jun Baik, *The History of Protestant Missions in Korea* (Korean), 151.

7. J. Herbert Kane. *A Global View of Christian Missions*, 265.

8. Nak-Jun Baik, *The History of Protestant Missions in Korea* (Korean), 151.

9. Hee Keun Jang, *The Korean Church History* (Korean), 118

10. Leith Anderson, *A Church for the 21st Century* (Korean Translation) (Bethany House Publishers, 1992), 32.

11. Sung Hee Lee, *The Great Prediction of the Future* (Korean), 109-313

12. Frank R. Tillapaugh, *Unleashing the Church* (Regal, 1982), 20.

Christian Focus Publications

publishes books for all ages

Our mission statement –

STAYING FAITHFUL

In dependence upon God we seek to help make His infallible word, the Bible, relevant. Our aim is to ensure that the Lord Jesus Christ is presented as the only hope to obtain forgiveness of sin, live a useful life and look forward to heaven with Him.

REACHING OUT

Christ's last command requires us to reach out to our world with His gospel. We seek to help fulfill that by publishing books that point people towards Jesus and help them to develop a Christ-like maturity. We aim to equip all levels of readers for life, work, ministry and mission.

Books in our adult range are published in three imprints.

Christian Focus contains popular works including biographies, commentaries, basic doctrine, and Christian living. Our children's books are also published in this imprint.

Mentor focuses on books written at a level suitable for Bible College and seminary students, pastors, and other serious readers. The imprint includes commentaries, doctrinal studies, examination of current issues, and church history.

Christian Heritage contains classic writings from the past.

For a free catalogue of all our titles, please write to
Christian Focus Publications, Ltd
Geanies House, Fearn,
Ross-shire, IV20 1TW, Scotland, United Kingdom
info@christianfocus.com

For details of our titles visit us on our website
www.christianfocus.com